Crossing An Ocean Under Power

Second Edition
By: Ken Williams
ISBN 1-4116-1918-8
Copyright by Ken Williams, 2004

Publisher: www.lulu.com

Photos in this book were taken by the Rally participants, the author and David Shuler (http://www.yachtphotography.com), a professional Photographer. Photos are included by permission of PAE Inc.

The author may be contacted at: Ken Williams (kenw@seanet.com)

INDEX

<u>Prologue</u>

If someone had told me that I would someday be the author of a book on ocean crossing, I never would have believed them. I am not a writer, and much less so someone who might ever attempt anything that could be considered dangerous. My wife Roberta and I have owned increasingly large boats throughout our 30+ years of marriage, but have never attempted a run of more than eight hours. We've cruised some of the greatest places in the world, including the Pacific Northwest, and even the Mediterranean, but always limited our cruising to short day-time runs, on calm seas.

Our boat, a 62' Nordhavn, is a serious boat, meant for crossing oceans. We bought it, not because that was our intent, but because we wanted the safest possible boat that could be run by two people. Our thinking was that if we had a boat that could handle huge waves, it would REALLY be safe for coastal cruising, or should we ever get surprised by an unforeseen storm.

At least, that's how things were prior to my receiving this email from PAE (the makers of Nordhavn):

Dear Ken:

Planned for the summer of 2004, Pacific Asian Enterprises, Inc. (PAE) will sponsor the adventure of a lifetime for NORDHAVN owners and their guests. In convoy with escort support, a fleet of NORDHAVNs will sail from New England to Gibraltar, via Bermuda and the Azores.

PAE will staff specifically selected escort NORDHAVNs to lead and follow the group. The finest of the PAE staff and associates will provide assistance to the fleet including the following:

* Mechanical and technical support with mechanics on lead and chase vessels for en-route repairs
* Emergency fuel reserves with boat-to-boat transfer capability
* Towing capability
* Diver for underwater repairs
* 24-hour monitoring of designated VHF and SSB frequencies
* Daily roll calls

* Daily weather briefings
* Physician for medical emergencies
* Shore side staff at Hamilton, Horta and Gibraltar to assist owners with government formalities, provisioning, fuel and shore side group activities
* Preferred group rates for transatlantic return aboard specialty yacht carriers

The Rally will kick off with a rendezvous at our Portsmouth, Rhode Island office beginning in May. Each vessel participating will be required to pass a comprehensive inspection for condition and meet minimum equipment requirements.

The fleet will travel within two groups dictated by the vessel's speed capability and the owner's desire. Larger NORDHAVNs may elect to travel up to 9 knots while the smaller vessels will run slower - particularly on the mid-Atlantic passage. The two groups will stay together with their respective escort vessel. During the day, vessels may run close together - sometimes closing to within 100 yards. At night, in reduced visibility or during periods of rough weather, greater separation will be maintained. The distance between lead and trailing vessels should not open up to more than 7 or 8 miles; this will ensure complete VHF radio coverage. Varied departure times for each group will allow the entire fleet to arrive at each destination together.

May 15th will be targeted as a weather permitting departure date for the 600-mile voyage to Hamilton, Bermuda. PAE staff will await arrival of the fleet and provide assistance with government formalities, provisioning and refueling. PAE will provide technical and mechanical assistance as needed by members of the fleet as well as acquire and ship any parts required. The escort vessels will inventory a wide variety of spare parts and have the tools on hand to deal with most problems that might occur. The fleet will enjoy approximately one week in port with numerous group activities planned.

June 1st will be targeted as a weather permitting departure date for the 1,800-mile passage to Horta, located within the Azores Island Group. This passage will be completed by the larger NORDHAVNs in as little as eight days while the smaller boats could take up to 11 days. As done in Bermuda, PAE shore side staff will be on hand to assist and welcome our fleet into port and to arrange for on-shore activities and fleet parties.

Weather permitting, the fleet will leave Horta on June 25th for the last leg across the Atlantic into the Mediterranean and on to Gibraltar - a distance of 1,100 miles. After lots of celebration and fun, the official NORDHAVN Atlantic convey will be complete and each NORDHAVN will be in position to enjoy the Mediterranean individually or within groups.

To make the Rally even more exciting, renowned circumnavigating yachtsman and television and film director Bruce Kessler will be accompanying the fleet to create a documentary film of the voyage. Bruce, together with t.v. producer Jo Swerling Jr., hopes to generate television network interest in the documentary. The film will not only cover the transatlantic voyage but will focus on the individual experiences of the participants and how they perceive this great adventure as it unfolds.

Finally, PAE has negotiated discounted return shipping rates for transatlantic shipping service from Europe to Ft. Lauderdale, Florida. The commitment will include multiple sailings, which can coincide with each individual's return itinerary.

Non-NORDHAVN Participants
The event will be open to other qualified vessels. A criterion will be established in the months to come, which will define the term "qualified". Some preliminary requirements are very basic. For instance, each vessel must be capable of at least 2,500 miles at about 7 knots (deck fuel will not be tolerated). The slow fleet will probably run below 7 knots (possibly around 6.5 knots on the Bermuda to Azores passage - 1,800 nm).

Additionally, minimums will be developed for glass thickness vs. surface area (this can be rectified with storm plates) and we will probably require auxiliary propulsion on single engine vessels - adequate to maintain 4 knots in calm weather. Each vessel will have to pass a survey for condition and suitability for a long ocean passage. This will include a stability study which will require an inclining experiment to determine the relationship between the vertical center of gravity and the vessel's meticenter (a minimum safe number will be developed). This relatively easy study which takes only a couple of hours, will ensure that each vessel has adequate stability for such a voyage.

The Rally will be officially introduced at the Miami International Boat Show, February 13-18, 2003, where participants can pick up a preliminary brochure. More information will be posted on the Nordhavn website (www.nordhavn.com) as it becomes available. Interested participants will be put on the Rally mailing list and will receive periodic updates via e-mail.

Cordially,

Jim Leishman

Roberta and I had already been talking about stretching ourselves as boaters. Specifically, we were planning what seemed to us like a major undertaking; circumnavigating the island of Corsica. We had spent the previous three summers cruising the south of France, jumping from island to island, but had always feared going to Corsica, as this would require us to make a crossing of over 100 miles. When I received the notification of the Atlantic Rally, I almost hit the delete button, but instead forwarded it to Roberta. I was confident that we wouldn't really participate, but knew it would make for some interesting dinner conversation.

I was wrong. What started as dinner conversation became a major project. We had a chance to do something extraordinary, and historic, but in a way that seemed relatively safe.

This book started as a series of daily emails to my family and friends. As the trip progressed, my emails started being forwarded to other participants' families, then to their friends, and then to their friends. The level of interest in the rally, and in Nordhavn was amazing. During the course of the rally, daily distribution of my emails grew to nearly five thousand people!

Why did so many people read these emails, and why would you want to read this book?

Trust me, it's not because I'm a great writer. What I am is a happily retired software entrepreneur. My suspicion is that most people were reading my emails because they were curious to see if we were going to sink. It's somewhat like when cars slow as they pass accidents.

As to why you should read this book, I'll tell you what the book is about, and then let you make your own decision. This book answers questions about long distance cruising that you won't find answered anywhere else.

- What is it like to live in a very small space, for a very long time, with complete strangers (our crew)?
- What do you do at night in the middle of the ocean? Is it scary?
- Can you really swim in the middle of the ocean?
- What are flopper stoppers? Stabilizers? Thrusters?
- What do you do with your trash?
- What happens when you encounter a fleet of fishing boats? How do you avoid their nets?
- Do they wear clothes on the beaches in Europe?

- What happens when you are 1,000 miles from shore, and the toilets stop working?

The crossing was an extraordinarily amazing learning experience. At the start, Roberta and I were nervous at the idea of not seeing land. At the conclusion, we felt confident enough to tackle a four day crossing of the med essentially alone. We are now planning a crossing of the Pacific, and have started talking about circumnavigating.

If you have ever wondered what it might be like to spend serious time on a boat, then you will find that this is the closest you'll ever get, without casting off lines, to doing so. And hopefully, you'll discover what Roberta and I now know: long range cruising is addicting. There's a magical feeling "out there" that once sampled never lets go of you.

-Ken Williams

December 16, 2004

AN IMPORTANT NOTE BEFORE YOU BEGIN

*This is not a guidebook, and I am not a professional mariner. I do not guarantee the accuracy of anything here. Ocean crossing is serious business, and I cannot overstate how critical it is to prepare, prepare and then prepare some more **before** you leave the dock. This book contains my thoughts, opinions and events. Your results may vary. Whereas I have tried to be accurate in what I say, it is your responsibility to verify everything you find here, and its relevance to you.*

Day 1 - Fort Lauderdale

Hello, my name is Ken Williams and this is the first of my daily postings about the NAR Cross Atlantic Rally.

We had a LONG night of packing, preceded by a longer week of packing. Then, yesterday morning – May 9th, 2004, the day had finally arrived. We were on our way!

The boat is parked at the Bahia Del Mar Marina in Ft. Lauderdale. It had been in France for the last four years, but was shipped here to Florida for six months of MAJOR overhaul. The electrical system went through a huge transformation including new batteries and invertors. I can now run the entire boat off the invertors, and shouldn't need the generators more than an hour or two per day. Also, the front cabin, which used to have the invertors and batteries under it, is now useable. Before, the invertors were throwing out so much heat that the cabin was completely useless.

Anyway, enough of that...

The people around us are at least as interesting as the boats. The original premise of the rally was that a large number of powerboats would be crossing the Atlantic Ocean together. Originally I heard that approximately 70 boats would be involved, which was then reduced to 50, then 30, then 22, then 21 – and, now, I think we are down to 18. I'm not sure I know why the shrinking number of participants. My guess is that as the realities, and expenses, of crossing an ocean became a reality for people, their willingness to participate dwindled. I know there were several boats that planned on participating where the owners, or crew, had medical problems preventing them from doing so.

The participating boats range from 40' to 90'. Most are around 46 feet. There are three 62' boats, including our own Sans Souci, and only one 90'. Nordhavn has manufactured all but 3 of the boats - the others are built or designed by Seaton, Krogen, and Monk-McQueen.

With respect to boating experience: I'm not sure yet about the other boaters. If our table at dinner last night is any indication, there is a LOT of boating experience here. Roberta and I were feeling like total wimps. We have spent a lifetime on boats, but in small bursts. Other than one three-day trip that I had participated on when Sans Souci was first delivered, we've never done a run of more than 10 hours. Roberta and I have taken Sans Souci to virtually every port and island in the Puget  Sound and the South of France – with JUST the two of us. But, these are always day trips, done when the weather looks calm. I describe myself as a person who likes boating for the anchoring, not the boating. I like being anchored in some bay, just off a remote island, tendering ashore from time to time, having dinner (and, perhaps some wine) on the back deck, swimming, playing with my computer, etc. That's my idea of boating.

Now, let's contrast Roberta's and my boating experience with those at the table. First, the Stricklands. A reasonably young couple, mid-40's I'd guess. He's a software developer. They picked up their boat just six months ago (a 47 foot Nordhavn), and immediately took it from San Diego to Vancouver, alone. They talked about being anchored off Sucia, an island near Seattle, watching it snow. From there, they headed south, through the Panama Canal, and here to Florida. Once again, frequently with just the two of them aboard ship, although sometimes with one extra crewmember. Scott Strickland spoke about the "fun" of watching thick smoke pour from his engine room 200 miles at sea running off of Nicaragua. As it turned out, it was "only" an alternator belt that had fried, so he was able to continue without it. Then we met another couple that lives in Switzerland (he is English and she is Brazilian), who also brought their boat around to Florida from San Diego. They talked about making one four-day passage with just the two of them. This sounds dangerous to me. We chatted about how much better it is to run your own boat than to have crew. Rip, our captain for this voyage, was sitting there, and didn't seem too happy with the discussion. And, lastly we met the owner of one of the other 62's on the trip, Bill Smith. He has taken his Nordhavn 33,000 miles, completely around the world, over the past three years.

I have to cut this short, as I need to get ready for class. Today, I will be learning about fuel systems, and spending an hour filling out paperwork. Tonight we have planned to take the tender and go exploring. Allegedly there are some great restaurants we can boat up to from here.

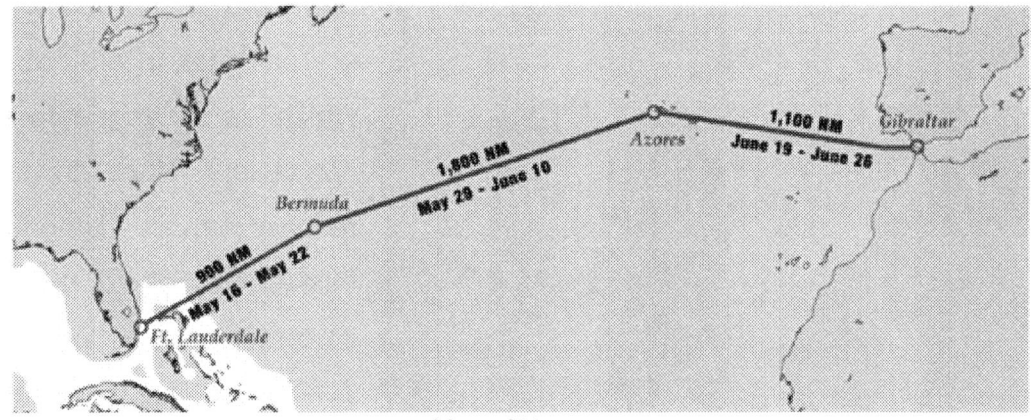

Map of Voyage.

Day 2 - Fort Lauderdale

A long day today...

Our day kicked off this morning with an overview of some of the operational details of the voyage. We discussed many topics which will hopefully never be an issue – such as the proper method for dealing with a man overboard situation, how to refuel at sea, how to rig a harness on your boat so that you are properly prepared should you need to be towed, etc.

This was followed with a course in how to use the onboard Skymate satellite-based

system for sending e-mails. Unfortunately, the process isn't pretty or cheap. Basically, there are satellites in orbit above us, which are frequently in a convenient place to send or receive e-mails. Unfortunately, this is only about 60% of the time most places, and perhaps 20% of the time in the middle of the Atlantic. To make a long dull story short, and hopefully more interesting, I'll summarize by saying that e-mails, and requests for weather information only go out about once per hour. E-mails sent to the boat are similarly only received about once per hour. For this, the cost for receiving an e-mail of about 1,000 characters (a couple of paragraphs) is around three dollars! Please don't take this wrong. Skymate is a wonderful product. Being able to send any e-mail from the middle of the Atlantic, as compared to where the state of the art was a few years ago, **IS A MIRACLE**, at any price. It just seems bizarre to pay $3 for a couple of paragraphs of text, when I stream video at home for $49 per month. If you see daily updates from me that say nothing more than "We're still afloat" during the long crossings, you'll understand that I was just being cheap that day – it isn't that I had nothing to say.

There were also courses today in "tuning your auto-pilot" and "fuel filtering" both of which I really wanted to attend, but instead I was bogged down working on some "issues" with the electronics on the boat.

There are a LOT of press along on this voyage. Virtually every major boating magazine is here. Roberta and I did take some time off for a video interview, as there is a documentary being made about the voyage. One of the other boats, Zopilote, is owned and piloted by Bruce Kessler, a television director who is well known and respected in the boating community. Bruce has taken Zopilote around the world (actually its

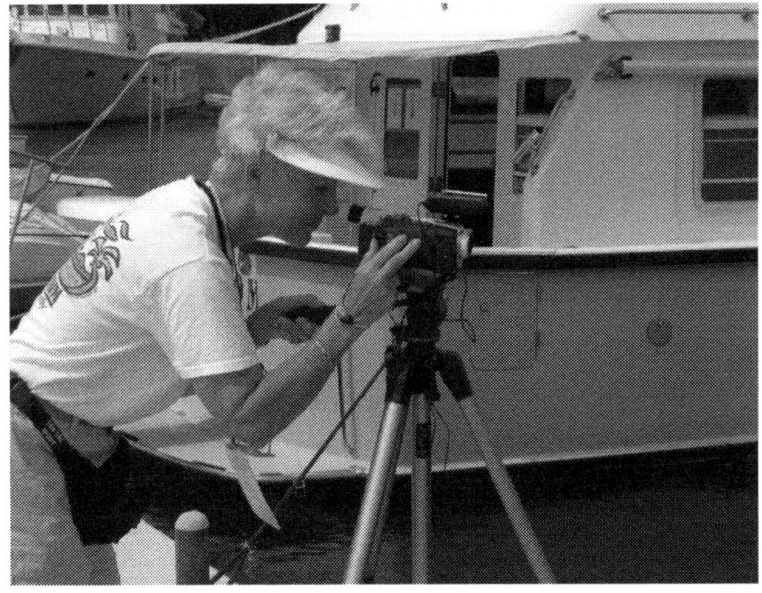

predecessor – the original Zopilote had an unhappy ending), and is going across the Atlantic with us, AND, he and his wife Joan are making a documentary about the voyage. Although powerboats have crossed oceans before, this is a VERY different trip, in that 18 powerboats are crossing at once, most of them captained by their owners who in many cases are not veterans of the sea. I'm not sure I could describe exactly what history we are making, but many times today I was assured that this was an historic undertaking –hence the documentary. Now, here's the twilight zone part. We actually had a meeting where Bruce encouraged us to keep our video cameras charged up and laying around, so that if something interesting happens, like smoke coming from the engine room, or a boat that doesn't respond to roll call, we would be prepared to videotape the crisis as it occurs. I understand and commend his responsibility to good documentary filmmaking, but hopefully he will forgive me if I ever see smoke, and grabbing the camera is not the first thought that leaps to my mind! It was very interesting to watch Bruce in action. As he spoke, you could see him mentally

 running through the documentary in his mind. Because the "actors" in his drama are scattered across 18 boats, he has logistical problems making his documentary that most directors don't face. He NEEDS us to film ourselves at moments when we least want to be filmed. He struck me as a VERY sharp guy, and I'm convinced that he can do about anything he sets his mind to. That said, I very much hope that his documentary is 100% dull, and that nothing interesting ever happens as we wander out into open ocean.

After Bruce finished his talk, we had a lecture from our "photo grunt". We have one person, whose "job" it is to collect all of our pictures for compositing onto one or more photo CDs at the end of the trip. As he said, it is impossible to take a good picture of your own boat, while it is moving. I have lots of pictures of the bow of my boat, while we are moving – but no shots that I'm really happy with. Our solution: take great pictures of each other's boats, and pool them at the end of the voyage. It was fun watching Dean, the photo grunt, explain the concept of mega-pixel digital cameras to an audience of boaters. I suspect that boating skills and computer skills are taught at different universities, as some in the room didn't seem to understand when Dean explained why jpgs use lousy compression, and what this means. One interesting part of the talk for me was when he talked for a moment about how to handle anyone who was shooting a true "film" camera, and I looked around the room, and didn't see a single film camera. I hadn't realized how pervasive digital cameras have become. I should have known.

14

We had the good fortune of having Dan Streech, the CEO of PAE, the manufacturer of Nordhavn yachts, such as our own Sans Souci, along at dinner. Dan and his wife

Marcia are wonderful and charming people. Dan will be accompanying us aboard Sans Souci on the run from Florida to Bermuda. For Roberta and I, this was our chance to ask all of the questions we were too embarrassed to ask in front of the whole group, such as "How long does sea sickness last?" and "Is it ok to throw paper plates overboard in the middle of the ocean?" Dan answered all our questions, and more. It will be awesome having him  aboard for the first leg of our grand voyage. A very real goal for Roberta and I is to move ourselves "the next step" towards becoming "real boaters", and I can't imagine a better way then being able to get private lessons from people like Rip and Dan.

Day 3 - Fort Lauderdale

Today was another day of preparing for the trip. Phil, the boat's chef, spent the day shopping for the voyage. We did some quick math, and for the roughly 70 days that the voyage will last, there will be approximately 210 meals – not counting snacks. We'll have eight people aboard most of the time, so this translates into over 1,600 meals! Even planning for drinks is a huge undertaking. Who is going to carry 2,000 cans of coke onto the boat, and where will we put them? Thus far Phil seems pretty mellow and confident about the whole undertaking – so I guess that if he isn't worried, I won't be worried. There are other complex issues we have to deal with. For instance, Bermuda has notified us that they will inspect all food on the boat. All vegetables and fruit that we arrive with in Bermuda must be destroyed. This

isn't a huge deal as any vegetables we bring on in Florida are likely to be mush by the time we get to Bermuda anyhow. Overall, this is not an area I am spending a lot of time thinking about. The rumor is that food is irrelevant on a long passage. No one eats, and those that do can only enjoy it for a brief period before the food becomes colorful decoration for the side of the boat.

Most of the people aboard ship have a connection with Seattle one way or the other, so coffee was on the agenda today. Roberta gave lessons on "how to run the espresso machine". She also shared with the group the location of the nearest Starbucks. Roberta was a big hit.

Speaking of Roberta, I should comment a bit on the demographics of those that are here. I believe, but I am not yet sure, that most of the boats are owned by couples. Having said that, you wouldn't know it attending the seminars. During the classes I've been to, I'd say that 90% of the attendees are male. About 2/3rds of these appear to be between 50 and 70, with the other third under

about 25. I know that its not politically correct to notice or comment on these things, but I've never been a big believer in political correctness – so, with that in mind: My guess is that most of the owners fall into the older age group, and the younger people were generally crew or in many cases employees of PAE, the "hosts" of the rally. There are exceptions to this, but as a generalization I don't believe I'm far off the mark. Generally speaking, the types of people who are crossing oceans seem to be retired couples. Another attribute that seems to bond the group is tougher to define. These are not average retirees. The grey hair is the least important part of the story when it comes to describing this group. These are people who are self sufficient, multi-talented, courageous, self confident, adventurous, smart, and just about every other adjective you can imagine, except stuffy. I have trouble imagining anyone in this group driving a BMW on their way to some yuppie event. I began this paragraph talking about Roberta, because there are clearly more men here than women. Even on our boat, we have eight men, plus Roberta (Marcia, Dan's wife bailed on us). I'm not sure I understand that one yet. At dinner tonight the owner of the restaurant said that he wanted to buy a 90-foot trawler, but was having trouble convincing his wife. I always have thought of boating as something couples do together, but obviously it's some kind of a macho thing (and, no one told Roberta or I)

Our boat, Sans Souci, is one of three boats that are leading the expedition. This seems to be in spite of the boats French name, which seems to be causing some confusion. I'm not saying this for any kind of political reason, but it has become apparent that NO ONE can pronounce these particular French words. In virtually every speech, Sans Souci is referred to for one reason or another. For the record, here's where the name came from, and how it is pronounced: The words Sans Souci literally translate as "no

worries". I chose a French name simply because I love France and wanted to spend time cruising the Med aboard her (which we have done). For us, the name Sans Souci is reminiscent of France, and also captures the spirit of the old Bobby McFerrin song "Don't worry – be happy!" The boat represented a chance for Roberta and I to take a few years off after a 20+ year career and enjoy traveling around the world. No worries. By the end of today, I was convinced that I am the one who doesn't speak French. I have heard Sans Souci pronounced (just today) as "San Sushi", "San Suzy", "Sahn Sushi", "San Suki" and more! Here's how I believe it should be pronounced: sahn-seuss-ie (the seuss is like Dr. Seuss)

I attended only one class today, and then spent the rest of the day aboard the boat problem solving. The class was very interesting. The theme was "what is most likely to go wrong, and how do you fix it". Even though there will be other boats around us, we need to be prepared to be self-sufficient. Things tend not to break when the sun is shining and the water is flat. Nope. Instead, things go wrong when the waves are 20 feet tall, lightning is striking in all directions, and the radar is a useless green flicker of white, due to the lightning and squalls. When things get bumpy we will be running AT LEAST a mile apart. There will be no way to transfer a mechanic from one boat to another.

So, what do you think was the #1 problem? The group consensus was that the majority of problems at sea had been fuel related in one way or another. Sans Souci carries enough fuel to go thousands of miles (from 1,500 to 5,000 depending on speed), but this fuel is spread across six different tanks. I'm not sure exactly why it's not one big tank, but my hypothesis is that if you have 2,500 gallons of gas in one big tank, and the boat starts rocking side to side, you could have a lot of momentum from all the sloshing. Also, if you take on some bad fuel, it's nice to think that you still have other tanks you can run on. Anyway, there is a simple, but reasonably complex system of switches that

specify which tank to pull fuel from, and which tank to return fuel to (on diesel engines, not all fuel gets burned on the first try). It can happen to even the most seasoned veterans that when the boat is rolling around and you are worn out from days of around the clock cruising that the switches get set wrong, and the engine runs out of fuel, even though there is plenty in other tanks. We went through the process to bleed fuel lines, with the understanding that we never want to actually do this at sea, with a hot engine, in ocean conditions. Roberta and I did actually run out of fuel once in the Mediterranean about 50 miles off of Toulon France, in really bad weather. It's a long story I'll save for another day…

The balance of the day was spent crawling (literally) through the engine room of Sans Souci. Today was "inspection day", which meant a team of inspectors was aboard checking out all our emergency equipment. We had checklists prior to their arrival, and had ensured that everything was in its place – so we passed on the first try (with a couple of small things to fix up). In addition to the inspectors I spent the day debugging the internet connection on the boat (which isn't looking promising) and then spent another couple of hours meeting with mechanics to go through all the renovations that has gone on with the boat over the last six months. By the end of the day I was starting to feel very good about things.

Hopefully tomorrow will be easier…

Day 4 - Fort Lauderdale

Not much to report today.

We spent six hours working on the paperwork, and vet visit, required to get Shelby, our dog, into Bermuda. We faxed 16 pages of information to Bermuda, and with a little luck will be issued a permit prior to our departure. Another of the owners, Bill Smith, aboard Autumn Wind, another Nordhavn 62, is going through the same hell with their two poodles. Hopefully it will work out – if not, we're not sure what we'll do.

The late afternoon was spent working on installing an XM radio system. It will give us 100+ channels of radio, and weather information, until we reach Bermuda. Given that we'll only be about five days to Bermuda, and then out of reception range, it was hardly worth doing – but I've always been curious to play with XM radio, and there is a add-on (at a huge price) that let's you get marine weather – so, this gave me the excuse I needed to buy a new toy.

Because I felt guilty about not having anything new to say, I did snap a few pictures – but, quickly discovered that it is impossible to shoot pictures of boats while they are on shore. I'll post better pictures as I get them. Visit http://www.trawlerweb.com and click on the **Nordhavn Rally** menu item. From there, select any of the Photo pages to see the pictures. I've also added a few electrical panel pictures at one person's request.

Sans Souci's Main Electrical Panel

Sans Souci's Inverter Control & Battery Monitor

I wasn't on the boat much today, as we spent much of the day at the veterinarian's office. When we were at the boat, only Phil (the chef) and Rip (the captain) were aboard. I'm not sure where everyone was. There were classes all afternoon having to do with medical emergencies at sea. As we have St. John onboard, who is an emergency medical technician, I let him represent our boat in the classes.

Overall, the boat has come together nicely. Other than buying fuel, we are ready, and impatient, to go to sea. There's still some shopping to do, but I suspect that we'll have lots of time to kill between here and Monday when we depart.

More tomorrow…

Day 5 - Fort Lauderdale

First off, we received some great news today. Shelby (our dog) has been approved to enter Bermuda!!! I uploaded a copy of her permit to the website (under Misc. Images). That's a huge load off our minds.

We have only two more days to go before we head to sea!!!! It's starting to get scarier and scarier. It has been extremely windy every day here in Fort Lauderdale. When I look at the sea and see all the whitecaps and waves, it seems hard to imagine that we'll soon be out there.

The group of 18 boats has been split into two halves – those who will be doing 7 knots and those who will be doing 8.5 knots. Sans Souci is leading the "fast" group.

To give you a perspective on this speed, 8.5 knots is about 10 miles per hour. It's not exactly a blazing speed.

Some of you who are reading this already understand why we'll be going so slowly, but my guess is that many don't. For those who really don't know much about boats, let me give you a quick super-high level overview. Basically, boats break into two categories: planing boats, and full-displacement boats. There are some hybrids, that are half way in between, but as a rough way of looking at it, this will suffice. The difference between the two has to do with how deep the bottom of the boat is beneath the surface of the water while cruising. Most powerboats have planing hulls, meaning that they plane above the water while moving. Most sailboats have a full-displacement hull, which means that they do not lift up while moving through the water, they push the water aside as they move through it. Most sailboats have hulls that run 6 to 10 feet below the water.

Whether or not a boat planes, or is full-displacement, makes a huge difference with respect to how much energy it takes to move it through the water. Planing boats require a huge amount of energy (lots of horsepower equates to lots of fuel) to lift them above the water and let them plane from point A to point B. Once above the water, they are not slowed down, and can run at fast speeds. On the other hand, there seems to be an exception to the law of physics, which is exploited by sailboats. An object in the water can be easily moved through the water (meaning without much energy expended), BUT ONLY up to a certain speed. The length of the boat makes a difference. The longer a boat is, the faster it can move through the water without consuming much energy. As crazy as it sounds, a boat 60 feet in length can be moved through the water with as little as 100 horsepower, up to about 5 knots of speed. To move it at a speed of 10 knots may require 10 times as much power. There is a math formula that can compute the speed that a given length boat can move through the water before it starts needing a HUGE amount of energy (fuel). If Sans Souci were half as long, and weighed half as much, its maximum speed would be MUCH LOWER, even with the same motor!

Lets put this into something closer to English. Have you ever tried to push a boat by hand? I can move my boat, and have done it many times, by pulling on a rope that leads to shore. I guarantee you that I do not exert even one horsepower. Having said that, there is no way I could pull the boat very fast. If I were to do an experiment, I would find that no matter what I do, I can't move the boat above a certain speed. Sailboats consume almost no fuel, even when running with a motor. Most sailboats have a backup motor in addition to having sails, and this backup motor is typically only 20 to 50 horsepower, and burns perhaps 3 or 4 gallons of fuel per hour. A similarly sized planing boat might consume 20-30 gallons of fuel per hour, but would go MUCH faster.

This is where range becomes important. Range is the distance that a boat can go. Most personal planing boats (which is essentially all non-commercial powerboats) are limited to a range of less than 500 miles. There are fishing boats with huge tanks, and some semi-displacement (meaning half way in between) boats, that can go farther – but generally speaking, 95+% of most boats you see are limited to range of less than 500 miles. The really big multi-million dollar powerboats that you see are able to cross oceans because they have REALLY big fuel tanks, not because they are defying the laws of physics. You can either go slow and not use much fuel, or go fast and REALLY burn it fast. It's not a straight-line co-relation. A planing hull boat could easily burn 5 to 10 times the amount of fuel while going only 2 to 3 times faster.

Sans Souci is a trawler. So, what is a trawler? Trawlers are powerboats that are designed more like sail boats, with full-displacement hulls. They do not plane above the water, and they do not go fast. They have motors with limited horsepower, and use very little fuel. For instance, Sans Souci only burns about 6 gallons an hour, and could burn as little as 3 gallons per hour if we slow down. At 5 knots, Sans Souci's range is over 5,000 miles! At 9 knots, this drops to around 2,000 miles. To accomplish this we are carrying only about 2,100 gallons of fuel.

Trawlers are recent inventions. Oceans have been crossed before, but only by sailboats, or huge commercial ships and mega yachts. The first trawler to complete an around-the-world trip, otherwise known as a circumnavigation, occurred within the last decade, and in just the last five years, trawlers have really started to catch on. My guess is that over the next decade we will start to see sailboat sales decline rapidly and sales of trawlers pick up – for people interested in retiring and seeing the world via a boat.

Anyway.… That's why we're going so slow… (and besides – once you are retired, why rush to get anywhere?)

P.S. - I received several enquiries from people asking what we do at night. The answer is, we keep on going. I'm wiped out after a long day. I'll explain how our 24-hour "watch" system works sometime in the next few days. We're tying it down now.

<u>Day 6 - Fort Lauderdale</u>

Preparations continue…

This morning was spent in a class on diesel engine troubleshooting. Sans Souci actually has four diesel engines aboard: the main engine, the backup (or, wing) engine, and two generators: a 12kw and a 15kw. Much of the discussion today was devoted to engine room checks. Several times per day, while underway, we will be going into the engine room to inspect the various engines and other systems. There is a LOT that can go wrong. My favorite comment of the day was when the representative from Lugger (which manufactures the engines aboard Sans Souci) said that special attention should be paid to the engine mounts. He said that whereas engine mounts shouldn't be a problem, and wouldn't be under normal circumstances, these are NOT normal circumstances. He said: "This is not a Sunday day cruise. Those engine mounts will be carrying a 3,000 pound load, which is being slammed violently from side to side, and pitching forward and back, for days on end." The seriousness with which he said, and pantomimed this, had my stomach complaining already. We discussed how to spot wear in belts, chafing of wires and hoses, how to spot exhaust leaks, bleed the fuel system, etc. Roberta was a true champ and sat through all of this – constantly elbowing me, saying "did you write that down?" or "Do we have one of those?" I assured her that not only did we have several of those (various diagnostic devices), but I was also writing things down as fast as I could.

Although - I did forget to write about yesterday's radar class, so I'll highlight a few things from it here. This was a very worthwhile class. At the class they passed out a great book on Radar usage, which I also plan on reading. There were several surprises, at least for me. For instance, we have a 72-mile radar – which I assumed meant we could "see" boats 72 miles away. Not true. The curvature of the earth kicks in long before this and stops the radar from seeing other boats. I've always assumed we had a few hours of notice before being surprised by another boat (or, an oil tanker) out at sea. I should know by now, that "assumed" is one of the most dangerous words in the English language. Here are the facts: There is a math equation that provides the maximum distance your radar can see, and it's much less that you might think. I don't have the formula here in front of me, but I remember that it took into account the height above water level for your boat, and also for the object you are trying to see. Assuming two normal 50' boats, this distance is around 6 miles. This means that a boat approaching you at 20 knots would only appear on radar for about 20 minutes prior to reaching you. If you are running close to shore, you might be able to spot mountains from 50 miles out – but, mountains are usually not a factor while at sea. Its other boats and floating logs that I worry about.

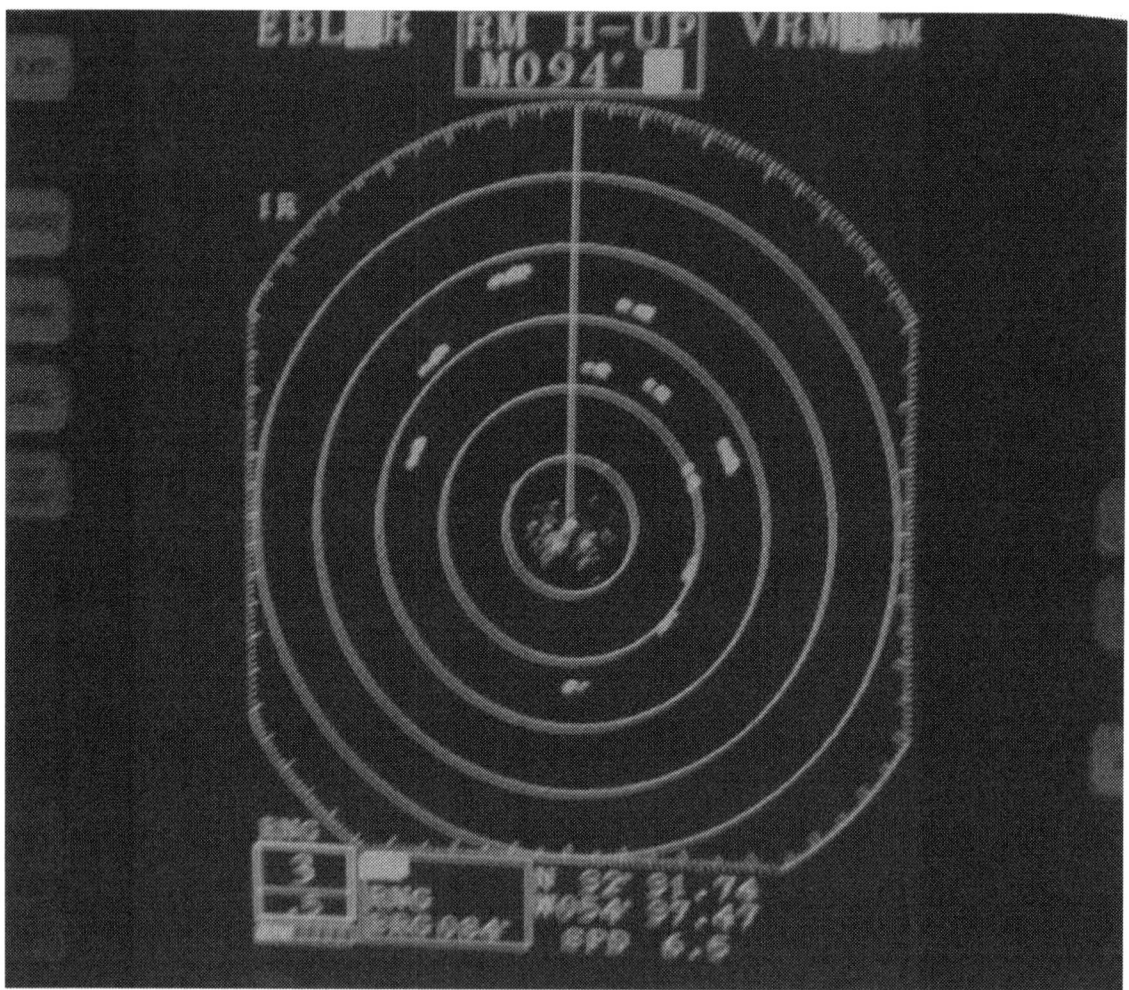

Radar image showing multiple "targets" representing other boats in the rally.

We also discussed how to adjust your radar for maximum visibility. Once again, there were several handy tips. For instance, most radars have a mode called "ES" that they say many people leave on, without really understanding what it does. I confess that I had never heard of it. The ES processor causes very small objects to be amplified on the radar, so that they are easier to spot. Normally this is beneficial. For instance, a small fishing boat might show up on the radar as a single dot, and be too small for you to notice. The ES processor would automatically scale this up to something that can easily be seen. This is not necessarily a good thing when it rains. The raindrops, and resulting splashes, get amplified on the radar. The radar is trying to help us see them better. I've noticed that when squalls are coming in (storms), I have a miserable time seeing anything in the radar. I'm planning to do some experimenting during this trip with various options on the radar to see if I can't materially improve what I am seeing.

Meanwhile back on the boat...

We're having more electronics problems than I would like. We've been fighting problems with our hailer all week (the loud speaker system which is handy for barking orders to the crew during docking). We had an electronics guy onboard today who identified our problem as being with the microphone. He also spotted that the microphone on the VHF radio isn't working. And, then they found, and fixed, a problem with the single side band radio. I spent the afternoon troubleshooting problems with our satellite internet connection. (Note: check out the picture on this site of all of us using the wireless network! We're sharing a 40k bad satellite connection eight ways – but

thrilled to do so. As far as I know, we're the only boat in the whole rally that can actually surf the internet) Our last semi-major issue has been with one of the fuel tanks. We have five fuel tanks, all but one of which have fuel gauges on them. To read the tank without a gauge, you look at a little thermometer, which is mounted on the side. This sounds easy, but is nearly  impossible. The tank is mounted behind the starboard generator, and you need to crawl and use a mirror to see it. We have five tanks, so I always just ignored that one tank. On this trip, we'll not only be using all five tanks, but I'm also thinking to put fuel into a 100 gallon extra tank I have on board for used oil. Rip was still fixing the site gauge on the fifth tank when I spoke with him at 10:30pm tonight. With 3,000+ miles to go, you can't have too much fuel aboard. Who knows what the ocean has in mind for us?

As I look back on today, I can't escape mentioning Rip, our captain. For those of you who don't know the full story, I believe that our boat is the only boat that has a captain along. Roberta and I have had boats our entire life, and have run the boat ourselves for the last four summers in the Mediterranean. Having said that, if I were to rank myself, I believe that I am not up to the same level of experience as many of the boaters here. My idea of great boating is a six to ten hour cruise to an island, where we drop anchor, swim / hang out for a couple days, after which we pull the anchor and boat our way to the next island. If the weather looks bad, we stay in port.

Other than a three-day trip when we first took delivery of Sans Souci five years ago, we've never run the boat for more than 10-12 hours at a stretch. By some standards we are experts, having had boats all our adult lives, and cruised extensively in the U.S. and Europe, but this is not coastal cruising. Crossing the Atlantic Ocean is the real thing. It's the big leagues. There is no safer way to cross the Atlantic in a small boat than to do it aboard a Nordhavn in the company of several other boats. For our first crossing, I thought it would make sense to have a veteran skipper in command – with the caveat that this is a training mission for us. Roberta and I will run the boat as much as any other member of the crew. If the oil needs changed, I want to be there with a wrench in my hand. Yes – we are out of place to have a skipper on board, especially given the fact that we have run the boat for years alone – but, for this particular run, I'd much rather be safe than sorry.

With that background, I noticed that Rip was looking a bit ragged today. He hasn't said a word, and I could be way off base. But, it's my sense that he is having some tough days. Traditionally, on a boat, the captain has a crew he can depend on. That isn't completely true in this case. Of the eight people who are aboard during the first leg, two are PAE employees who are not being paid (at least not by Rip or I). One of them is

Dan Streech, who is the CEO of Nordhavn, the manufacturer of the boat. Also aboard is Christian Fittipaldi, a friend of Dan's, who is a Nascar driver. Next up is Saint John O'Neil Dunne, an emergency medical technician who is participating in the rally, who came to us via Nordhavn. Then we have Phil, who Roberta and I hired to be the boat's chef. That leaves Rip, our Captain. As you can see, if you look closely at the first part of this paragraph, none of these people were recruited by Rip to be his crew. Those of you who have ever tried to manage a loosely assembled team know how hard it can be. There is a lot of work that has to occur to get the boat ready, and Rip has a crew that is hard for him to manage. Simple things like loading equipment onto the boat can be challenging when there is no one around who you can clearly give orders to. Rip has done an amazing job of pulling things together. Hopefully, once we leave shore things will get simpler for everyone.

I am not planning to do an update tomorrow. The boat is essentially ready to go. We'll be taking it out briefly to take on fuel, but that's about it for excitement. There is a big dinner to honor the "slow group" of boats that leaves on Sunday morning. We don't leave until Monday – but as we will be moving faster, the plan is for us to arrive together in Bermuda. It will be a strange feeling watching half our fleet vanish into the ocean on Sunday, and know that we follow them 24 hours later. I will definitely have pictures on the website (http://www.trawlerweb.com). Unfortunately, the weather has decided to make our send-off a bit more interesting as thundershowers are predicted for the next few days.

Days 7 and 8 - Fort Lauderdale

It's departure day for the Division 2 boats. We have split into two divisions, Division 1, which departs tomorrow, and Division 2 that departed at 3:00pm EST today.

This morning started with a 10:00am Captains briefing. What follows are a few highlights from that briefing:

> The Flagship, traveling independently, is a Nordhavn 57, Atlantic Escort

> Our boat, Sans Souci, is the Division 1 escort vessel

> Division 2 is lead by Autumn Wind, another Nordhavn 62

> The weather report from Fort Lauderdale to Bermuda looks good. The first 12 hours are expected to be the worst as the boats proceed north to go around the Bahamas. Waves are estimated at 5 - 7 feet, with an average of 7 seconds of separation, descending to 2 - 4 feet as we approach Bermuda.

> The doctor reviewed with us the process for dealing with medical emergencies. It was made clear that if weather conditions are such that support vessels cannot approach a boat in distress without endangering additional persons, the distressed boat will be on its own.

> We reviewed the communications plan (twice daily roll calls, radios always on channel 16, single side band on 1282)

> We went through the arrival procedures in Bermuda

> We will be running in the following formation: each boat will run initially ¼ mile behind and to the port side of the boat in front of it. Our departure will be filmed from a helicopter, so we want to look sharp (as we are being beat up by the waves).

1) Division 1 (Fast Boats – Mostly Nordhavn 57's and 62's)
   - #18 Sans Souci
   - #16 Grey Pearl
   - #15 Sea Fox

32

- #14 Emeritus
- #12 Goleen
- #11 Que Linda
- #19 Crosser
2) Division 2 (Slow boats – mostly Nordhavn 46's)
  - #20 Atlantic Escort
  - #17 Autumn Wind
  - #10 Four Across
  - #9 Sundog
  - #8 Strickly For Fun
  - #2 Satchmo
  - #3 Envoy
  - #4 Egret
  - #6 Stargazer
  - #5 World Odd@Sea
  - #1 Uno Mas
- ➤ During the day, it's ok to run close together, but at night we should spread out.
- ➤ There will be another meeting tomorrow morning for the Division 1 boats

The departure was almost delayed when a giant cruise ship caught fire, just off shore, and had to be towed into the port. We were listening to the action on the radio, and it became quite exciting when the towropes snapped, and also when the captain of the cruise ship admitted that the boat did not have a fire suppression system in the engine room.

Roberta and I watched the boats depart, until the last of them was out of site. The boats will be motoring nearly 100 miles north before making the turn to the east to go around the Bahamas. I'm not sure why, but I put on music as we were watching – the soundtrack to Titanic. It was almost certainly in poor taste, and not one of my brighter moves...

Division 2 departs from Ft. Lauderdale.

Autumn Wind leads Division 2 out to sea.

Within 30 minutes of departure, we had our first incident. Autumn Wind, the escort boat for Division 2, a Nordhavn 62, suddenly had to shut down. Massive amounts of Diesel fuel was spraying everywhere in the engine room. A couple of days ago, we had discussed that fuel frequently seems to be the culprit when things go wrong. I haven't heard the whole story yet, but my understanding is that one of the return lines, bringing unburned diesel back to the tanks from the engine, had inadvertently been left closed. All of the hot, unburned fuel that wasn't consumed by the engine, was being pumped under high pressure into a hose that was capped. Fortunately, the crew of Autumn Wind was able to quickly diagnose the problem, make the repairs and resume their place in line. I feel very sorry for whoever had to spend hours, in a sloppy sea, mopping up the mess in the engine room. Autumn Wind, like Sans Souci, has a small backup engine. My assumption is that they were able to slow down and run on it, while making repairs.

Five N46's head out to sea.

As I type this, I am uploading a lot of new pictures to the site, mostly of the boats leaving the dock. I had staked out a place from which to take pictures of the departing boats, but everyone took off at least 30 minutes early, and I missed the great shots. The pictures of the departure can be found on the http://www.trawlerweb.com/ website under the **Nordhavn Rally** menu item. From there, select **Photos – Part I** followed by **Departure**.

The afternoon was spent doing some final tweaking on electronics, and washing the boat. We put a net across the back of the boat so that Shelby (our dog) won't fall off. I'm looking out the window now watching the Division 2 boats running about a mile off shore. They really look like they are getting tossed around. The wind is supposed to subside a bit over the next 24 hours. I have my fingers crossed.

Tonight, we went to dinner in Miami with the whole crew, with a stop by Christian Fittipaldi's house, where Rip made his final departure speech to the crew. We spent an hour discussing man overboard procedures, and reiterating about 20 times that safety is priority #1.

Tomorrow morning will be busy with final details. There will be a kick off briefing, which I assume will be largely redundant to the briefing this morning. I have to return our rental car, etc. My guess is that I won't send another update until we are at sea.

P.S. - In Friday's e-mail I mentioned that there is a correlation between the length of a boat, and its maximum speed (on full-displacement boats). Here's the formula: maximum speed = 1.3 x the square root of the length of the boat at the water line.

Day 9 - We are at sea!!!!

We have been at sea for about four hours now. I uploaded four pictures from our departure, which can be found on the website http://www.trawlerweb.com – under the **Nordhavn Rally** menu item. From there, select **Photos – Part I** followed by **Departure - May 17th, 2004 – Division One**.

Division 1 departs Ft. Lauderdale.

Autumn Wind surfs down a wave.

Thus far, we have no problems. Two of the boats in Division 2 have reported problems, although nothing serious. One of the boats has a broken stabilizer. They were able to disconnect one of the two stabilizers, and just run on one. One other boat has a leak in the stabilizer system, which they are watching closely. Here aboard Sans Souci, all is well. I'm having a heck of a time typing while getting slammed from side to side. Hopefully, the wind will die down at some point and I can write more.

Our departure from the bay was a bit of a mess. We were supposed to get onto our course and then line up for picture taking. However, Sans Souci, as the lead boat, goofed in setting our course, and veered way off course to the east. Some of the boats were good soldiers and followed us deeper to sea, others stubbornly held to the previously agreed to heading. This caused a bit of anarchy as we briefly insisted that the error was theirs, and they insisted that the error was ours. We were quite embarrassed when we turned out to be the guilty party. All of you reading this will now know "the rest of the story" when you see the pictures someday (that were taken by the helicopter) and Sans Souci is NOT in lead, as we had anticipated. Oops....

Helicopter hovers ahead of Sans Souci.

We've been lucky so far − no one sick, and dinner went well. I experimented with throwing my paper plate overboard, and discovered that throwing a Frisbee shaped object loaded with food is best done downwind. Double oops...

Otherwise all is well. We just had the roll call, and everyone reported in. We're all talking to each other frequently, as it's totally dark, and the waves are too high for the radar to be as effective as I'd like. We had a bit of excitement during the roll call when we discovered that the single side band radio was interfering with the autopilot. None of us knows why, but the boat would make a hard turn to starboard every time that we pressed transmit on the SSB!

More later, when things calm down (hopefully!)

Day 10 – En- route to Bermuda

It is now Tuesday morning, and all is well.

We just did a fire drill as Roberta rang us up to let us know that the master stateroom was full of smoke! That immediately caught everyone's attention. When we opened the door into the master cabin, there was indeed white smoke. Rip launched himself into the engine room, and the rest of us each grabbed a different part of the boat. I checked behind the electric panels and checked the batteries. The battery banks around the boat are located under beds and floors. The good news is that after 15 minutes of searching we were left scratching our heads. Our best guess is that somehow the air conditioning system in the master cabin is sucking exhaust fumes from the engine compartment. We just had the exhaust from the main engine checked for leaks, and I believe they put new wrapping around the exhaust. Perhaps we have developed a small exhaust leak? We couldn't find one, but we'll be watching it VERY closely now. We've now given up the search and opened the door to the master stateroom to get rid of the smoke smell.

It is now 15 minutes beyond when I wrote the last paragraph. The smell and smoke came back with a vengeance. We all rushed back to our stations, and this time we found the problem. The 24-volt alternator was frying!

I'm a software person, not hardware, so if you will keep that thought in mind, I'll do my best to give the readers of this log enough information to understand what happened and why.

Sans Souci has a constant need for electricity. We have all the ships electronics, lighting, refrigerators, air conditioners, electrical outlets – even a power-hungry espresso machine. Just prior to this trip, I had the boat rewired to solve problems with the electrical system. The boat had been in Europe where the electrical standards are different than the U.S. In order to keep the boat running, I had to use shore power to run a European battery charger. This worked when we were in port, but when at sea, I had to depend on the invertors.

So, what you might ask, are the invertors?

An inverter converts DC current into 110v AC current. The boat requires a combination of 12v DC power, similar to what you run in your car, and 110v alternating current – identical to what you have at home. Unless we are in port somewhere, our only option for getting 110v electricity (actually ANY electricity) is to make it ourselves. Perhaps you have noticed that your car battery, if the car isn't run for a few weeks, will run down. This is because the alternator, which generates electricity, requires the car's engine to be running to enable it to work. There is a belt attached to the front of your car's motor, which is then attached to the alternator. When the alternator spins it generates 12v (or, in the case of Sans Souci, 24v) DC current.

And what are generators?

Sans Souci is equipped with multiple alternators, and two invertors. We also have the ability to generate our own 110v AC current directly, via generators. A generator is a completely separate diesel engine that has a self-contained alternator and inverter such that it is a "plug and play" solution for generating 110v electricity. This 110v electricity can then be used to power the boat AND to power battery chargers, which provide the 12v and 24v DC needs of the boat.

At the briefing prior to our voyage, it was said that one way to diagnose any problem aboard a ship is to think of it as a sprinkler system, like you have in your front yard. You have a source of water, and then a distribution system that delivers the water to where it is needed – typically the sprinkler heads. If you notice a sprinkler head that isn't spraying water, you check the source to see if the water is coming in, and then you start tracing the system to find out where the water that should be flowing, is escaping from the system. Sans Souci has many systems that can be thought of in this way - the fuel system, the water cooling system, the fresh water system, the electrical system, the hydraulic system, and who can forget one of the most important of all – the septic system!

Aboard Sans Souci, the electrical system has MANY possible sources: the batteries, the 12-volt alternators, the 24-volt alternator, the 110v AC generators, and shore power (when we are in a marina). All of these sources of power feed into the invertors, which perform a bit of a traffic cop function on the AC side of things. The invertors are intelligent. They look at all the potential sources of power and make decisions about where to get power from, and what to do with it. For instance, if shore power is connected to the boat, then this is given priority #1 to power the boat, and all other sources of power are ignored. In the absence of shore power, if the generators are running, the inverter is smart enough to stop inverting, and just use the electricity put out by the generator. When the generators aren't running, the inverter shifts its thinking towards the alternators.

Our current problem is that we do not have shore power, and the generators aren't running, so, the inverter made the decision to take 100% of the boat's power needs from the 24-volt alternator. This is fine, so long as you don't try to take more electricity from the alternator than it has to give. In our case, we overloaded the alternator. The system was sized such that we can do essentially everything we want to do using just the 24v alternator. That said, we have been running three large air conditioning units, and weren't sure how to measure the amount of power drain we were pulling from the alternator. I consider this an important lesson learned. Mickey Smith, the engineer behind the re-engineering of San Souci's electrical system, did give me a walk-though of the boats electrical system. Another lesson I should have learned is to write things down. When Mickey walked me through the systems, everything seemed simple and obvious. Now that he is 150 miles away, nothing seems obvious.

Which brings us to the problem at hand. We asked the alternator to produce more electricity than it was capable of producing. The alternator tried to make us happy by working harder and harder, until it started burning itself up. Once we determined what was happening, we shut down the alternator, and fired up a generator. However, nothing on a boat is ever as easy as it sounds. The alternator in question takes its power from a device (called a PTO, which I assume means Power Take Off) attached to the back of the engine. Our first reaction was to shut down the PTO, but within seconds we realized that this would be a dumb move. The PTO on the back of the engine is also used to power the hydraulic system, which runs the water pump that cools the stabilizer system. In trying to solve our electrical problem, we were putting our water-cooling system and stabilizer systems in jeopardy. We reacted immediately and found a cut out for the generator at the front of the engine room (on the voltage regulator for the alternator).

Shutting down the alternator requires us to bring a generator on line. This is literally as simple as pressing a button. This raises the further question of why we don't just run the generator all the time. The answer is that generators consume fuel. We're not sure exactly how much, our sense is somewhere around one gallon per hour. That means nothing on this run, but a great deal on our run from Bermuda to the Azores. I'm still not completely comfortable with the math on our major crossing. We have to run 1,800 miles and have 2,100 gallons of fuel on board. At 8.5 knots, we'll be running around 210 hours, and are currently consuming over 9 gallons of fuel per hour. If you divide these numbers, the result is that we are cutting it closer than I'd like. All will be well if nothing goes wrong – but, on a boat, things do go wrong from time to time. I'd like to make the big pass without using the generators at all. This certainly means no usage, or limited usage of the air conditioners, which will not be popular. In rough water we close all hatches, doors, portholes, etc – to keep water out of the boat. Unfortunately, this also keeps air out. Enough gets in such that we can breathe, but it's at best an "adequate" airflow. We are currently discussing how to put extra fuel onboard for the big trip. There is one tank on board that is reserved for putting old, used, engine oil. We think this tank holds 200 gallons, and are now planning to put supplemental fuel into this tank. Alternately, we can always cut our fuel consumption by slowing down. Even a 1 mph drop in speed can result in a 10% fuel savings.

Our top question now is whether or not the alternator can now be brought back on line, or if we have destroyed it. We've brought it back online a couple of times, and it does seem to be working. We need to make a decision so we know whether or not to fly parts to Bermuda. I'll also sleep better once I've spoken with Mickey and gotten a better handle on how to measure electrical consumption. I guarantee that our days as electrical bingers are in the past.

On to other issues...

Most people are holding up well. Our chef Phil is looking green. I noticed our EMT (St. John) running through the hallways with medical supplies in hand. He mentioned yesterday that he has a refrigerator full of suppositories should the pills not work. Yuck. Sea Fox, the Krogen 58, has taken to referring to itself as the hospital ship. They have several people who are "down" with seasickness.

And, in that vein...

Before we left dock, I went aboard the Nordhavn 47, Strickly for Fun. It's a new boat, and I couldn't help noticing immediately that everything is being kept immaculate – even the bathroom floors. As part of their efforts to keep the boat in pristine condition, there is a very official sign posted in all heads that reads: "Gentleman are kindly requested to keep seated throughout the entire performance." I'll let you figure it out.

And continuing on the lighter side...

Each boat seems to be trying to express its individuality through their radio communications. One boat called out last night to invite us all over for a cocktail party (they were kidding unfortunately). One Nordhavn, a single engine boat, announced that they were now running on two engines and might fire up a third to go even faster. There was also a lot of discussion as we attempted to decide on which boat would take the lead in mooning the helicopter. No one ever went for it. Our hope was that if the documentary had an "R" rating it might be a lot more fun to watch.

And now returning to the serious issues...

During our battle with the smoke, we dropped the ball on filming. Bruce Kessler, our filmmaker, will be disappointed with us. I did briefly film a discussion of Dan and Rip where they were discussing the possible roots of our problems, but put away the camera about 30 seconds later. I felt like a total loser standing there with a film camera as smoke floated around me. Oh well... The other important lesson we all learned is that you must NEVER stop looking for a problem until you find it. We knew there was smoke, and made a decision to ignore it. That was a bad decision that shall not be repeated.

Lastly...

The wind is better today, but the seas are far from calm. We are running straight into the wind with non-stop 4-6 foot waves. The weather report is saying that the waves are going to continue for many days to come. Crap.

Hopefully today will be a bit calmer on the crew front. Yesterday, everyone's tempers were on edge. Some comments were made in anger, and some feelings may have been hurt, although you'd never know it today. Now that our excitement has passed, everyone has scattered around the boat to read and enjoy.

The Dan Streech Report #1

We have been at sea for about 27 hours now and are beginning to settle down to a routine.

The departure from Ft. Lauderdale was CHAOTIC to say the least. We had a well-rehearsed departure plan, which had been discussed in several meetings. It was important to leave in a prearranged formation because there were 3 different helicopters in the air for magazines and the documentary.

While circling in the turning basin, we delayed the departure several times waiting for traffic to clear while the helicopters were hovering. Just as we were committed to the path towards the harbor entrance, we realized that a ship with assisting tugs was entering and coming towards us. We all squeezed past the ship (which was in the middle of the channel) and entered the very choppy and bumpy Atlantic. Right away, things went awry. We (Sans Souci) were to be the lead boat, but we headed out on the wrong course due to a temporary case of CRS. Some followed us, and some proceeded on the correct course. Our formation was thus mixed up. After 30 minutes or so, we got reformatted and back into a proper line-up - except Sans Souci ended up in second place.

The filming commenced and I am sure that some incredible shots were taken as the brave fleet pounded into the 6-foot seas. The helicopter pilots are amazingly skilled. With a 20-knot head wind, they were flying sideways within 50 feet of the boat. The confusion and noise together with multiple radios and a cell phone call caused a case of TMI (Too Much Information). Also, I should add that at the very crescendo of the chaos, the refrigerator in the pilothouse flew open and a dozen soda cans poured out. One of them exploded and drenched us. Undaunted, we stayed the course and smiled for the cameras....

After a bumpy 24 mile ride into head seas to our first way point, we cracked off for a more comfortable ride to our next way point about 160 miles north. This gave the crew a chance to relax and settle in.

We are quite pampered aboard Sans Souci with 3 professional crewmen.

Rip Knot (I'm not kidding) is our courageous Captain. Several years ago, Rip moved Sans Souci from Seattle to Florida and later spent time on Sans Souci in Europe.

Phil Strable is our chef and is in charge of the galley. In his real life, Phil is a chef aboard private rail cars, so he is quite comfortable in the spacious galley of Sans Souci. He is very gracious and "at our service" 24 hours per day. Last night's chicken Caesar salad and this morning's scrambled eggs and bacon were served with a smile. Phil's mysterious persona is enhanced by his collection of brightly colored tattoos…

Our EMT is St. John O'Neil-Dunne. "Singen" is a student from Tulane with a wry sense of humor and is a look alike for Kramer on Seinfeld (especially the hair). Singen took great delight in telling us that extreme seasickness is best cured with suppositories and that he has them safely stored in the freezer…

Also aboard are:

Owners Ken and Roberta Williams. Ken and Roberta purchased Sans Souci 6 years ago after selling their software company. They have used their boat in the Pacific Northwest, Mexico, Florida and Europe, but until now have not made any open ocean passages. They are a lovely couple and easy to get along with. With their software background, they are very "techy" and thus have Sans Souci equipped with some nice gadgets. The gadget I like best is the "always on" Internet connection purchased thru Stratos net. That Internet connection is distributed throughout the boat by a common wireless system, so I can use my laptop anywhere on the boat and get my e-mail. Is that good? The cost of the Internet connection is based on usage and will probably amount to several thousand dollars or more by the end of the passage.

Christian Fittipaldi. Christian is a world-renowned race driver who has competed in Formula 1, CART and NASCAR and most recently was a winner in the 24 hours of Daytona. As a racing fan, I had followed Christian's career for many years before meeting him when he called our Dana Point office several years ago with interest in a Nordhavn. Christian and I have formed a friendship and Marcia and I have been his VIP guests at several races. Christian has owned several boats and is very passionate about boating and the sea, but until now has not made an offshore passage. If Christian gets hooked on passage making, we already have the headline of the ad figured out… "Fast guy learns to go slow" or something like that.

Garret Severen. Garret is a fine young man who has worked for PAE for about 3 years. He started with the commissioning crew on the docks in Dana Point and moved to Stuart Florida when we opened the office there. Garret is "First Mate" aboard San Souci and as part of the PAE response team is prepared to help with problems on any of the boats in the fleet. A small inflatable is at the ready to take Garret and the EMT to the other boats if an "event" takes place in open ocean.

SEVERAL HOURS LATER...

I just finished a great two-hour afternoon nap and am gradually getting caught up on my sleep. When Marcia and I flew out to Florida on a Jet Blue "red eye", I lost one night of sleep and couldn't ever seem to catch up during the busy week in Ft. Lauderdale prior to departure.

The seven boats in our group have drifted apart somewhat. All but Emeritus are within radar and VHF range. Emeritus turned to starboard last night and has taken a different track. When Emeritus didn't answer this morning's radio roll call, we called them on the satellite telephone and found that they were 90 miles from us (VHF radio range is about 30 miles). We conduct a roll call each day on the radio at 8:00AM and 8:00PM to check on the condition of each boat. It is now about 4:30 PM, and afternoon will soon turn to evening. All of the boats will close in a little for the night. It is very comforting to look out and see your compatriot's running lights.

We cooked our main 24V alternator today in a smoky event. At this point, we are not quite sure what happened but think that it might be the regulator. Despite the fact that parts of it were glowing red, we think that it might still work. Mickey Smith and I are going to have a post mortem e-mail chat about it later to try to figure out what happened.

In a radio chat with Seafox, we learned that Tom Selman has been battling with seasickness. We told him that we would launch the boat and rush over with the suppositories. He has miraculously recovered.

The seas have calmed somewhat and a lovely long swell is starting to dominate. Chef Phil is going to produce a magnificent dinner tonight.

Best Regards from the happy ship San Souci,

Dan Streech

Day 11 - Three more days to Bermuda

The seas have calmed down. It's still tough to walk or read, but overall we're quite happy, and hoping it stays this way.

We heard last night that another of our boats, Sea Fox, lost a stabilizer. For those that don't know what stabilizers are, here's a bit of background:

Stabilizers are small "wings" that protrude from the side of the boat, about three feet beneath the surface. When you see a boat out of water the stabilizers are easy to spot. They look like short wings that one might see on an airplane. On Sans Souci, they protrude approximately six feet on each side. Unlike airplane wings, the entire fin (the nautical word for the wings) moves to counteract the movement of the boat. The stabilizers do nothing to prevent the nose of the boat from rising and falling, but can greatly diminish side-to-side rolling. The fins are controlled by their own computer and gyroscope. Aboard Sans Souci, we do nothing to manage the stabilizers other than to turn them on. When we have guests on the boat, it's always fun to turn the stabilizers off for a minute in rough seas. It only takes a few minutes without the stabilizers for our guests to understand why they are amongst the more critical components on the boat.

Just as stabilizers can make your life comfortable when they work, they can make it hell when they don't. Here on Sans Souci, when we hear reports about boats that have "lost a fin", we know that what we are hearing is a very condensed version of what really happened. Performing surgery in the hot engine room of a moving boat is serious stuff. My guess is that in order to work on the stabilizers, the first step is to shut off the stabilizers – which causes even more rolling about. I overheard Dan's reaction when he first heard that one of our boats was going to try to "pin a fin" (disable it). He said - "I wish them luck, because if you aren't very careful, you can easily lose a finger" The fins are trying to stabilize boats that are extremely heavy. Sans Souci weighs 120,000 pounds. To access the stabilizers you need to crawl your way through a hot, constantly rolling, engine room. Then you need to diagnose the problem, and try to take one fin offline in such a way (I would assume) that it can free float, while the other can be brought back on line. Dan assures me that San Souci's stabilizers are of a type that are much less likely to fail.

During the night, we had a close encounter with another boat from our own group (whose name I shall not reveal). We still do not know the whole story, but last night at about 2:00am they suddenly shifted course to start coming straight at us. Garret and St. John were on watch and noticed the other boat coming closer. Normally at night, we run with at least a mile of separation from each other, for safety reasons. When the other boat closed to under a third of a mile, and a collision was starting to look possible, Garret took prompt action. Above Sans Souci we have a powerful searchlight. Garret pointed it at the other boat's pilothouse and hit the search beam. That got their attention and they immediately turned away from us. I asked him why he didn't call them on the radio, and he just shrugged.

For this morning's roll call, Dan decided to add a little more drama. We have an XM Radio onboard, with 120 channels. We found one with just the right type of music, and after transmitting a burst of loud rock music, Dan came on the radio to do his best "Good Morning Vietnam!" impersonation.

During the roll call we discovered that the slow division of boats is currently about 90 miles ahead of us. They were 110 miles ahead yesterday. We're closing on them at the rate of slightly over 1 mile per hour. Once we catch them, we'll hand the helm over to Christian Fittipaldi, our Nascar driver, so that we can appropriately blast by them. As soon as we have them looking at the back of our boats, we'll strategize further action. Hopefully they have a sense of humor…

Several people have sent us e-mail. To all of them I say thank you! Several have asked for more pictures. I'll try to make that a priority this afternoon. Unfortunately, our internet connection isn't good for much beyond text. I did manage to upload four pictures right after we left shore, but do not know if I can repeat that success. If I am successful in uploading, I'll put the pictures under the **Nordhavn Rally | Photos – Part I** section, with a heading that says **May 18 – 22 – Fort Lauderdale to Bermuda**. Once we get to Bermuda and get a high-speed internet connection, I'll post MANY more pictures. If anyone sees a picture that they would like at much higher resolution, let me know. I'm shooting with an 11 mega pixel camera and have been reducing the images for upload to the website. Once I get to Bermuda, my plan is to take my favorite shots and post them in full resolution.

Ken & Roberta Williams – owners of Sans Souci, and their dog Shelby.

We have eight people on board, which we have divided into three teams of two. The remaining two people are Rip (our captain) and Phil (our chef). Rip has been helping out whenever and wherever needed, and doing most of what needs done in the engine room. We have rotating shifts on watch, with two people in the pilothouse at all times. At night, the watches are three hours, and during the day, four hours. Roberta and I will soon be commencing our 10:00am - 2:00pm watch, after which, we'll be followed by

Roberta at the helm.

Dan and Christian who will take the boat from 2:00pm – 6:00pm, and then finally Garret and St. John who will take the 6:00pm – 10:00pm shift. After this we start again, with Roberta and I doing a three-hour shift from 10:00pm to 1:00am.

The Dan Streech Report #2

We are now in that wonderful "sweet spot" of a passage where routine, comfort and relaxation have taken over. Those prone to seasickness have their sea legs, running jokes and pranks abound and everyone is in their own world of reading, sleeping, fishing, eating, listening to music or playing with their (wretched?) computers. There is no sense of "when do we get there". In many ways, we are there...

Ken works on an update (or is he just playing a game?).

Sans Souci is on a rhumb line course for Bermuda which now lies 530 miles ahead and we will be sipping Pina Colatas at the Bermuda Yacht Club within 3 days. She is running sweet and is perfect in every way. Once again, I am reminded of Jeff Leishman's design genius and Ta Shing's fine craftsmanship as the 5-year-old Sans Souci conquers this open ocean passage with ease.

Our gaggle of boats (6 of us) answered roll call this morning with extra gusto as I suspect the sense of well being has infected the entire fleet. Bob Rothman (the 7th of our group) continues on his own special course and is about 40 miles away. The only known mechanical problem is on Sea Fox. One of their stabilizer fins made "an expensive crunching noise", so that fin was secured and they are running on one fin, which will still give adequate stabilization.

Jim initiates from Escort.

Leishman the Roll Call Atlantic

I spoke with Jim this morning by SSB and got fairly good reception on the 4 meg frequency. His "slower" group of 11 boats are all well and are now about 90 miles ahead of us. We are closing on them at about 1.5 knots, and will thus catch them in about 60 hours.

At this point, it is self evident that the entire group of 18 boats will arrive safely, on time, and together in Bermuda, and that the fundamental concept of NAR is sound. Hats off to the entire NAR planning committee and especially to Jim for making this event possible. Their hard work and attention to detail is paying off big time. I know that history is being made. Thanks also to the participants themselves who have invested their time, money and effort to be a part of this rally. Without them, there would be no rally.

The seas and wind have settled down and are about as good as you can expect on an open ocean passage. As we learned on the ATW (Across the World) in the Nordhavn 40, there is nearly always the "lumpiness" of multiple swell patterns present in open ocean. As long as they are allowed to soften in light wind conditions, the motion of the boat and the speeds are fine.

The sky is bright blue and is dotted with puffy clouds and the crystal clear water (15,000 ft. deep at this location) is a deep cobalt blue. The sun glistening off the deep blue sea is more beautiful than I can describe in words.

Chef Phil continues to be a joy. Last night's dinner was halibut wrapped in fila dough (aka halibut "en croute") and this morning was an especially delicious omelet with ham, bacon and cheese. Could someone check for me and see if a cholesterol reading of 756 is OK?

Contented,

Dan

Position at 1:00PM EST May 19, 2004
30 00.2 N 74.51.9W

For more NAR/Sans Souci news go to http://www.trawlerweb.com. This is a web site maintained by Sans Souci owner Ken Williams. Ken is keeping a daily log of the voyage and is also uploading photos.

Day 12 - En- route to Bermuda - Two days to go!

The quote that best describes boating - "Hours of boredom punctuated by seconds of terror"

After days of bouncing around, Grey Pearl and the rest of the participants enjoy the calm seas.

We're in absolutely calm seas as I write this. Sail boaters would not be happy, but as power boaters, we're loving it. Yesterday we saw our first whales. I saw the spout, and sounded the alert, but then no one else saw anything during the next 30 minutes. Just as people were convincing

themselves that I was crazy, Braun Jones, from Grey Pearl, announced that he had a whale on his port side. Instantly, we all were sighting whales and porpoises in every direction. The calm seas revitalized the crew. Christian and St. John took folding chairs out to the front deck and spent the afternoon sunning and reading. Smiles had become the dominant facial feature. A perfect day!!! Blue skies, sunshine, flat water! Fishing poles are springing from the backside of each boat.

Our boat is very laptop and internet centric. With the flat water, everyone got their laptops out to catch up on e-mail. The pilothouse table didn't have a square inch free for me to plop down my laptop, so I went downstairs. No luck. The downstairs table was wall-to-wall laptops. We had achieved 100% laptop usage! Sans Souci has a wireless network and satellite internet connection. We're all sharing an internet connection that is slower than most dial-up modems, but no one is complaining. I even uploaded a few pictures. If anyone has a particular person or boat they want me to take pictures of, let me know. My original vision was to take thousands of awe-inspiring pictures. Reality has differed. The other boats are separated from us by about a mile. We do feel a sense of team spirit as we talk, via radio, all day – but no great pictures have emerged.

Dinner last night was incredible as usual. Phil is a huge hit on the boat. Last night: Caesar Salad, Mashed Potatoes (both regular and low-carb), Meat Loaf (once again regular and low-carb). Cheese cake and fresh cherries for desert. I've never been much of a Meat Loaf eater, so I fed mine to some hungry fishes, but everyone else raved about it. All signs of discord had evaporated with the high seas. We have a no-alcohol policy here aboard Sans Souci, but I made the decision that one bottle of wine split eight ways couldn't do too much damage. I made a conscious decision not to load any wine aboard ship. We have a few bottles on board that have been here for years. The boat was in France last year, for the hottest summer recorded in many decades. My assumption was that all we had on board was a few bottles of vinegar. I'm now happy to report that at least one bottle did survive.

Our group, Division 1, consists of seven boats, one of which we haven't seen in two days. Emeritus made the decision to split from the group and take a "short cut" across the top of the Bahamas. We've touched base with them once a day via sat phone, but they have consistently been out of VHF radio range. I noted early on that boaters have strong independent personalities and each day reinforces that opinion.

Our daily update had nothing but good news. No new mechanical problems. No one is seasick. In Division 2, they dropped a tender (dinghy) and were traveling from boat to boat, transferring crew. They are talking about fishing from a tender today. Interestingly, we have closed to within 45 miles of the Division 2 boats. By tomorrow we could be close enough to see them.

We are still running without an alternator. To get by, we are running a generator every few hours to keep the batteries charged. My hope is that a new alternator will be waiting for us in Bermuda. I'm still nervous about our fuel consumption, and have set a goal to make the long passage from Bermuda to the Azores without running the generators. We have two water makers on board; a small one that only makes about 10 gallons an hour, and a large one that consumes roughly the same amount of electricity as Las Vegas at the height of tourist season. I've been running the little water maker around the clock for the past few days, and it seems to be keeping up! If we continue to run the little water maker non-stop, and our new alternator shows up, the generators will get some serious rest – and we'll arrive in the Azores with a huge fuel surplus.

Lastly, we had a small bit of excitement last night – which helps explain why you always need to be on your guard aboard a boat. At around 4:00 am, during Garret's and St. John's watch, Grey Pearl called to say that we had a UFO dead ahead (Unidentified Floating Object). It did not show on our radar, but was coming at us from about two miles out, and was moving at .5 miles per hour. Rip kicked off the trip by telling us a story, which may or may not be true, but is likely to have been in our watch team's minds at the moment. The Atlantic is constantly being crossed by freighters, which carry railroad-sized containers on deck. Usually the ships arrive at their destination with all containers exactly where they were put, but from time to time, during a storm, some fall off. In Rip's story, most of these sink, but some of them don't. The others are floating just below the surface waiting for us. This particular UFO refused to reveal itself, in spite of our team's scouring the ocean with a giant searchlight. They were guided by radio from other boats whose radar did show the UFO. As Murphy's Law would predict, this is the exact moment that our autopilot chose to go crazy. I had noted on my watch earlier in the evening that the autopilot had developed a nasty habit of making giant "S" turns. It

Sans Souci Pilothouse.

would suddenly veer left, only to veer to the right a few minutes later. Sans Souci does have a steering wheel, but it really isn't meant to be used under normal cruising conditions. The computer does a far better job steering than the average human. Theoretically, we could make an entire passage with just hand steering, but it wouldn't be much fun, or very pretty. Sans Souci has a backup autopilot, so I made the switch to the backup, and alerted the incoming watch team to the problem (Dan and Christian). During their shift all was well, but Garret and St. John discovered that this would change at the worst possible moment. Sans Souci made up its own mind that an unscheduled right turn would be good. This put us on a course to intercept Goleen. Instantaneously, Goleen was on the radio to announce that we had invaded their "space." Garret and St.

John handled all of this without missing a beat. The autopilot was brought offline immediately, and they were able to circumnavigate the mysterious UFO, which still remains unidentified. We are now running with the autopilot, but in a completely different mode. Hopefully it holds no further surprises for us. Mr. Kessler, our filmmaker, will be disappointed to hear that no one grabbed a camera (not that a picture of an invisible object is very exciting…)

I'm going to work now on uploading a few more pictures. As I type this, Grey Pearl is within a hundred yards of us on the starboard side, with Crosser just behind. Time to get the camera out!

Talk to you tomorrow!

The Dan Streech Report #3

Each day just gets better… It is Thursday morning as I begin to write this. We are cruising along on absolutely glassy seas and Jimmy Buffet is playing on the sound system.
Crosser glides through the glass-like seas.

Few things in this world can match the simple wonderful pleasure of a night watch in calm seas. My watch last night was from midnight to 3:00 AM. The bridge of Sans Souci was set for night running and the various screens, gauges, plotter, GPS units etc emitted their soft red and green glows. The doors were open and the pleasant 75-degree breezes rustled the papers from time to time. Except for the occasional sound of water past the hull, it almost seemed as though Sans Souci were floating on a cloud. Best of all was the music. We have "XM" radio on board and I had it tuned to channel 7 for "70s" music. Every song was perfect for the moment and brought back many memories.

After roll call this morning, the boats came closer together for a photo shoot. About that time Crosser reported whales on their port side. We saw them and turned over to get a closer look. It was a pod of 4 sperm whales and we were able to get right along side of them for quite a long look. I have never seen a sperm whale (that would be Moby Dick) and the site of them diving into the crystal clear water is a memory that I will have forever.

The folks on Sea Fox are having quite a time. They claim to have caught the same fish 3 times. They first reported it last night and claimed it to be 4 feet long and that it got away. They said that they landed it and it slipped thru the scuppers and overboard. We protested that a fish, four feet long, wouldn't fit thru the scuppers, and they then changed their story and said that it jumped through their transom door taking their prized lure with it. They then landed the same fish later and recovered their lure. They decided that it was too big and released it. Then they claimed to have caught the same fish AGAIN. This time they released it again, but not before scolding it and telling it not to bother them any more. See anything "fishy" in that story?

Here's the fish that Sea Fox caught ...four feet? Perhaps they meant four inches!
I should take a moment and introduce our fleet AKA group 1, AKA the "fast" boats. We consist of:

Sans Souci – A Nordhavn 62 Hull #9 with a crew of 8, including Ken and Roberta Williams and your author.

Crosser - A Monk-McQueen 90 with a crew of 9.

Grey Pearl – A Nordhavn 62 Hull#8, with a crew of 5, including owners Braun and Tina Jones.

Sea Fox - A Krogen 58 with a crew of 6, including owner Dennis Fox and VIP guests Kurt Krogen and Tom Selman. Tom is owner of a Nordhavn 50 in his other life.

Goleen – A Nordhavn 57 Hull#29, with a crew of 4, including owners Chris Samuelson and the lovely Sonia.

Emeritus – A Nordhavn 57 Hull#21, with a crew of 4, including owners Bob and Janis Rothman. Unfortunately, Emeritus "turned early" and has not been part of our happy fleet.

It has been really fun and rewarding to see how the dynamics of the fleet have developed. Having never done this before, we didn't know for sure how (or even if) the travel as a fleet would work. As it has turned out, it has been quite easy to stay together. The twice-daily radio roll call is the "campfire" time as we chat and each vessel reports on their situation. Numerous running jokes carry over from time to time and we have gotten to know each other better through these chats. I start the roll call each morning with 30 seconds of rock and roll music and then my best Robin Williams impersonation of "Goooooood Mooorrrrnnnning Group 1!!!!"

At noon today, we had a BIG event - we changed the clocks. We "sprung" forward to Bermuda time so that when we arrive, there won't be any mix-ups.

Go NAR!!!

Dan

Day 13 - Almost to Bermuda

Everyone aboard Sans Souci is likely to remember yesterday for the rest of their lives.

 Those of you who have been to the website have already seen the pictures, so this will be old news, but we had a very close encounter with sperm whales. We stopped the boat when we saw the whales swimming, and were lucky enough to have them swim directly in front of us. We had four sperm whales within a few feet of the boat. The pictures do not do justice to the experience. Everyone was blown away by the experience.

The entire fleet had an incredible day. No reports from anyone of anything except fun and silliness. Sea Fox was on the radio periodically proclaiming their status as fishing gurus. We suspect that we were being fibbed to, but I will dutifully report their claim as it was told to us. Early yesterday they caught a four-foot fish that they threw back as too small, only to have it bite again. They re-returned it to the water with a firm reprimand. Later in the day, the fish came back, but this time it just stole their lure and ran off. Sea Fox asked the rest of our fleet to try to recover their lost lure. I confess that I have expended zero effort on this quest. However, should you see a four foot fish carrying a bright yellow lure, let me know and, I'll pass along its location.

Later in the day, a call came in from Que Linda that their espresso machine had broken and they desperately needed us to stop at the nearest Starbucks. In a true departure from life in Seattle, I realized that there actually are places on earth where it is possible to rotate through all 360 degrees without seeing even one Starbucks. Sans Souci, and our emergency medical technician St. John, did not want to see anyone go through caffeine deprivation, so we immediately fired up our espresso machine, dropped the tender, and sent a crew over to hand deliver steaming-hot lattes to the Que Linda crew, who were waiting for them in their rooftop hot tub. Yes – it was decadent and silly, but it was that kind of day…. Trust me, we're not always like that.

St. John and Garret rush the lattes to Hal & Linda of Que Linda, who enjoy them while sitting in their Hot Tub!

To make the coffee delivery, we had stopped Sans Souci in the middle of the ocean 400 miles from the nearest land. The water was the bluest as I have ever seen it. I have no idea how far beneath the surface I could see, but would like to believe it was at least a mile. It certainly seemed like it.

Christian used this opportunity to jump off the top of the boat, which reminded me of a conversation I had with Rip just before we left land. Rip had told me about a crossing he did a few years back where they stopped the boat in the exact middle of the Atlantic for a swim. I asked if they hadn't worried about sharks. His response: "Of course! But, we had someone circling the swimmers at all times, from a tender, with a shot gun pointed at the water." I wished I hadn't asked. Christian's dive into the water prompted Garret and St. John to do the same. I know this is crazy, but my guess is that we are all going swimming when we get to the center of the Atlantic. There are no guns aboard Sans Souci, so I'm hoping our luck holds.

Looking out the window as I type this, the seas today are rougher than yesterday, but far from rough. We have perhaps 1 to 3 foot waves, and a light 10-knot breeze.

Everyone is excited that we'll be seeing the rest of our group today. Both Emeritus, which has been running independently, and the Division 2 boats should be with us before nightfall. On watch last night, I kept hearing our Division 1 boats trying to contact our friends in Division 2 via VHS radio. There were no responses on my shift. We could at any time use our sat phones to call the Division 2 boats, but that doesn't seem as aesthetically pleasing. Radio contact means we are close, whereas calling them on the phone says nothing about distance. Roberta and I did the 3:00am to 6:00am watch last night, so we slept through the 8:00am roll call, but my guess is that we are within 20 miles of Division 2.

We're now 150 miles from Bermuda, and should arrive sometime tonight. The actual approach to Bermuda is difficult, or so it appears on the map, as a giant reef surrounds Bermuda and we must pass through a narrow access channel. I will be studying the maps today and will know much more about what is ahead of us later this afternoon.

My apologies for my lack of response to everyone who has sent an email, or posted a message on the website. I've been neglecting my inbound e-mail, but have received a number of questions and requests to say "Hi" to people. As soon as I can, I will pass along all the requests for greetings from friends and family. Where I have been able to do so, this has already been done.

Many people have asked about Shelby, our dog. One person asked whether or not Shelby could have just stayed on the boat, had we not gotten her entry permit for Bermuda. I do not know the answer to this question, but assume that she could have. The officials in Bermuda have been pleasant but firm. They return phone calls, and have gone out of their way to help us immigrate (temporarily) Shelby. They had a long list of hoops we had to jump through, but it was a fair list, and really the toughest part was the final timing. Shelby had to have a health certificate within ten days of our arrival in Bermuda. We couldn't submit our application until everything was assembled including this final health certificate. Our fear was that we would submit the paperwork and then not receive our import permit until we were already at sea, or that our departure would be delayed due to weather, and the health certificate would no longer be valid. We were very impressed when Bermuda faxed us approval within two hours of application. My sense is that they were happy that we followed every single rule, and got it all right on the first try.

The other major Shelby question has been "where does she go?" Lots of people seem curious about this, and rightly so. This was a big question for Roberta and I. Our human children have grown and moved away, so Shelby has become an integral part of our immediate family. We perhaps take this a bit too far, and suspect we're not the only dog or cat owners to do so. Shelby is well known to many of the restaurants in Cabo, our primary land-based home, where she usually dines with us. Getting Shelby trained was a bit of a project, and something we knew we HAD to do. She's a Norwegian Lundehund, which is a rare, and not particularly domesticated breed. To train her was a yearlong process that started with an enormous tray on the back deck of our boat filled with sod. Shelby had a yard of her own, complete with real grass! To make a long story short, over time the grass was replaced with Astroturf, and eventually taken away completely. She now understands that the back deck is "the place." We even asked Nordhavn if they could build Sans Souci with a doggy door. Unfortunately, they thought this was impossible, and perhaps that is for the better. When the seas are high, no one should go out alone. This way, we have a bit more control over where she is.

I've also received questions about Christian Fittipaldi from his fans. Someday I'll have to watch him race, to see another side of him. Before meeting him, I had tried to imagine what he might be like. Nothing I envisioned compares to the person who is here. He is intelligent, shy, polite, considerate and very serious. Last night while the rest of us were checking our e-mail, Christian was watching a National Geographic DVD on his laptop. He is now on the back deck reading. At 4:00am this morning, Roberta and he were deep in discussion about the subtle distinctions between some similar, but different, Portuguese and Spanish words. He also seems to have no fear. When we were stopped yesterday to do our coffee delivery, he was the first to dive off the boat. While I was wondering if there sharks in the water, he was swimming. He loves the sea, and you could see the passion in his eyes as we looked at a map of the Bahamas and he showed us his favorite cruising grounds. After talking to Christian, do not be surprised if Sans Souci winds up in the Bahamas someday…. I received an e-mail asking what he has on his iPod play list. According to Christian, he listens to older groups like Supertramp, and Prefab Sprout (which I've never heard of), After Hours music, New Age and techno.

On an unrelated to anything note, during watch last night, I was able to chat with our son Chris, who is living and working in Tokyo. Chris loves challenges, so I just typed in our latitude and longitude with no explanation whatsoever. Within a few seconds, he responded "Boring. There's nothing there but water." I'm not sure why this struck me as funny, but it did. I am also not so spoiled by technology that I can't still be awed by the idea that a dad on a boat in the middle of the Atlantic can chat with his son in Tokyo.

I received an email from one person correcting the formula I posted a few days ago. Thank you to Henry Rothberg for this clarification:

" ... I do believe that it should be stated as: Hull speed (NOT maximum speed) in knots = 1.3 x the square root of the length of the boat IN FEET at the water line. THIS formula is not valid if the length is expressed in meters/metric - Henry Rothberg hbrothberg@yahoo.com ... "

Lastly...

I inadvertently stirred up a bit of controversy when I mentioned tossing my paper plate overboard in an earlier update. Dan Streech answered the gentleman far more eloquently than I could have, so the original e-mail, and Dan's response follow.

Dan:

I LOVE reading your reports and the San Souci weblog ... And I DON'T mean to sound like a "know it all" or "holier-than-thou," but ... reading comments such as:

"We've been lucky so far – no one sick, and dinner went well. I experimented with throwing my paper plate overboard, and discovered that throwing a Frisbee shaped object loaded with food is best done downwind. Double oops..."

I am reminded that while LEGALLY, throwing paper plates into the sea may be "OK" when you reach the legally specified distance from land, I note that good sailors & cruisers THROW NOTHING over the side unless they have eaten it first ... and even then it should be "treated / macerated" first, if possible.

A GREAT cruiser's guideline: Save & hold ALL trash and dispose of it at the next port of call. (aren't trash compactors just great !)

We can (still) legally litter and pollute the sea ...but that doesn't make it right ...!

It would be nice if you could diplomatically relay this message to the entire NAR fleet ... I'm not very diplomatic so I'll leave it to you to ignore my message or relay it to the entire NAR fleet, and everyone else you meet and cruise with.

Not trying to be a pain-in-the-butt, I'm just doing my small part looking out for the seas...

Henry

Hello Henry,

Thanks for your (provocative) email. It is going to provide some interesting debate for our readers as I am going to post your e-mail and my response on the web site.

First I want to say that the pollution subject didn't pass un-discussed on board Sans Souci. The 8 of us on board range from college student knee-jerk liberal to Bush conservative, but we all share one thing in common - a love of and respect for the sea and the need to protect it.

The experience yesterday with the sperm whales and a speechless awe at the deep blue crystal clear water was a reminder of the priceless pristine beauty that still exists and our collective responsibility to protect it.

The pollution enemy (of course besides oil and chemical spills) is PLASTIC. Wretched hateful plastic takes years or a lifetime to disintegrate. In my travels over the years, I have walked remote beaches from Borneo to the Bahamas, and my pleasure of the moment is nearly always spoiled by a Styrofoam cup, plastic bag, 6-pack holder, or worse. I have never seen a paper plate, magazine or an apple core washed ashore. I have not wanted to mention it in my reports, but we have seen numerous floating objects during this passage - all of them plastic. In an amazing confirming coincidence, Crosser just came on the radio to report a floating plastic barrel.

I have never been one to practice silly robotic PC perfection and prefer to act sensibly and responsibly. I will continue to throw paper and organic garbage into the open ocean as well as pump the holding tank without remorse. I know that these things are eaten by the marine life or absorbed easily by the sea.

As mentioned above, I am going throw this debate on to the web site and see how people react. I could be convinced to give up my paper and garbage throwing if it would help foster a better ATTITUDE towards protecting our precious seas.

Yours humbly,

Dan

P.S. - Prior to departure from Ft. Lauderdale, it was discussed in a Sans Souci crew meeting that the paper plates could go overboard but the plastic utensils DEFINITELY could not. Not one molecule of plastic has gone overboard. Also, we DO NOT use any holding tank treatments (which contain formaldehyde) aboard Sans Souci. The chemical treatments are worse than the sewage itself.

We arrive in Bermuda later tonight

As I write this we are within 6 miles of merging the two groups of boats. As many of you noticed, I did not post any new pictures today.

I'm not sure why, but I was seasick ALL day. I couldn't get up the energy to power on my computer. I could have put on the patch, but with land practically in sight, that seemed wrong.

On the positive side, tomorrow morning we arrive in Bermuda. This should give me some great photo opportunities, as well as lots to talk about – and hopefully a high-speed internet connection with which to upload the pictures. The approach to Bermuda looks tricky on the map (narrow, and shallow). Goleen has just e-mailed a list of THIRTY-SEVEN waypoints for the approach. That did nothing to make it sound any easier.

The Dan Streech Report #4

It was another magic night aboard Sans Souci. After chef Phil's delicious dinner of Chicken cordon bleu, we conducted the evening roll call. These roll calls are becoming ever more fun as the jokes, pranks and outrageous fishing stories seem to grow. Goleen now claims to have caught Sea Fox's 4-foot fish and (wouldn't you know it) it got away again with a lure. Crosser

was boarded by a giant squid, which they fought and killed with dental floss. They are now enjoying calamari. While discussing the rather tricky routing in the final approach to the Bermuda Yacht Club, Grey Pearl wanted the Lat/Lon of the nearest bar. And much more... Emeritus has finally come within radio range and will join tonight's roll call.

My watch last night was 9:00PM to midnight. The moonless sky was breathtaking with stars from horizon to horizon. The running lights of our faithful fleet blended with the stars as we floated along on the surreal "Lake Atlantic".

I spent much of my watch standing at the Portuguese Bridge enjoying the balmy air and counting shooting stars. It was so beautiful, that several people who didn't want to waste the experience by sleeping stayed up. We chatted about nothing and everything in a way that just doesn't seem to happen in "real life".

The pleasant melodic and reassuring purr of the dry exhaust was a backdrop to the above scene. Our faithful Lugger engine located two flights below us has of course run non-stop since we left Ft. Lauderdale without a hiccup. These magnificent engines are designed to run 20,000 hours or more and are superb pieces of machinery. Our trip around the world on the Nordhavn 40 in 2001/2002 put 3,500 hours on the Lugger engine, so you can see that most of us will not live long enough to see our Luggers "wear out".

I talked to Jim last night and this morning by SSB and he was euphoric about the wonderful day that they had in Group 2. They launched their RIB and played, fished and moved from boat to boat conducting video interviews for the documentary. Group 2 was 24 miles ahead of us as of this morning, so we plan to catch them sometime this evening.

This morning has dawned with an imperceptible shift in mood and weather. As predicted by weather router Walt Hack, we now have light winds and seas from the west, which means from astern. Following seas and winds are of course a "sailor's delight", but the glossy "oily" seas which so captivated us yesterday and now gone. The radio chat and activities on board have now turned to preparation for tomorrow morning's arrival. Reality has intruded on the special bond that has formed among the 6 vessels of NAR Group 1 over the last 4 days...

It may sound strange to some of you readers, but I almost wish that Bermuda were further away than the 147 miles now showing on the GPS...

Love being at sea,

Dan

Dan,

Since you were so quick to respond...

I have a comment on garbage disposal.

If someone such as Henry were to walk around a selection of Caribbean islands and see the garbage problems that they have now because of the flood of cruisers to the island, he would realize the need to dispose of as much of the vessels garbage at sea as possible.

I have seen many times, the disgusting dump sites on these poor islands, the rotting food, the papers blowing around in the wind, the flies, dogs, cats, pigs and rats that are ripping apart the plastic garbage bags that are full of scraps and waste from the cruising folks.

I came to the rapid conclusion that all paper, food, tins, glass and basically anything except plastic, should indeed be cast into the depths (of course not the shallows) to become part of the planet again. The plastic containers, bottles and bags should be washed out and taken ashore at the larger islands, as they are more capable of dealing with the garbage problems.

Anybody that suggests anything to the contrary, should try cruising the islands, walking the islands, smelling the islands and checking out the local garbage disposal plan!

Back to work,

James Knight
Commissioning & Service Manager
Nordhavn South East

Day 14 - Arrival in Bermuda!

Arrival went smoothly, although it didn't seem like it at the time.

The Bermuda advance team asked that the larger ships arrive first, so that we could unload our tenders and help the smaller boats come into the marina. You can't imagine how happy we were to hear this. Even though we were 10 miles behind the lead group when this news came in, with only 10 hours left, we jumped on the opportunity. We rocketed to 9.5 knots, and stayed there until we were comfortably in front of the slower group. Although this is not what many think of as high-speed, it sure felt like it. We had a 20-knot tail wind that kept the autopilot in a confused state, as we slid back and forth, surfing the 3 to 5 foot seas and working our way through and around the slow group.

Autumn Wind arrives in Bermuda under a cloudy sky.

I didn't like how Sans Souci's engine sounded at 1,800 rpm, and was anxious for the moment when we could slow down. Dan assured me that the Lugger wasn't working hard at all, which should have calmed me, but my nature is to be cautious. Accidents happen when you get in a hurry. As usual, there was nothing to worry about EXCEPT: Rip and I were on watch as we got into range to see the lights of Bermuda through the binoculars. We were running with Crosser, Autumn Wind, Grey Pearl, and our group was lead by Goleen. About 10 miles from Bermuda, Rip and I started noticing that we were drifting to the right of the other boats, but that the computer mapping system showed us as needing to turn farther right. For about 15 minutes Rip and I were highly focused on finding the problem. There was a temptation to believe the computer mapping system. Through thousands of miles, it had never failed – but, something felt wrong. Either Sans Souci was off course, or the other boats were. In this case, we had plenty of time to search for the error. We were running further south than where we felt our track should be, but as there was only open-ocean to the south, we felt no need to correct anything until the problem had been identified. After comparing the boat's GPS with what we were seeing on the computer, we realized that the computer map was off by a full six miles! We rebooted the computer, which accomplished nothing, and then switched to a completely different chart which immediately corrected the problem. Had we been running alone and approaching Bermuda from the north, it could have been a dangerous situation. Once things calm down, I will be investigating how this could have occurred. The one thing I know for sure is that we have a chart with erroneous data.

The actual arrival in Bermuda was far simpler than I had anticipated. We had to run our way through a narrow channel, but nowhere near what I had expected. Even the actual Med mooring of Sans Souci was anti-climactic. Perhaps when we head to sea again, I'll devote an entire daily update to the Med tie. The short story is that generally in Europe there aren't boat slips. Marinas are much more crowded than in the US. You back the boat to a wall, and attach yourself in the front either to a mooring buoy, a line to the bottom of the marina, or drop your own anchor prior to backing to the wall. Usually, you are parking in a space that is narrower

than your boat, and you have to force your way to the quay by rolling your boat forcefully against the fenders of the neighboring boats, pushing them aside slowly. Even backing into the slip can be interesting, as there is rarely adequate space to turn, and winds often add to the excitement. All of this taken into account, even though Roberta and I have run the boat alone in Europe for the last four years, I made the decision to have our Captain, Rip, bring the boat in. As we approached the Royal Bermuda Yacht Club, I saw immediately that we were backing to a bare wall with a huge bay to position ourselves in. With 20/20 hindsight, I should have pulled rank on Rip and brought the boat in. He wouldn't have been happy, but I think he would have understood.

I've been typing this while awaiting the arrival of customs. I've been watching the other boats arrive, and want to get out and shoot some pictures. I'm not sure when I'll be able to get anything uploaded but assume that by tomorrow I should have our arrival pictures on the site, as well as more pictures from the first leg of the trip.

Happy to be here!

P.S. - I wish I had a picture of Shelby's face when she saw grass for the first time in five days. We have a very happy dog!

Day 15 - In Bermuda

Roberta and I have now moved off of Sans Souci, and into a hotel. We're in port in Bermuda, and will be here for at least nine days. This is my last "daily update" until we get ready for the big run to Horta (around June 1st). I will continue to take pictures of the boats, and to rummage through my existing photos for images worth posting, but 99% of our time here in Bermuda will be spent "just being tourists."

Sans Souci demonstrates a Med tie in Bermuda.

The crew is staying on Sans Souci. We moved into a hotel for a couple of reasons: a) I wanted a high-speed internet connection, and b) we're living with strangers on Sans Souci for over two months. Thus far there hasn't been any serious conflict, but the possibility certainly exists. I think the best way to ensure long-term peace is to give each other the maximum amount of space when possible. Actually, everyone has bound together VERY well, and is having a great time – however, we're all from very different backgrounds. Outside of this trip, I would be surprised to see this group hanging out together.

The next leg of our journey is the one that worries me most. Weather-wise, it has the potential to be the most perfect. We've spoken to several people who have done the crossing recently (between Bermuda and the Azores) and all have experienced perfectly flat seas. What concerns me about this leg is the overwhelming distance involved. 1,800 miles is nothing in an airplane, and not even much of a drive, but for a small boat it's a serious distance. The smaller boats will be at sea for a full two weeks, and we'll be out there for eleven days. It's unlikely that anything will go wrong, but if it does, help will be a long way away. Based on our fuel consumption on the first leg, we're in great shape as far as range is concerned. We burned roughly 1 mile per gallon - 900 gallons for a 900-mile passage. We were even a bit wasteful on fuel, as we knew that we had plenty of fuel on board. We ran the generators (gensets) far more than we will be running them on this next leg, partially because of the failure of the hydraulic alternator, and partially because there was no reason not to. The washer and dryer were running quite often, a luxury that we may not have on this next leg. With the hydraulic alternator, we can do quite a bit without powering the generator, but not everything at the same time. There will be tradeoffs to be made, and we'll have to be smarter about understanding these on the next leg than we were on the first. Sans Souci carries 2,400 gallons of fuel, which implies that we can arrive with 600 gallons left over. We can also take at least an extra 100 gallons in an oil drum we use for holding used oil.

Exhaustion will be a major factor on this next trip. Our crew is dropping from eight persons to seven. Many of the boats are running with four or five, so I'm not complaining, but it means that we won't have a spare person on the watch rotation as we had on the first leg. Christian Fittipaldi and Dan Streech are leaving us here in Bermuda. Another PAE employee, Kirk White, will be joining us. I'm not sure of Kirk's position at PAE, but it's clear watching him in action that he knows the boats systems better than almost anyone. He will be a huge positive for us. We have split the crew into three teams of two persons

who will be doing "watches". Chef Phil has a more than full time job keeping us fed and full of coffee, so he doesn't do watch. For those not familiar with "watches", I should give a quick description. 99% of the time, Sans Souci drives herself. It is entirely possible, and quite likely, that during a watch, the person piloting the boat will never do anything to actually drive the boat. The person on watch needs to be qualified to run the boat, in case action is needed, but most watches really consist of not much more than "watching". The autopilot knows nothing about logs that might be floating, or sailboats crossing your path (sometimes running at night without lights) or even large freighters that don't slow down or change directions for anything. The person on watch needs to constantly monitor the radar and the radio. Additionally, the instrumentation needs constant monitoring, and the engine room needs visiting periodically. We do engine room visits at least every 2 to 3 hours. I have remote controlled cameras in the engine room that allow us to see what is occurring, and even zoom in on specific gauges, but there is nothing like being in the engine room, using your senses of touch and smell, to tell you if everything is as it should be. A proper watch shift is not a relaxing experience. It's 3 or 4 hours of having to be very alert, and ready to make serious decisions quickly under pressure. Each team does two or three shifts per 24-hour period. We split the watch shifts to give some time for rest, so that you are never on watch for more than four hours straight. Nighttime watches are 3 hours long, and daytime watches are 4 hours. The luxury we have that most boats don't is being able to run two person teams. This means one person can watch the other. Falling asleep while at watch is a serious concern, and has resulted in many accidents at sea. The extra person can also fetch snacks, do engine room checks, and cover during the inevitable bodily function breaks (which can't really be delegated). I am sure that for those of you reading this who have never done a passage, it doesn't sound like much work to spend only eight hours per day watching the boat, and rest the other 16. I wish this were true. It fatigues you in a way that I can't explain. The boat is in constant motion. You can't generally do such simple tasks as walking without holding on. Exhaustion leads to errors, and I have no statistics, but am convinced that more accidents have occurred as a result of human error than as a result of mechanical failure.

On another topic, I sent my son Chris a note asking whether or not he was receiving the daily updates. Chris is a super-intelligent, but sometimes-gruff person. His response: "Why would I care about the experiences of a bunch of old rich dudes?" Chris is way off base with his question, and I'm responding to him here, in case there are others that have this misconception. First off, the owners of these boats are not dudes. They are mostly retired couples, and in many cases, couples who are still working and taking some time off, or who have found a way to work from their boats. As to his contention that we are old, I'll partially agree to this, although it depends on your perspective. Chris is only 25. I remember being 25 and thinking 30 year old people were old. Now that I'm in my late 40s, I'd happily swap ages with a 30 year old. Most of the owners are in their 50s or 60s (my opinion, although I must admit that I'm terrible at judging ages). I know of at least one owner who is running his own boat, in his 80s. I know of at least a couple of others who are in their 40s, and know of some who are self-schooling young children while boating around the world. We don't have a lot of people here in their 20s and 30s mostly because it takes a while to save up enough money to buy a boat, and because most people can't take time off for world cruising while they still have a job. As to Chris' contention that this is a crowd of rich people, I suspect that he would be quickly thrown overboard if he were to say such a thing anywhere near this crowd. There are some well off people here, and perhaps some that qualify as "rich," but Chris is completely wrong in his characterization. I don't know any of the people here well enough to know their finances, or even to render an opinion on their finances, but a lack of knowledge has never stopped me from commenting, so I'll continue in that tradition. My sense is that most trawler owners have saved most of their lives to have a trawler. It is not something they bought with spare pocket change. Many of them have thought long and hard about the costs of living aboard a boat, and have their monthly budget thought out almost down to the dollar. One of the tough realities of retirement is that your money needs to last you for the rest of your life. Every dollar counts, because you really don't know how long you will live, what interest rates will be, how much you need or what inflation will do to the value of savings. I overheard several of the rally participants complaining about the cost of receiving an email while at sea, and some even passing on having email because of the potential cost of receiving an unwanted email. I watched a group of owners enthusiastically band together to negotiate a better price for fuel. Techniques for minimizing expense are a big issue for essentially all of the rally participants. Most do the maintenance of their own boats, and can talk for hours about how to minimize operating costs aboard their boats. Sans Souci is very unusual in having a chef on board. I've heard of only one other boat that has done this. It's a controversial comparison (and I may be alone in my opinion), but I think an accurate one, that motor homes and trawlers are similar. The kinds of people that generally buy them are people that want to travel, and take their home with them. For the most part, it's a lifestyle decision, not a rich-person's plaything. Roberta and I are boating people. We knew long ago that living aboard a boat was part of our future, and have always had boats. And, as this rally shows, we are not alone....

Talk to you in a week!

The Dan Streech Report #5

Here is today's update from Dan Streech. With Dan leaving the rally here in Bermuda, his updates will stop. I'll miss both him, and his updates. Dan said that he is hoping Kirk White (who is replacing Dan on Sans Souci) will take over for him, and continue the updates. Hopefully, he will!

-Ken Williams

Approaching Bermuda

With the theme song from the Tom Cruise movie "Cocktail" (Bermuda ..., Bahama,... come on pretty momma...) playing in the background, I say:

Good morning from Bermuda! We made it!! The fleet arrived yesterday (Saturday) morning exactly on schedule with pride and satisfaction bursting from everyone on board.

Our last night at sea (Friday night) was filled with excitement as the two fleets finally came together. We first saw group 2 on the radar, then one by one, their stern lights began to appear. It was a wonderfully satisfying moment, which validated the endless hours of planning that have gone into this event. For the first time, radio roll call was a combined event in which all 18 boats (including Emeritus) reported their position in order of their size. Throughout the night, the radio was busy with questions and answers about the various issues of arrival.

Around midnight, we began to see the lights of Bermuda. At first, it was just an indistinct sky glow, but then individual lights began to show themselves. Several of us marvelled at the oddness of this little rock of land sitting out in the middle of the Atlantic Ocean.

Entering the channel.

Our well-crafted arrival plan turned to benign anarchy when we arrived at the entrance to the "Narrows" passage thru the reef. We were to all enter together to give dramatic effect for the people waiting at the yacht club. However, the faster boats ended up about 45 minutes ahead of the slower boats and just proceeded on to the club. In the end all was fine because the staggered arrival actually helped the docking process run more smoothly. I was very proud of the participants as they deftly manoeuvred their vessels into their "Med-moor" positions. Anchors were dropped and the powerful ABT bow and stern side thrusters were barking out their presence as each boat was manoeuvred into position. Joan and Bruce Kessler were on the docks filming and Milt and Judy Baker with radios in hand were directing the various activities.

The Royal Bermuda Yacht club is PERFECT. It is exactly what one would expect. The building is old and the floors creak, and it reeks with history and British decorum. One expects HRM the Queen Herself to appear at any moment. In fact, she has visited the club twice (in 1953 and in 1994) as evidenced by the photos on the wall. The striking dissimilarity between the pretty smiling young Queen of 1953 and the dour stooped Queen of 1994 is amazing and reminds us that "time waits for no Queen". The walls are covered with old photos of schooners, steam yachts and various yachting characters going back over 100 years. The lobby and trophy room (where the temporary PAE NAR office has been re-established), open on to the outdoor bar and eating area. As one comes and goes from the slips, they must pass by the bar area... thus this "watering hole" has quickly become the social center for the participants. In a strange juxtaposition, the bar area is also an internet "hot spot", so the 100 year old edifice steeped in tradition has been invaded by laptops. While in Bermuda, I will be doing my internet business from the yacht club to give some relief to the expensive system aboard Sans Souci.

I can only describe Bermuda in superlatives. I LOVE this place. The air is balmy, the weather is perfect and the mood is friendly and relaxed. The rocky shoreline of the lovely bay that we are located in reminds me of Maine. The pastel colors of the building and houses remind me of a Mediterranean scene, the beautiful lush greenery and flowers reminds me of Singapore. With the knee high socks and the "British" décor and accents, one at first thinks that this place is stuffy. There is however an almost imperceptible wink that says "hey relax, we don't really mean it..." A local guy came into the club last night wearing a blue blazer with tie, short pants, knee high socks and shiny black shoes. I said to myself... I LOVE this place.

Within a few hours of arrival, we headed up to Smatt's to rent scooters. PAE now has 10 scooters under contract for cruising around the island (no car rentals allowed - only locals are allowed to drive). As our valiant young PAE men roared off (on the left side of the road), Jim turned to me and said that open ocean passage making was child's play compared to the dangers that we are facing here in port...

Ken and Roberta have taken a hotel room for a few days to get some privacy and Christian has taken a hotel room. Christian's very lovely and charming wife Andrea arrived yesterday afternoon and the 3 of us had dinner last night at a quaint Italian restaurant. We hadn't had pasta during the entire passage and Christian said that he was craving it. When we arrived, the *best outside tables were all taken. Christian began rattling in fluent Italian and a table magically became available. During the passage, Christian has had non-stop questions about the technical aspects of a passage maker. The dinner conversation was about steering and the interplay between the stabilizers, the rudder and the bulbous bow. He would not quit until he understood it. One can imagine that there have been many similar episodes after practice or qualifying in which the sensitive interplay between down force, gear ratios and tire pressures were discussed to the nth degree.*

While wandering the docks, I ran into Bob Rothman of Emeritus and asked him about his wayward course. He finally admitted that he is a loner and a "contrary" guy who isn't comfortable traveling in a group. Thinking to myself, then why did you join a group? I told him that there wouldn't be much opportunity for him to deviate from the plan for the next leg since it is a straight line from Bermuda to the Azores. With a twinkle in his eye, Bob said: "ahhh, but you are wrong... there is the rhumb line route and the great circle route". With that, Bob and Janis his lovely wife of a lifetime walked away towards the yacht club.

I could not be happier with the rally situation at this point. Leg 1 went perfectly and frankly turned out even better than I had thought. In all of our planning of the details, we had not anticipated the simple FUN and JOY that would come from this rally. I have not done well in naming the individual boats and their owners and crews, but they all have a story to tell and I am proud of each and every one of them. Without exception, the boats (Nordhavn and non Nordhavn alike) have been well prepared and have been well operated. The competence and confidence of the participants is high and will only grow as the rally proceeds.

This will be my last report, as I must head home soon. Business and personal pressures are calling me and I must heed. Kirk White of PAE will take my position as group 1 leader for the final two legs. I wish the rally group well and know that they will complete this undertaking with great success. This first leg to Bermuda has shown me that the NAR management and the participants themselves are first class and will cope with whatever befalls them.

I will stay here in Bermuda for a few more days, but won't post any more reports. All they would say anyway is: I LOVE this place and we are having fun.

Satisfied,

Dan

Day 16 and 17 - In Bermuda

I'm currently taking a one-week hiatus from doing the daily update, as we're actually not on the boat this week. Roberta and I are spending the week doing standard Bermuda tourist activities, while staying in a hotel that is literally in front of our own boat.

Roberta and I were briefly on the boat yesterday in order to pick up a few extra things – like more dog food – and, while there, we spent some time on another 62,the Grey Pearl, getting to know her owners/Captains, the Joneses. Roberta was telling me about her time on Sans Souci, and I talked her into adding her comments to my weblog:

 Yesterday afternoon, Sunday, while Ken and I were visiting our crew on the boat after a relaxing night staying in an air-conditioned hotel, Dan Streech told us an amusing story about the housekeeping service that I had arranged to clean the inside of the boat upon our arrival the day before. Several days prior, while still at sea, I had called the Royal Bermuda Yacht Club for recommendations about a boat cleaning service for inside the boat. They recommended a cleaning service and gave me the phone number. I had called the service and arranged for them to be at the boat around 2:00 p.m. on Saturday, giving us plenty of time to arrive, get through customs, 'kind of' clean things up a little bit, and pack our suitcases for our weeklong hotel stay. (By the way, we're staying at a wonderful little hotel, the Waterloo House, which is right on the harbor and overlooks our boat.)

A couple of hours after our arrival at 9:00 a.m., Ken and I left the boat, bags and dog in hand, with cleaning instructions for Rip to give to the cleaning crew once they arrived. They came, all 6 of them, ready to clean the interior of the boat from top to bottom. One guy even wore the vacuum cleaner as a backpack on his back! According to Dan, they spent about three hours on the boat, and they literally rubbed and scrubbed every inch of the inside of the boat. It was spic and span indeed! Here's the 'humorous' part: Dan had kindly offered to pay for this cleaning as a sort of 'thank you' for letting him and his crew spend this past week on Sans Souci. I had taken him up on this offer. Had I known though, that the bill would have come to $435.00 – that's American dollars, not Bermudian money! – I wouldn't have let him pay this cost, or at the very least, I would have warned him of the price. However, I had neglected to ask the particulars of this cleaning job, and so, just trusted that it would be one or two persons, and would probably come to 'around' $100.00 or so. Dan was very nice about it, though. He cheerfully paid the bill, and then thought it kind of funny to tell me this story during our Sunday afternoon visit. The moral of the story though is this: When calling for any service, ask the particulars first, and approximately how much it will cost before contracting the job. Normally I do this, but didn't even think about it in this case. I don't know that we had needed 6 people to do the job, but, at least the boat was nice and clean; they did a good job.

Another Sunday note: after gathering a few things (dog food, etc.), we spent an hour on Grey Pearl drinking cocktails and getting to know her gracious owners. We shared laughs and stories about our crossing and mused about what we might do once we arrive in the Med. Immediately afterward, we all attended a barbecue sponsored by P.A.E and the Royal Bermuda Yacht Club. It was a very nice get-together for all of us. Plenty of food! Thank you P.A.E. and Royal Bermuda Yacht Club!

Today, Monday, is a National Holiday here in Bermuda. It's called Bermuda Day and I'm told it's similar to our Memorial Day in the U.S. as it semi-officially starts off the 'summer' season. Everybody has the day off and there are boat races, picnics, and a big parade in Hamilton, the 'big city' of Bermuda. As I write this on Monday morning, Ken and I are looking forward to our participation in Bermuda Day!

… and now back to Ken …

Parade participant plays the Sax while on horseback

We have started to talk to some of the other rally participants about "what happens next" after the rally. There is starting to be some momentum towards a few boats running together to France. Grey Pearl has spoken of tagging with us, as has Strickly for Fun. I had assumed that everyone already had firm plans on what to do after we reach Gibraltar, but if the few people I've spoken to about life after the rally are an indication, then in true boater style, "no formal plans have been made."

I speak French, and know some very cool places to drop anchor in the south of France. Roberta speaks Spanish, and we've also done some cruising in Spain (Mallorca, Ibiza, Barcelona and Formentera) – all of which were incredible. The great thing about the Med is that things are so close together. A trip from Gibraltar to Mallorca is only a day's run. From there to Barcelona is under a day as well. And from there, its less than a day to France, and then Corsica is only a day away, as is Italy! We have a lot of Atlantic to cross before we start to think these thoughts however, and perhaps it's bad luck to think beyond this particular passage, but as we get closer, I can't help remembering all my favorite places...

Day 18 – Bermuda

I said that I would not be doing updates this week, but Roberta is asleep, and all is quiet, so....

I'm sitting on a terrace at my hotel, and it's 7:00am. The hotel does have a high-speed internet connection, but it is only in the "common areas," so I am spending a lot of time sitting here on the terrace working my way quickly through my first pot of decaf.

Yesterday, Roberta, Shelby and I decided to see Bermuda from the water, with the goal to try out our new tender. When we first bought Sans Souci, they asked what we wanted for a ship's tender, and I didn't understand the pros and cons of the different options. We decided to go with a 15 foot Boston Whaler and a 13' inflatable boat. The second tender was meant to be a backup for the primary, and over the past six years, it has been used exactly ZERO times. In fact, when we decided to make a major change prior

to the start of this trip, the backup tender was sold without every having been used. What a horrible waste of money and deck space. Our primary tender, the Boston Whaler, was also a problem. The Whaler is a fine tender, but it wasn't right for us. The davit on Sans Souci is rated at 1,500 pounds, and the Whaler weighed around 1,200 pounds. We thought we were well within the safety limits, and it is possible that we were. However, no one who ever heard the sounds our davit made as it raised or lowered the Whaler would have leapt to that conclusion. For those not familiar with the Boston Whaler, it's a solid fiberglass bottomed boat. It's a "real" boat, with a "real" outboard motor. Roberta and I run Sans Souci alone 99% of the time. This meant that I would work the screeching Davit (via its remote control) while Roberta tried to keep the tender under control. Sometimes we would have nice calm seas to drop the tender in, but we never seemed to get that lucky, that often. We have dropped or raised the tender on seas where we should not have. Because raising or lowering the tender was such a major project, we tended to wait until some triggering event forced us to drop the tender. I've towed the tender hundreds of miles in order to avoid raising or lowering it. To understand what I'm talking about, you have to imagine me working a remote with my left hand, my right hand on the tenders bow, and the 5' Roberta stabilizing the back of the 15' tender as it bounced back and forth on a rolling sea. All of this while the tender dangles from a single cable attached to davit that is doing its very best to tell us, in a very audible way, that we should NOT be doing what we are doing. We experimented many times with attaching ropes to the tender, and trying to stabilize it from afar, but were never successful with this. You can't, or at least we couldn't, hold onto a rope that is attached to a bouncing tender from six feet away.

One of the first rules they tell you about tenders is that you MUST NOT ride in the tender as it is raised or lowered from the water. My personal observation is that we are not the only ones who have broken this rule incessantly. There are a couple of problems with dropping the tender without someone in it. 1) It bangs into the side of the boat, gouging the fiberglass as it does so, and 2) On the 62, there is no way to get into the tender after you drop it (the geometry of the 62 is such that you are about eight feet off the water at the bow, but at water-level in the center of the boat). The problem with raising or lowering the tender with someone in it is that it is extremely dangerous. If something goes wrong while the tender is dangling off the side of the boat, and you are in the tender – you will have a very bad day.

After six years, and many attempts to reinforce our davit, I finally admitted I made an expensive mistake and swapped tenders. Just prior to this trip, we sold off both our tenders, at an enormous loss, and bought a new Caribe 15' rigid bottomed inflatable. The Caribe weighs about 800 pounds, with motor, fuel, and everything. The davit still squeals a little as the tender goes up or down, but these sounds seem much more natural. Because the tender is an inflatable, it does not require fenders. If it bounces into something while dangling from the cable, it's no big deal. We also swapped the cable on the davit so that it has plenty of length. By attaching a line to the stern of the tender, we can drag it backwards after it drops to the water, for easy step-in from the side of the boat. Roberta doesn't need to ride up and down in the tender anymore (which she shouldn't have been doing EVER).

Our question was: how did the Caribe feel on the water? We ordered it from a picture, and had low expectations. To our surprise, we had a great time! It was at least as comfortable as the Boston Whaler, and seemed faster, based on how we ran it. I

suspect the Whaler is faster after getting on a plane, but the Caribe didn't seem to be as binary as the Whaler was. The Whaler seemed to have two speeds: slugging through the water painfully, and planing at high-speed. It really didn't feel comfortable at speeds like 15 knots. The Caribe felt great at all speeds.

I'll try to upload some pictures from our cruise. Shelby was funny to watch, as Roberta put a bright pink life jacket on her, and a bright red hat. After about 15 minutes I took pity on Shelby and helped her out of the hat.

Tendering around Bermuda was trickier than I expected. I'm sure that once you've done it a few times it's no big deal, but as a complete novice, we weren't sure where to go, or where we could go. We weren't even sure how fast we could go. I had a marine map of Bermuda with me, but no speeds were indicated. I wasn't sure if I could directly cross the harbor, or was supposed to follow some sort of "keep to the right" rules. We watched others, and decided that if there were rules, they were a well-kept secret. Everyone seemed to be going every direction, at every speed. We also weren't certain where we wanted to go. I had no idea where to start. While taking a taxi, we had seen a bridge that was described as the smallest draw bridge in the world. That seemed a fun destination, so we went there. I was puzzled because on our map, virtually everything on the other side looked too shallow to run. This meant a challenge, and challenge is

opportunity! The bridge itself was a pleasant surprise. It was short and narrow. All traffic under the bridge was one way only. Across its span were 10 or so kids who were leaping off the bridge into the water between the boats. I wanted a picture of one jumping, but Roberta yelled at me for potentially  encouraging an activity that was almost certainly unsafe.

After the bridge, we discovered a wonderful bay and marina. Through an opening on the far side of the bay, we could see open ocean. For at least a mile out, the surrounding ocean was shown on the map in a scary looking yellow color, with little plus signs in it. A large span had the message "This area inadequately mapped" written across it. As we were thinking that we had gone as far as we could, a family in a small tender headed

 out into the shallow waters. They had one person on the bow to watch for rocks, and were moving slowly. We decided to do the same. As I watched for rocks and Roberta drove, we worked our way through a couple of miles of water only 6 to 12 feet deep. The depths were nothing for the tender and we could

have blasted our way through at any speed, but we didn't know that at the time. Perhaps it was high tide. All we knew was that the other tender, who we assumed were locals, were moving slowly and carefully – so we did the same. Our quest was rewarded by entry to a great anchorage. We found hundreds of boats all anchored together, many rafted together and lots of barbecuing, swimming and general merrymaking going on. We also found a shortcut back, and after a bit more sightseeing, called it a day – a very fun day....

When we returned to Sans Souci, St. John and Garret were eagerly waiting for us. Actually, they were waiting for the tender, so that they could take it out for some scuba diving. The crew from various boats, mostly young men, seems to be VERY HAPPY here in Bermuda. I've noted an increase in the number of young, attractive ladies hanging out in front of the boats. It will be difficult to get everyone focused on the preparations and repairs that need to be made before the next leg of our voyage, although I have been assured that the "work" starts today.

As I am sitting here, I have noticed several of our boats leave the dock. Today is the first of several "bunkering" days (the nautical term for taking on fuel). Each boat has been assigned a time slot at the fuel dock. Ocean crossing powerboats are a rarity here in Bermuda. I'm sure the fuel dock is struggling to deal with 18 boats, each of which wants a thousand gallons or more of fuel.

Our slot is at 1pm today. I might tag along, and bring Scott Strickland with me, the owner/captain of Strickly For Fun, a Nordhavn 47. We've been discussing the need to practice running the boat without thrusters. For those not familiar with thrusters, these are optional equipment that can be added to your boat to help you with slow speed turns. They are literally small props that are mounted sideways, through the hull of your boat. A bow thruster has the ability to turn the nose of your boat to port or starboard. I have a small joystick at each of the control stations for Sans Souci, which controls a small hydraulic motor attached to the bow thruster. I also have a stern thruster at the back of the boat. This allows me to move the back of the boat directly to port or starboard. By using the two joysticks together I can easily sidestep Sans Souci, theoretically parking her in a space her own length. As good as this sounds, and it is, the thrusters have no effect on the boat when it is moving more than about 1 knot. They also have no effect when there is more than about 15 knots of wind. I have come to rely on them, and avoid situations where there is high wind, when I need to maneuver the boat in or out of a boat slip. Unfortunately, there will come a day when the winds are too high, or the thrusters fail, and I need to be prepared for this. There are techniques for turning a single-engine boat at slow speed, and sail boaters tend to be experts at them. I've read the books, and done some experimenting, but must confess that this is an area where I need more study. Perhaps this afternoon, or if not today, sometime this week, we'll take Sans Souci out for some practice.

Day 19 - In Bermuda

We're still here in Bermuda waiting for the next leg of our voyage. We're not going sight-seeing until the afternoon, so I thought I'd answer a bit of my email (I'm receiving a LOT of email. I apologize for not responding to each of you individually)....

A lot of people seem very curious as to how it is working out to have eight quite different people all living together on the ship, and would like me to comment more on how we are all getting along. There are a few answers to this. The one that leaps to mind first is that I really don't know my shipmates that well. They all seem to be perfectly charming people, but we really haven't spent much time talking. I've gotten to know Dan Streech, Christian Fittipaldi and Rip Knot at least a little, but the balance of our crew I really haven't spent much time with. When we are underway, it is difficult to talk. It seems to be different for others, but I've found it impossible to hold a conversation while bouncing through the waves. Plus, I'm not generally someone given to hours of small talk. I spend most of my non-watch time sleeping, working with my computer, or when the water is flat, reading. There's also a recognition that our lives might depend on having a good working relationship. I'm concerned that we are all very different people, and there is the possibility that clashes could occur. It is critical that we avoid this. Recently though, I've become convinced that this is a non-issue. The more I learn about our crew, the more I like, and respect, them.

Speaking of which, I'm getting a LOT of email asking for more information about the crew....

St. John is our emergency medical technician. He's a young college student, who I would guess is around 25. He blows me away! He already has seven years of experience working in ambulances, and has a clear vision of his career plan (he wants to be part of a helicopter emergency rescue team). He's quiet, highly focused, serious, and likes to sleep. I do what I can to make him smile, which is funny – because he is the funniest person aboard ship. He has some great lines!

Garret works for PAE, but I'm not sure in what capacity. I haven't spoken with him that much, but the first word that leaps to mind when I do is: capable. It doesn't seem to matter what I ask, Garret can do it. When a call came in from Goleen asking if we had anyone aboard who knew water makers, it wasn't a surprise when Garret said "I guess that would be me." When we were discussing who would install the electronics for the new alternator, Garret said: "Well, I guess that would be me." Once again, he is a young man in his 20s, but also someone who is clearly going places.

A true stand-out on our crew is Phil, our chef. I remember thinking we were taking a chance bringing him on board, because he had no boating experience, and limited cooking experience. I don't know the whole story, but Phil has an entire career behind him as an electrician. He then decided to go to culinary school and become a chef. He has been cooking over the past year aboard a high-end dinner train that runs the west coast. I think I remember that Phil said his long-term goal was to become a personal chef. His reputation is expanding by the day. Whoever gets him will be very lucky, in that not only is his food at the highest level imaginable, his personality is so dynamic that you just like being around him.

Rip, our Captain, I've known on and off for many years. Rip's name tells you a bit about him. He lives for the sea. His whole life revolves around boating. When not at sea he earns his living repairing boats, and my recollection is that he lives on a boat. I've seen Rip both as a fierce taskmaster, and also as a friendly companion. He takes the sea seriously, and understands how serious any mistake can be. He has thousands of hours experience at sea, and has a mastery at operating Sans Souci that comes only from decades of experience.

During this next trip, my hope is to collect some feedback for my daily report from the crew. I'm quite curious what they are thinking....

Here's a comment about the problems I had with electronic charts towards the end of Leg One:

" ... *Your chart error is not unusual. Read Niegel Calders new book "How To Read A Nautical Chart". There he spends considerable time discussing the increasing problems with the inaccuracies of electronic charts. The problem is simply that GPS is extremely accurate but the charts are not. You are trying to blend the accuracy of GPS with charts that may have been first compiled in the 1800"s. Always have paper in front of you. Duane "*

I agree!

" .... *How do you handle watches when you and Roberta are running your boat alone 99% of the time? Thanks so much for the regular messages. They're great. Capt. Steve Larivee Longmeadow MA. "*

I apologize for having been a bit confusing in my writing. Historically, Roberta and I have always boated alone. We have had Sans Souci for six years, and with one exception, a dinner cruise, we have always run her alone.

We are extremely private people, and don't like the idea of living in a small place with other people. When we were designing Sans Souci, we deliberately designed in crew quarters, and even added a refrigerator and stove to the forward cabin. We knew that we did not want crew, but also thought it was possible that Sans Souci would turn out to be too large and complex for Roberta and I to run alone. Nordhavn was assuring us that several 62's were being run by husband/wife teams just fine, but we weren't convinced. Also, our original vision for Sans Souci was that we would take three years to circumnavigate. We thought we would fly in crew, or family, as needed, for the long passages, and run the boat ourselves on the short runs.

Please do not interpret this as a reflection on Rip, or any other Captain. Rip has been impressive on this voyage, and I would hire him again in an instant. Rip and I have discussed the possibility of his continuing as the captain of Sans Souci, but with the understanding that this means that 99% of the time Roberta and I will run her alone. Rip would be responsible whenever we are not onboard, and for assisting us on long passages, or for delivering Sans Souci when we decide to "cheat" and fly to Sans Souci's next destination. I'm not sure how these discussions will evolve, but want to go on record as saying that Rip is a great captain, and that this is not a Rip, or any other Captain, issue. We have family that we love, that I'm not sure I'd want to share a 70 foot long space with for several months each year. Sans Souci is our home several months per year, and we'd rather live alone.

Overall, we've had no problem running Sans Souci alone. That said, there are times when having more people on board would have been nice. Raising and lowering the tender has been complicated at times with just the two of us (I discussed this yesterday). Going into strange ports is something we've been reticent to attempt. Frequently we anchor out, and tender into a port, just to avoid trying to slide Sans Souci into a tight parking place with just the two of us. I've watched crews of ten people each working a fender to bring a boat into a tight berth at St Tropez, on many occasions (remember: in Europe, there are no "finger" docks.) Even anchoring out can be problematic. I am always nervous to leave Sans Souci at anchor unattended. Winds in the Med can rise quickly, and if we are ashore enjoying dinner, we might not be able to tender back. I've seen many anchors come free in high wind, and it's never a pretty site. An unattended boat with a dragging anchor would be disastrous.

As to our desire to circumnavigate, I'm not sure what the status is. We bought Sans Souci six years ago, with the intention to take her "around the world." After cruising in the Pacific Northwest for a couple of years, we continued to talk about circumnavigation, but it was becoming apparent that it would be impossible for us to commit more than three months per year to boating. Our lives may change over the next few years, but for now, three months per year of live-aboard boating is the absolute maximum. As we thought about leaving Sans Souci alone for nine months a year, in foreign countries, reality started setting in. Thus, we decided to follow an alternate approach. We shifted our thinking to moving the boat somewhere where we could feel good about parking the boat for months at a time, and then using that as the hub for our cruising. In 1999, we had Rip deliver Sans Souci to France (on its own bottom from Seattle to Florida, then freighted to Toulon France.) We have had Sans Souci in a boat slip in France, just outside Monaco, for the last four years. From this hub, several countries can easily be reached, none requiring a long passage. We've had four great summers exploring France and Spain. We had planned to circle Corsica this year, and to run the boat to Greece next year.

However, we have decided that it is time to bring Sans Souci back to Seattle. Once we complete this voyage, and do a few weeks of exploring the Med, we will be freighting Sans Souci to Seattle, and run her in the Pacific Northwest for a while. We have had problems with keeping Sans Souci properly maintained in France. We have a very nice gentleman who has been looking after Sans Souci in France, but overall, the depth of experience in maintaining trawlers in France isn't the same (today) as it is in the US. The war has also made it a bit more awkward to be an American in Europe. France has a large Muslim population, and although we've never personally experienced a problem (with Muslims in France), it is an understatement to say that relations are "strained" between our two cultures. There are discussions of choosing a new "hub" for Sans Souci. Our goal would be to find somewhere that is central to a wide range of cruising opportunities. Whereas we've cruised extensively throughout the Pacific Northwest, we've never ventured north to Alaska, as have many of our friends who are quite passionate about cruising there. My guess is that we will cruise for a year or two between Seattle and Alaska, take the boat to Cabo for at least one season, and then move it to a new hub. My discussions with Christian have me thinking about the Caribbean or the Bahamas, although I have a strong sense that Greece and Turkey are part of our future. We'll see.

I really need to kick myself to stop thinking beyond the Azores. We still have a lot of water to cross on this current crossing that I need to focus on...

Day 20 - Division Two (the slower boats) leave tomorrow

I just received the weather report for the next leg of our voyage. I had heard that this next leg is normally the smoothest, but the weather report seems to think otherwise.

Specifically, the weather report is now predicting 4 - 7 foot seas and wind for the next week. As I sit here in Bermuda looking out at the water, it's hard to imagine going to sea. We have 30 knot winds here in the harbor. Sans Souci is being pushed into the wall we're parked against, and we've put fenders on the back to try to keep us off the wall. I tried to play golf this morning, and the ball either went 200+ yards, or nowhere, depending on if you were hitting into the wind, or against the wind.

It will be interesting to speak with the Division 2 boats at this time tomorrow to see how rough the waves are. Our group doesn't leave until Tuesday, but as you can see from the weather report it isn't much better. Nothing scary, but also nothing that looks comfortable. The patch worked well during the first leg. I guess it shall get another chance.

The good news is that the wind should be behind us, helping to push us onward, and providing a smoother ride, although, we did have a problem arriving in Bermuda with the wind behind us. The autopilot did a poor job keeping the boat straight when being pushed by the sea.

Oh well...I shall just be happy to get on with the voyage. Bermuda is a lovely place, but it's time to get moving!

P.S. – I am sending our latest weather report from Walt Hack...

Weather Report from Walt Hack

We do note weather fronts associated with the low center will extend WSW across and just south of Bermuda Sunday - Tuesday with some "sloppy" conditions departing Bermuda on Sunday. There is the risk of some showers/thunderstorms, some of which could bring locally gusty winds late Sunday/am-aft which would affect the "SLOW GROUP"

For the SLOW GROUP departure Sunday/30th along this route expect:

Sunday/30: N-NE 10-15kt at the outset, backing NNW-WNW 12-18kt during pm. Chance strong showers/thundershowers, Sea/swell WNW-NW 5-7ft, to 8ft, 8-10sec periods.

Monday/31: Backing WNW-W 12-18kt am, then WSW-SSW 8-16kt pm. Becoming SSE-SE by midnight. Swell WNW 4-6ft, 8sec, mix ESE-SE, 3-4ft, 7sec. periods.

Tuesday/01:Veer SE-SW 10-17kt am. Swell SE 3-4ft, 7 sec & developing SW 3-5ft. 7-8 sec during Tuesday/am. Freshen SW 17-25kt, gusty pm. Swell: SW & WNW 6-8ft., period 7-8sec.

Wednesday/02: SW-WSW 17-25kt am. Swell WNW to NW 7-8ft, 7-8 sec period. Ease WSW 15-21kt, WNW-W 6-8ft, 8-9sec period pm/hrs.

Thursday/03: WSW-SW 12-20kt, Swell: W-WSW 6-7ft, 7-9 sec period.

Friday/04-Saturday/05: Ease WSW 10-17kt. WSW 5-6ft, mix WNW 4-6ft Friday. WSW-W 08-15kt, WSW & WNW 4-5ft on Saturday.

For the FAST GROUP departure Tuesday/01st along this route expect:

Tuesday/01: SW-WSW 17-25kt, Gusty in near Thunderstorms pm/hrs. Swell WSW 5-6ft to WNW 6-7ft. 6-8sec periods.

Wednesday/02:Chance veer W-WNW 12-20kt early am. Otherwise remain WSW 15-21kt. Swell: WSW 5-7ft & WNW 4-6ft, 7-9 sec periods. Chance am showers/thundershowers.

Thursday/03: WSW 12-19kt, Swell: WSW 6-7ft, mix WNW-NW 4-5ft. 7-8sec period.

Friday/04: WSW 11-16kt, WSW 5-7ft.

Saturday/05:Veer WSW-WNW 10-15kt, WSW 4-6ft am. Back WSW 10-17kt, WSW 5- 7ft pm.

Day 21 - Departure of Division Two For Horta (the slower boats)

Earlier this morning I watched the departure of Division 2. Their number has grown from 11 to 12, as Sea Fox made the decision to run with the slower boats. My guess is that the decision was mandated for fuel conservation reasons, not speed. On the first leg, Sea Fox did seem to have some trouble keeping up, but that won't be an issue on this next leg as we're all running significantly slower. The slower boats will be running at 6.3 knots, and the faster boats, which still do not leave for another two days, will be running at around 7.8 knots. I will be very curious to see what our "Miles Per Gallon" is on this next leg. During the first leg we averaged almost exactly 1 mile per gallon, giving us an approximate 2,500 mile range. My guess is that our 10% speed reduction will boost our range by at least 20% or more. Everyone will be pleased about the idea that we should have PLENTY of fuel, because I was stingy about running the generator, which is required for the air conditioners, on the first leg.

Sea Fox's mutiny reduces Division 1 to only six boats, or perhaps five, depending on what Emeritus does. During the first leg, Bob Rothman on Emeritus chose to run his own course, 40 miles or so away from the balance of the Division 1 boats. It will be interesting to see if he makes the decision to run independently again! On the first leg, we had no idea until the moment he came on the radio to say that he had made the decision to cut a corner. We didn't see Emeritus again until just before landfall in Bermuda. The only explanation I've heard is that he values his independence.

Last night, we all gathered at the Royal Bermuda Yacht Club for a last dinner before Division 2's departure, pictures of which have been posted on the website (http://www.trawlerweb.com). Everyone seemed excited and ready to go. I was lobbied to join the slow group, and thought about it for a few minutes. It would be fun to continue to

hang out with our friends in Division 2, and we even discussed using tenders to swap crews amongst the boats while underway. The downside would be that we'd be on the water a couple of days longer. After agonizing over the decision for under 30 seconds, I decided that 10 days at sea is more than adequate, and Sans Souci WILL be staying with the fast boats. Realistically, we couldn't swap allegiances under any circumstances, as we are the escort boat for Division 1. And besides, we've also been strategizing crew swapping, inter-boat high-seas piracy, swimming, and possibly even some random acts of hot tubing within the Division 1 boats. We'll see...

Roberta and Rip (Sans Souci's Captain) had a "discussion" about the watch schedules. On leg one, we had three teams, each consisting of two people, with the same two people staying together throughout the cruise. Rip mentioned that he wanted to have the teams rotate on this next leg, so that each watch shift would have a different pairing, and the teams would constantly be mixed up. That didn't go over well with Roberta, as she likes the idea of her and I doing our watch together. She is now envisioning a 10 day cruise where we hardly see each other, and is lobbying me to "fix it" with Rip. I don't like giving her and I special treatment while under way, and I also hate the idea of pulling rank on my own captain – but I suspect I will be doing so soon as Roberta is right. It would really be confusing to have us working completely different shifts. We should stick together not because we own the boat, but because we are a couple, and the only couple aboard ship. That does make us different any way you look at it.

Here's a memorable moment from last nights dinner, which political correctness implies I should NOT have noticed. The Commodore (I hope I have her title correct) of the Royal Bermuda Yacht Club was a very proper English lady, who welcomed us to the club, and as part of her greeting took the opportunity to say something to the effect of "And, as a British Citizen, I would like to salute the U.S. President, George W. Bush." During normal times, no one would have paid much attention to the comment, but these are not normal times. I have never seen one comment divide a room so quickly. I am confident that she had no political purpose whatsoever for making the comment, it was just the proper thing to say. At our table, there were some sullen faces, with no effort whatsoever to applaud, while others applauded enthusiastically. This division seemed to be replicated throughout the room at each table. The whole incident only lasted a few seconds, but I thought summarized how different the people are that have been brought together on the various boats. Most of the boats are running with far more people aboard than normal. In some cases, these extra bodies are press people who are completely unknown to the rest of the crew. I met a reporter this morning that had just joined up with Atlantic Escort for the next leg. There are also boats such as ours with several Nordhavn employees and some who hired professional crew just for this trip. I've heard some rumbling that our little social experiment (combining multiple strangers in a 50' space for 10 days of cohabitation) has had mixed results. On Sans Souci we have just said our goodbyes to Dan Streech and Christian Fittipaldi, and have gained a new Nordhavn person, Kirk White, for the next leg. If first impressions mean anything, Sans Souci will continue to be "for the most part" a calm and happy ship.

If there was any "late night" partying, I saw no sign of it. What I did see was lots of people with patches behind their ear, each of which knew they had to get up early this

morning to prepare for departure. I wanted to say goodbye to everyone this morning, so I was at the dock early, with my camera in hand, to watch everyone untie. I wanted to watch reactions during the final 10 seconds after the lines have been cast off. Most people were so busy with physically getting the boat away from the dock, that they were just consumed by the process. They'll shift into passage-mode an hour or two later. Others seemed to really understand that they were seeing land for the last time for two weeks. I uploaded a picture of Georgs in the section called "Departure of Division Two for Horta", as he stares off the back of the boat, and it's not hard to guess what he is thinking. In the picture, Division 2 has just left the dock for 1,800 miles of open ocean at roughly walking speed, in boats that average only about 47 feet long. And two days from now, it will be our turn…

-Ken Williams

Sans Souci, 6209

http://www.trawlerweb.com

P.S. - The wind seems to have subsided today. The latest weather report follows…

WE CONTINUE TO SUGGEST AN EASTERLY COURSE FROM DEPARTURE BERMUDA TO NEAR 55W, THEN THE RHUMB LINE TO APPROACHES HORTA Mostly following wind/sea conditions will help maintain speeds and provide a more comfortable ride, while adding only a minimal amount of distance

For the SLOW GROUP departure Sunday/30th along this route expect:

Sunday/30: WSW 15-22kt, gusty at the outset, then shift NNW-NE 10-15kt by/around midday. Backing NNW-WNW 12-18kt during pm. Chance strong showers/thundershowers at the outset, ending by midday or so. Sea/swell WNW-NW 5-7ft, to 8ft, 8-10sec periods.

Monday/31: Backing WNW-W 12-18kt am, then WSW-SW 10-18kt pm. Swell WSW 4- 6ft, 8sec, mix ESE-SE, 3-4ft, 7sec.

Tuesday/01: Freshen WSW-SW 15-21kt am. Swell WSW 5-7ft 7-8sec during Tue/am. Freshen SW 18-26kt, gusty pm. Swell: SW & WNW 6-8ft, period 7-8sec.

Wednesday/02: SW-WSW 17-25kt am. Swell WNW to NW 7-8ft, 8-9 sec. Ease WSW 15-22kt, WNW-WSW 6-8ft, 8-9sec period pm/hrs. A secondary E-ESE swell 3-5ft may develop pm.

Thursday/03: WSW-SW 12-20kt, Swell: W-WSW 6-7ft, 7-9 sec. Ease WSW-SW 10-16kt, WSW 5-7ft pm.

Friday/04-Sat/05:WSW 10-17kt. WSW 5-6ft, mix WNW 4-6ft Fri. WSW-W 08-15kt, WSW & WNW 4-5ft on Sat.

For the FAST GROUP departure Tuesday/01st along this route expect:

Tuesday/01: SW-WSW 19-28kt, Gusty in near T/storms pm/hrs. Swell WSW 5-6ft to WNW 6-7ft. 6-8sec. Chance veer/ease W-WNW 15-22kt, WNW 6-8ft by midnight.

Wednesday/02: Back WNW-WSW 15-21kt. Swell: WSW 4-6ft & WNW 5-7ft, 7-9 sec periods. Chance am showers/thundershowers.

Thursday/03: WSW 12-19kt, Swell: WSW 6-7ft and WNW-NW 4-6ft. 7-8sec period.

Friday/04: WSW 12-18kt, WSW 5-7ft. Ease WSW-W 10-15kt, SW 4-6ft and NW 4-6ft eve-night.

Saturday/05: Veer WSW-WNW 10-15kt, SW & NW 3-5ft am. Back WSW 10-17kt, NW 4-6ft pm.

Day 22 - Final Preparations for Departure

We leave tomorrow!

The Division 2 boats left yesterday and reported this morning that all is going well. Sea Fox, which lost a stabilizer on the first leg, has already had to lock down one of their stabilizers on this leg. They will have a very uncomfortable ride running without a stabilizer. Division 2 reported that the seas are reasonably calm as predicted (5 foot or so seas), and that they are 140 miles due east of Bermuda. It amazes me how the slow group has moved so far, given their slow speed (6 knots), but these boats are relentless. They just keep ticking off miles.

On Sans Souci, we have a surprise mechanical problem. A visitor from another boat, to whom we were showing off our new 24-volt electrical system, noticed that a bolt on the front of our engine that had shaken loose and was poking out a couple of inches! The repair isn't a big deal, only an hour or so, but it's scary to think that we hadn't noticed it ourselves. I need to step up a couple of notches, the attention to detail during engine-room checks.

As soon as we finish the engine repair, we're planning to move the boat. Currently, Sans Souci is parked perpendicularly to the pier. Her aft is to the pier, and we have an anchor dropped 125 feet in front of the boat. The Division 1 boats received surprises when they raised anchor. I find this impossible to believe, but there are cables and other underwater junk along the bottom of the bay just in front of the Royal Bermuda Yacht Club. One of the boats hooked a  power cable and fortunately noticed before their anchor was fully up. Another boat partially lifted another cable. Bad weather is supposed to roll in tonight with 30 knot winds and possible thunderstorms. We don't want problems getting away from the dock when the time comes, and with the space vacated by the Division 2 boats, we can now shift the boat to be parked sideways to the dock. We can then tie ourselves to the pier and not need to drop our anchor, making the departure tomorrow fast and simple.

We had a pre-departure planning meeting today. The weather service is recommending that we avoid weather by going due east for a hundred miles or so, and then turning northeast for Horta. Kirk White, from Nordhavn, expressed his opinion that he thought a straight course to Horta made more sense, so the plan is to go for it. If the ride is too uncomfortable we'll re-evaluate. Kirk then shared his hope that we could get some flat water out in the middle of the ocean and try to raft the boats together. With a little luck, we can tie all the boats together and have a picnic!

My next email will be sent from at sea, and with a little luck, and smooth seas, I hope to upload some departure pictures.

P.S. - I am forwarding an email I received yesterday which I found flattering, but also very funny. I still haven't discussed the watch schedules with Rip Knot. We saw each other a couple of times today, but were focused on last minute customs clearing issues and the engine "issue". My guess is that for the first eight hours tomorrow the entire crew will be so excited to be underway that'll we'll all be hanging out non-stop in the pilot house. We'll do the final watch schedule planning then.

Ken,

I want to express my appreciation, not only for your web log that seems to be the best, and sometimes the only, regular update on the Rally, but also for the candor that it contains. You share the realities and apprehensions of the passage making life in port and on the sea. Sometimes you even share things with us before your shipmates know about them such as your decision about not rotating the watch crews.

This latter situation calls for some diplomacy and I suspect you're looking for just the right words. Maybe something like this: "Rip, as Captain, I know you expect to be the final authority on this vessel and I respect that. But when it comes to keeping Mrs. Williams, the wife of the owner, content, I'm Mr. Williams and you're Knot!"   :-)

Rick Austin in Austin

Day 23 – Start of Leg 2 - At sea again!!!

I'm late sending today's email, as I've been lying on the front deck for the last couple of hours wishing I could stand up. Luckily, the seasickness passed quickly. I waited to put on "the patch" until minutes before departure, and we hit waves immediately upon leaving Bermuda. As I'm writing this we're six hours into the voyage, and the ride has settled down to 4-6 foot waves, with a reasonably smooth ride, but for a while there we had 8-12 foot waves that were braking. Nothing even remotely scary, but my stomach didn't seem to like it. I never like it when I can see waves higher than the back of the boat chasing me from behind!

Five 46's docked stern-to, along with Uno Mas

Our departure from Bermuda was quite eventful. I mentioned yesterday that we were nervous about being able to leave the marina this morning, as there was a prediction for 30+ knot winds. To give us an easy escape, we side-tied ourselves to the dock, with two boats on the west side of the dock, two on the south side and two to the east. As predicted, at departure time we were looking at winds of 30 knots from the west.

The boats on the south side of the dock pulled away easily. We were on the east side, and were being blown away from the dock. Our only problem was that the wind had blown us far enough from the dock that getting on and off the boat was difficult. We were happily loading the tender, and had it on deck, when Kirk came running down the dock to tell us not to load the tender. Both Grey Pearl and Crosser were being pinned to the wall by the wind and needed help getting away. Grey Pearl wanted assistance with a line they had tied from their starboard side out to a mooring buoy, and Crosser was nervous that their thrusters might not lift them off the wall against the wind.

Garret jumped in our tender and went to their aid. In a couple of minutes Grey Pearl was away from the wall and moving through the water. She had used her front thruster to push the nose of the boat away from the wall, and then gunned the engine to get moving. Crosser tried the same maneuver with less luck – the front thruster wasn't strong enough to move Crosser away from the wall.

Crosser is the largest boat on the rally, at 90'. I missed the opportunity to go aboard, but everyone has been raving about it for days. One person described it as having a mega-yacht feel that put it in a different league than the rest of our boats. Heated granite floors, indirect lighting everywhere, modern art, a space age instrument panel, etc. Hopefully I'll get a chance to visit her in Horta.

Crosser has what I call high "windage". Whereas the 62 sits low to the water, Crosser has more vertical square footage to act as a sail. Crosser's thrusters couldn't overpower the windage to push Crosser from the wall. Our plan was to run a rope from Crosser's bow to Garret in the tender, and hopefully lift Crosser far enough off the wall that they could drive ahead, as had Grey Pearl. It seemed like a good plan, however, unfortunately it did not work. Once Crosser was at about a 10 degree angle to the wall, they gunned it. Although their bow was off the wall, their stern was pressed firmly to it, and the fenders started working themselves out of the gap that divided Crosser from the wall. Once some of the fenders had risen above the wall, the remaining fenders found themselves overloaded, and EXPLODED! Those of you who have no idea what I am talking about can study the pictures I uploaded earlier today to the website (http://www.trawlerweb.com). There's a great shot of the damaged fenders (and the damage to Crosser).

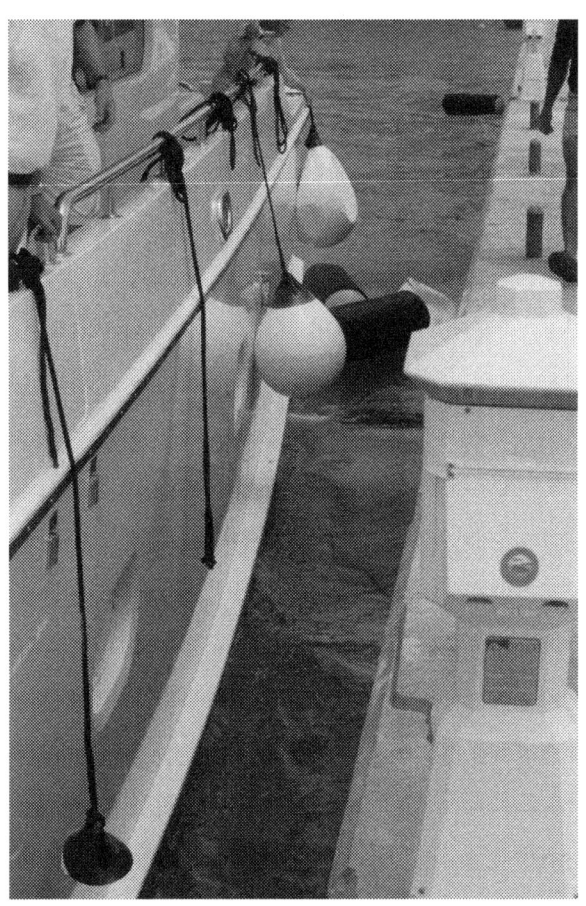

Once Crosser's stern was without fenders, it started digging itself into the wall, accompanied by a squeal of grinding fiberglass that I never want to hear again. This

immediately caused Crosser to straighten itself out, placing it once more parallel to the wall, moving forward while continuing to grind into the wall as it went. I'm missing the best photographs, because I, like everybody else, immediately ran to Crosser to push her off the wall. To my amazement we did introduce a couple of feet of separation, which allowed Crosser to "punch it again". This time she made it such that her bow was beyond the end of the dock, but her stern still against the dock. The wind then started turning Crosser to the port (left) side, and straight into the corner of the dock. Crosser was pivoting on the side of the dock, held there by the 30 knots of wind.

 This was being made more interesting as the corner of the dock started cracking, and parts started falling off. A power pedestal broke at the base, and was being pushed to a 30 degree angle. A lamppost on the corner of the dock was leaning badly. There was a fire hydrant inches away, and I knew that it was seconds from blowing (which fortunately it never did).

As all of this was happening, things started going really bad. I've said before that boating is best described as days of boredom punctuated by seconds of terror. This was to be no exception. A passenger on the back of Crosser stepped onto the swim platform and leaned into the water to retrieve the fenders that were being trailed through the water. You could sense the same emotion run through all of us at the same time. Crosser weighs perhaps 200,000 pounds, and a passenger put himself in a position that could result in his being between Crosser and the wall. A unanimous chorus (all of us on the dock) advised the passenger loudly, and unambiguously, that this was the wrong time to worry about the fenders, and he stepped back into the boat.

Meanwhile, at the front of the boat, Garret had repositioned himself to PUSH Crosser's nose to the starboard (right side). In my opinion, this was a courageous, but a very dangerous decision. Had Crosser been farther forward, and suddenly made a sharp turn to port, Garret would have been in a tough place. The tender weighs about 800 pounds, and has a 60 horsepower motor. It did help having it directly pushing on Crosser's nose. From where I was standing on the dock, pushing on Crosser's port side, I could see Garret to my left, with the tender's nose dug into Crosser, literally folding itself up under the pressure.

That's when Crosser punched it again, and Garret's engine quit. Crosser shot forward, and I was briefly worrying that the tender would somehow get sucked under Crosser, but the tender was pushed away nicely. Garret got the engine rolling, and life was good again.

Once out to sea, we all relaxed, and perhaps to counter the tension of minutes earlier, there was some mooning that ensued. As the other boat did not return the gesture, it is possible that offense was taken. Hopefully no pictures shall reach the internet!

As the mood whip-lashed from serious to jovial and back to serious, it was time to talk about our heading. Walt Hack, our weather forecaster had suggested that we proceed due east for roughly the next day and a half rather than heading directly to Horta. Walt felt this would give us a smoother ride by avoiding rougher seas to the north, and add only an extra 8-10 hours to the voyage. Walt knows his stuff and has been guiding many of us for years, including yours truly.

Our first sign of dissent was Bob Rothman, of Emeritus, jumping on the radio to say that he had made the decision to go straight for Horta. He was convinced Walt was being overly cautious, and put us on notice of his new heading. His opinion was echoed by a few more of our boats, forcing Kirk to put the issue to a vote. We called Hack to discuss the issue with him personally, and he held firm that going direct to Horta was a mistake. After much discussion the decision was made. We're going direct. I hope we know what we're doing.

Being an eventful day, the next hour had more surprises for us – Garret caught us a tuna, followed by our having to take evasive action to avoid a large tanker!

On a completely different topic, exercise was a topic today. Roberta is worried that sitting still for the next 10 days will cause her to turn to mush (which really isn't possible) – but her and St. John discussed an exercise program and Roberta kicked it off with 90 minutes of step aerobics/stretching/semi-yoga, all accompanied by ABBA (at maximum volume).

At 8:00 pm we had our standard evening report from the other division of boats. All was going well, and they are now 300 miles in front of us, also going direct to Horta. There was one concerning thing in their report, which was that one of the crew aboard Four Across appears to be passing a kidney stone. The doctor is monitoring him closely, and all is reported to be under control. The crewmember in question was not identified.

After the Division 2 update, it was time for roll call. Kirk, who has taken this duty over from Dan Streech, decided to put his own mark on the process. Roberta was assigned to the weather report ("it's dingy, windy and bumpy out there"), Phil was asked to do a cooking tip ("When preparing sushi, use a sharp knife as it's actually safer") and St. John was asked for a medical tip ("An apple a day keeps the doctor away – as constipation at sea could be serious") I suggested renaming Sans Souci to Avec Sushi to commemorate Garret's tuna haul, but no one got the joke and I felt a bit silly (it means "We have sushi" in French). All boats answered the roll call, without surprise, except Emeritus who unsuccessfully tried to convince us that they were already arriving at port in Horta.

Lastly, we finally settled our watch schedules. Roberta and I are a team, and stand watch from 8:00 am to noon, and from 8:00 pm to midnight. We couldn't be happier!

As my fingers are tired, and my stomach is rolling again, I shall quit typing now…

Day 24 - 240 miles east of Bermuda

Today was almost a perfect day! Not one person sick, and reasonably calm seas. Hopefully there will be more days like this.

That said, there were a few mechanical problems...

> Here on Sans Souci, we almost lost our steering system. Garret and St. John had a problem in the middle of the night. Sans Souci suddenly refused to steer on autopilot. Garret tracked the problem to a "collar" that connects the steering system to the rudder. The collar is attached to the rudder by four bolts, which had come loose. The steering system was limping along, but complete failure was imminent. After tightening things down (we are still missing one nut), we're going again.
> Que Linda has a leak in their stabilizer system. Fluid is pouring out, but they are capturing it in a bucket, and pouring it right back.
> Grey Pearl lost an alternator belt, but after a 30 minute slow down was going again.

On the good news front, I am happy to report that our new alternator is installed, and working fine. I believe that the frying of the first one was a result of our overloading it. When the trip is over I'd like to do a bit of investigating on this issue. It seems to me like there must be a regulator of some sort that should have been able to stop us from burning out the alternator. We are being very careful with the new alternator – even to the extent of taking cold showers to minimize electrical consumption. This is probably overkill, but we would like this alternator to last, and I still haven't heard a good explanation of why the first one blew.

We spoke with Division 1 (the slow boats), which is approximately 300 miles in front of us. They had no problems to report, and did not give us an update on the one medical problem that was reported yesterday.

Given that there was no action, we decided to create some of our own. Sans Souci organized a pirate attack on another boat in our fleet - Goleen. I've uploaded the pictures to the website (http://www.trawlerweb.com.) As you can see from the pictures, we had fun, and our attack was a huge success. Roberta had a fun question. While we were in the throes of our pirate attack, Roberta took me aside to ask if people would think she looked silly if she set up a jogging track around the pilothouse. I reminded her that most of the crew was on the front deck wearing pirate attire throwing water balloons. She was not in danger of looking strange.

With each mechanical problem that occurs here on Sans Souci, I've asked myself whether or not I could have fixed it, had Roberta and I been on the boat alone. Thus far, the one that scares me is the alternator problem. Would I have been able to figure where the smoke was coming from before it caught fire? Maybe. Would I have known how to take it out of the system and continue the voyage? Probably not. Unless we could have contacted someone at the manufacturer who could do some real-time diagnosing via sat phone, I think we would have been turning back, or worse. Luckily, Dan Streech of Nordhavn was on board and solved the problem.

This is an issue Roberta and I discuss often. We still have a lot of the world to visit aboard Sans Souci. The fact of the matter is that I am a retired software entrepreneur. I'm a software guy, not a hardware guy. If I can press a button, or write some code to fix a problem, I'm fine – but when the electric meters and torque wrenches come out, I start to sweat. My "fix" for this has been to duplicate all systems aboard ship. We have two engines, two radars, two generators, two GPS units, two water-makers, two autopilots, two VHF radios, two fuel filters, two water filters, etc. Do you see a pattern here? My primary repair strategy has always been to flip to the backup when needed, and this has served me through thousands of miles of cruising.

The right answer is to force myself to become a diesel mechanic, and develop a strong understanding of electrical systems. I'm smart and will learn quickly, but even smart people can't learn without making a concerted effort to do so. Aside from this trip, and until that day when I can honestly look in the mirror and see someone who could have diagnosed and replaced the alternator, my sense is that I'd like to confine my voyages to no more than 8-12 miles from shore when Roberta and I are traveling alone. I'm not sure how practical it is that I'll ever be fully self-sufficient. I've been watching Rip Knot and Kirk White in action. The odds that I'll ever possess their mechanical skills are somewhat comparable to the odds that they will ever be able to master computers or spreadsheets at my level. The question is where one draws the line to have a SAFE boating experience. What level of competence is needed, and what level is reasonable to expect?

As I sit here doing my watch in calm seas, with a totally dark sky, its the perfect time to think about boating, and about life in general. What else is there to do for the next nine days?

Thank you,
Ken Williams
Sans Souci, 6209
http://www.trawlerweb.com

P.S. – The following is a report from Jim Leishman from the Division 2 group. I'm also passing along several of the daily updates from the Web log of Georgs Kolesnikovs, the only journalist crewing on all three legs of the Nordhavn Atlantic Rally 2004. Georgs is having problems getting his daily updates posted to his website … so, I'm helping him "get the word out."

Wednesday - June 2nd
Position: N32-2' - W055-15'
Speed: 7 knots
Course: Due East

Its the third day at sea for Division 2 and the crew has settled in nicely to the passage-making routine. Aboard for this leg are Motorboating's John Woldridge, and Peter Swanson - writing for Yachting. Additionally, we have our normal crew consisting of Dr. Kevin and Kari Ware, Dave Shuler, Justin Zumwalt, James Leishman and myself. With a crew of eight and six bunks - things are a little tight but we're all enjoying the trip very much.

Since leaving Bermuda we've traveled about 500 miles east into the North Atlantic and have enjoyed moderate weather with winds mostly aft of the beam and under 20 knots. Our weather forecaster - Walt Hack predicts more of the same with some increased wind and seas from the northwest early next week.

We were all pleased to get underway last Sunday after a week of activities in Bermuda. A combination of working through boat problems, fueling, provisioning, diving, scooter riding, sight seeing and Bermudian night life all combined to drain our energy levels and pocket books. I have nothing but good things to say about Bermuda, however it is probably the most expensive of countries I've visited.

The highlight of our stay was the formal dinner Saturday night at the Royal Bermuda Yacht Club. Crews of the each Rally boats participated, and we were joined by the Commodore and Vice Commodore of the RBYC. Dating back to 1844 the RBYC has earned the reputation of being one of the most prestigious yacht clubs in the world and has hosted the biannual Bermuda Yacht Race for almost 100 years. The halls and meeting rooms of the RBYC are filled with yachting history and it was a heady experience to feel so welcome and a part of this establishment.

Our days at sea consist of morning and evening roll call where each vessel in our division (12 yachts) check in and give their latitude and longitude, speed and course and an estimate of their remaining range at the present speed and fuel burn. Additionally, any problems the vessel is experiencing are discussed and then any additional comments or concerns are reviewed. Generally this is all for drill now as every boat is in visual range and most issues are discussed casually through out the day. Generally speaking, the problems are very minor - today a loose belt was discussed aboard "Stargazer" and her owner quickly made an adjustment and the problem was solved.

The VHF provides entertainment as there is constant chatter amongst the crews. Calls are made on 16 and frequencies are selected for these discussions. At times numerous VHF channels are in use and the crews are developing the friendships we anticipated. There's heavy discussion about the daily fishing, weather, food preparation, onboard maintenance and dozens of other topics. I heard this morning Susan Spencer aboard "Uno Mas" announce that at 14:00 each day there would be "Chick Chatter" on channel 68 - I'll try to listen in tomorrow.

Today - Georgs Kolesnikovs, a man I had absolute trust in, suggested that we slow down "Atlantic Escort" and line our entire crew up on the starboard rail for a photo opportunity. Georgs encouraged us to move in closer for the perfect photo and then without warning he and his captain Scott Strickland, Terri Strickland and crew maliciously attacked us with a water balloon salvo. We will not forget this and vow revenge before this Atlantic Ocean is crossed.

More Tomorrow,
Jim Leishman

FRIDAY MAY 28 2245

I'm batching it tonight, feasting on baked potatoes and Mini Babybel cheese to replenish carbohydrates and protein after a 6-mile walk/run. The Significant Other is in town - actually, she's at Aqua, the high-end Michael Douglas restaurant - meeting a friend who is in her fifth year of working for Bank of Bermuda.

I saw the other side of Bermuda tonight along the former railway line running down the center of the island. It's the Bermuda of ordinary folk, black and white, living inland, a reminder where the heart of Bermuda resides. It's the Bermuda of roosters crowing, even at dusk, of hens and chicks scattering at my approach, of barbecues and Friday night gospel meetings, of tree frogs singing.

The Bermuda I saw certainly was not the million - and multi-million dollar "cottages" along Bermuda's coast line, the prim and proper business bustle of Hamilton, the capital, or the privilege of Royal Bermuda Yacht Club.

Tomorrow is the last day in Bermuda prior to departure Sunday at 0800.

It's been a hectic week, with me torn between getting pictures selected, cropped, uploaded to the blog, and working on my assignments for Power Cruising and Circumnavigator, and helping get the Nordhavn 47 Strictly for Fun ready for the passage to Azores, and spending time with Significant Other. As I'm going to be away from home for two full months, in my time management here, I have erred in favor of Significant Other.

SATURDAY MAY 29 2315

The smaller boats are ready to depart Bermuda at 0800 on Sunday for the Azores about 1,800 nautical miles across the pond. As you can see in the weather forecast from Walt Hack a few posts down, conditions will be a bit bumpy at first but then should improve.

This is the longest leg across the Atlantic, with the distance being what separates true passage-makers from poseurs.

119

We should be at sea about 12 days, our pace dictated by our smallest vessel, the Nordhavn 40 Uno Mas.

At the final briefing this afternoon, we heard that Uno Mas will start out conservatively, running its Lugger at 1,400 rpm which should produce 6 knots of boat speed with fuel consumption at 2 gallons per hour. The idea is to proceed cautiously for the first two or three days, recalculating fuel burn every 24 hours. Once real-world data for this stretch of ocean this week in this boat is in hand, we may be able to speed up a bit.

At the farewell dinner tonight, most folks seemed eager to get under way again. I am in that camp too, looking forward to my time aboard the Nordhavn 47 Strickly For Fun with owners Scott and Teri Strickland and one other crew, Jonathan Ehly.

Teri is the one who provided that great quote early in this weblog: "My husband is having a middle-life crisis, and he's invited me along."

SUNDAY MAY 30 1030

We're at Five Fathom Hole off St. George and turning east for the Azores. Actually, we're first heading to 55 degrees 00 minutes west longitude on a heading of 106 magnetic.

Weatherman Walt Hack suggested the waypoint to give us the smoothest possible ride between weather systems to the north and south of our route. Once we get to 55 00 West, in about 480 nautical miles, we'll pick up the rhumb line (shortest distance) to the Azores.

After the 25 knots of wind that blew through Hamilton harbor for much of the day yesterday, today we have perfect weather for starting a long passage. There is a light wind and gentle seas of 2 to 3 feet, with only the occasional bump, on our starboard quarter.

Uno Mas, the fleet pacesetter, is steaming along at 5.9 to 6.1 knots.

SUNDAY MAY 30 1520

Lat 32 22 North Long 63 51 West Speed 6 knots Course 106

We've had our excitement for the day: Teri spotted a round fender in the water ahead of us and Scott decided to call a man-overboard drill. The fender looked fairly new and Scott was determined to retrieve it. Thus, with the boat in neutral and alongside, he dove into 15,000 feet of ocean to get the thing.

MONDAY MAY 31 0230 during my night watch

Lat 32 22.3 North Long 62 53.2 West 403 nm from our waypoint at 55 00 West, Speed 4.8 knots because of an adverse current, Course 106, Light wind, gentle 3-5-ft seas

In the night sky, there are dim flashes of lightning so distant I cannot hear thunder.

120

I am alone on the 0200-0400 watch. With a four-person crew on Strickly For Fun, watches are stood solo - just the way I like it. Scott, Jon Ehly and I look after the three two-hour watches between midnight and 0600, with Teri standing the evening watch from 2100 to midnight. Between 6 a.m. and midnight, watch-standing is not a fixed schedule. Whoever feels like, he or she has the con. There is an informal attempt made to ensure no one is stuck on the bridge for hours without a break.

This is my first experience with free-form watch-standing during the day. It is ironic to find such an unstructured system on a boat as well and tightly organized as the Stricklands run Strickly For Fun. When I signed on, Scott emailed me a PDF file detailing the routine of the ship and what was expected of guests and crew. See preceding post.

Those who haven't been at sea at night will be surprised to hear how bright it is out here as a result of the moon being a few days from full. Despite overcast skies, there is the appearance of a silver dawn.

On the Furuno Navnet display, Scott has set the radar for night running: Black background. Red rings one-half mile apart emanating from the center where our vessel is. Bearing and course in green lines. Eleven red blips shows where the fleet steams eastward around us.

We are now 12 vessels in this division of smaller/slower boats. The Krogen 58 Sea Fox has joined us, preferring to run a long passage such as this one at 6 knots plus or minus rather than 8 plus with the larger/faster vessels. That division of six vessels still is in port, in Hamilton, scheduled to depart Tuesday at 0800. They should catch us up on the final approach to Horta where we are due to arrive on June 11.

Introduction for the 17-page document Scott and Teri have prepared for guests and crew aboard Strickly For Fun:

"Strickly For Fun" Pre-Trip Information
1. Purpose.

The purpose of this document is to help you understand what to expect while traveling on the Strickland Motor Yacht, "St f F". Reading this manual is very important. It will help you determine if the trip is right for you! It will let you know what to expect the trip to be like. Give you important safety information. This manual will describe:

- *Purpose of the Crew Manual.*
- *What to expect on the trip.*
- *Our Route.*
- *Safety Concerns.*
- *Food.*
- *Weather.*

- *Sea Communications.*
- *Harbor Communications.*
- *Work Effort.*
- *Watch Standing.*
- *Entertainment.*
- *Comforts.*
- *Seasickness.*
- *What to Bring.*
- *Clothing and Personal Gear Checklist.*
- *Rules.*
- *Conclusion.*

A general understanding of the trip, equipment, and responsibilities will make the trip more enjoyable for everyone.

This document is one of four documents you should read.

- *Crew Manual*
- *Emergency Manual*
- *Watch Standing manuals*

We also have:

- *Departure manual*
- *Underway*
- *Arrival Manual*
- *Shoreside (managing the boat at a dock without us!)*
- *Systems manual*

Conclusion of the 17-page document Scott and Teri have prepared for guests and crew aboard Strickly For Fun:

17. Conclusion.

This trip is not for everyone. The trip is not a common activity. No one else you know will ever do this. This trip is designed to be an adventure of a lifetime. It will not be perfect! If you don't want new experiences, take a plane. Since you will be involved with actually operating the vessel you will need to do your share of the work. If you are not willing to help, please stay home. This trip is for people who want to grow. You must be willing to learn new skills. We do not expect people to know these skills before they come on the boat. Part of the fun is teaching and learning new skills. Due to weather our times have to be somewhat flexible. If we plan on a two-week trip, plan for a couple of extra days. If you want to follow a rigid time schedule, take a tour. For everyone to have fun we all need to get along. If just one person is cranky the trip will be miserable for everyone! We have a gang plank are we are willing to use it! In short: this trip is not for the boring, lazy, stupid, inflexible or grumpy people!

TUESDAY JUNE 1 0700

Lat 32 22.6 North Long 59 30.7, Speed 6.4 knots, Course 107, Light wind, gentle 3-to-4-foot seas.

We are experimenting with a new watch system as the one we started with didn't suit everyone.

I am now on from 9 p.m. to midnight and from 6 to 9 a.m. In effect, I get my share of watch-standing - 6 hours out of the 24 hours the four of us deal with - done in one half of the day, thus, I should be able to look after my others chores, devote several hours to my work, as well as get a couple hours of sleep to augment the 5.5 hours I can get in between watches.

The other three crew stand two-hour watches between midnight and 6 a.m., in rotation from one night to the next.

At the roll call last night, our smallest boat, the Nordhavn 40 Uno Mas that is setting pace for us all, reported it had increased speed to 6 knots, so the entire fleet was able to bump rpm up 50 or 100. At 6 knots, Uno Mas reported burning 2.1 gallons per hour, meaning it had a healthy reserve in hand. (Aboard Strickly For Fun, we burn more, but our fuel tankage, at 1,400 gallons, is such that 1,800 nm is not a challenge, at least not from the point of view of fuel consumption.)

The latest weather report from Walt Hack indicates the light winds and gentle seas are likely to end in 48 hours, being succeeded by wind up to 22 knots and seas up to 8 feet. Some of the new weather may come from the east - right on the nose - but by the weekend, we could be enjoying blue skies and sunshine and mild conditions again.

Last night, I took a turn in the galley and served up the almost-famous Kolesnikovs Klops, a dish from my Latvian motherland made with ground beef, bacon, mushrooms, onions and plenty of sour cream, presented on a base of a creamed and buttered potato mash with green onions, with a side of dill pickles. So satiated were we that dessert of chocolate mousse with whipped cream has been postponed until later. If that sounds like a repeat of what I wrote from Autumn Wind, that is because it was.

Autumn Wind was a dry boat while under way. Aboard Strickly For Fun, we uncorked a Hawk Crest Cabernet Sauvignon to wash down the meal. Lest that leaves the wrong impression, I should note the bottle was not emptied.

Yesterday, I neglected to mention that Teri Strickland has named herself fleet DJ. At the beginning of the morning roll call, we broadcast Bad To The Bone by George Thoroughgood to the fleet on VHF 17.

Naiad stabilizer problems continue to pop up. The latest to be afflicted is Sea Fox, the Krogen 58, which has been running on only one fin for the last 24 hours or so. Yesterday being Memorial Day in the U.S., no sat phone calls were made to Naiad, but starting this morning, sat phone charges have been mounting, with no solution yet.

Also yesterday, Scott Strickland initiated a 12 noon "coffee klatch" on VHF 17 with a half-dozen vessels participating. Today, we plain forgot to get on the air.

Everyone aboard Strickly for Fun is anxiously awaiting the first shout of "Hook up!" from Jon Ehly who has two fishing lines out. Jon is quite a fisherman and he cannot believe how bereft of fish we have been since leaving Hamilton. That, despite the fact he invested $500 in new lures.

June 1 0700

Note to readers: I have given up on attempts to post to my weblog via Skymate. Henceforth, using SailMail and the single-sideband radio aboard Strictly For Fun, I will send reports to Ken Wiilliams aboard Sans Souci and Fred Wunderlich back in Fort Lauderdale for posting to their sites, and to Significant Other for keeping family and friends informed.

WEDNESDAY JUNE 2 1600

Lat 32 25.5 North Long 55 04.1 West, Speed 6.4 knots, Course 92, Light wind 5 to 10 knots out of SSW, gentle 2-to-3-foot seas.

Just short of our 55 00 West waypoint, we have turned for the Azores 1,351 nm distant. Coincidentally, Autumn Wind reached Goleen in the larger-boat fleet behind us. The four Nordhavns, one Northern Marine/Seaton, and one Monk/McQueen are 313 nm behind us, running on the rhumb line to the Azores at 8.5 knots. That means they could catch us in six days, that is, Tuesday.

The larger boats had better weather right from the start, thus, they have been on the shortest course for Horta right since departing Horta.

It has been an eventful day, eventful for the middle of the Atlantic at displacement speed.

World Odd@Sea reported catching and releasing a 90-lb marlin. Someone else reported sighting a whale.

We have fish, too, for dinner, sent over to Strickly For Fun by the Spencers on Uno Mas. We exchanged gifts while running about 30 yards apart and tossing a line from one boat to the other. We sent them a best-selling book on CD, Number One Lady Detective Agency, which Teri wanted to share with Sue Spencer. In return, we received yellow fin tuna, caught and frozen on the Pacific side of Panama.

As I write this in the saloon, Teri is in the galley preparing a mango salsa with cilantro to go with the tuna which Jon will medallion and lightly pan-fry. My mouth waters as I type.

Earlier in the day, under the ruse of wanting to photograph Jim Leishman and the crew aboard Atlantic Escort for Power Cruising, I asked Atlantic Escort to run along side Strictly For Fun, getting as close as they felt comfortable. They took the bait, and for their trouble were bombarded with water balloons by Scott, Teri and Jon on our flying bridge. As Escort pulled away, threats of revenge rang in the air.

At 1400, Sue Spencer on the Nordhavn 40 Uno Mas convened the first rally chick chat, a get-together on VHF 69 for the women of our fleet.

At 1200, I resurrected the daily coffee klatch that Scott started a few days ago on the radio, calling it NAR Net. Today we chatted about fishing and what lures were working. Tomorrow the theme will be filters.

This morning we heard that the larger boats had departed Hamilton on schedule. Crosser had an encounter of the unwanted kind with the dock on departure. More recently, Grey Pearl lost an alternator belt. Otherwise, all goes well with the big boys.

Must go now as it is time for an engine-room check.

--30—gxk

Day 25 - 410 miles from Bermuda

Rip spoke to me this morning about his concern that readers of my daily reports might be getting the wrong impression. His concern is that people will think that Sans Souci "breaks a lot" or that Nordhavn boats generally have problems. This could not be further from the truth. Roberta and I chose Nordhavn because we wanted the best, and after six years of ownership, we believe that more fervently than ever. I would be very surprised to see us ever own a non-Nordhavn boat. They have my strongest recommendation.

In the off chance that anyone reading my emails shares Rip's concern, I'd like to tell a little more of the story. Contrary to what you might think, I've been very pleasantly surprised by how Sans Souci has performed on this voyage. To tell you why requires a bit of explanation.

Personal powerboats capable of crossing oceans are a rarity in US marinas. When Sans Souci was at Roche Harbor, in the Pacific Northwest, we were somewhat of a tourist attraction. Not a weekend went by that someone didn't come begging for a tour of the boat. It took us a while to get used to the concept that there was nothing we could do about the constant stream of people wandering past our stern.

As unusual as Sans Souci was, we had no problem keeping her properly maintained. The Pacific Northwest, and Seattle, has some of the top maintenance facilities in the world. Several of the companies that built the systems aboard Sans Souci are based there, such as Lugger (the engines and generators), and Nick Jackson (the Davit).

For the past four years, Sans Souci has been in France, where it is an even rarer boat. There are plenty of top quality shipyards, but they aren't accustomed to boats such as Sans Souci. Seattle is a major fishing port, and the propulsion system that powers Sans Souci is more similar to an Alaskan fishing boat than the mega-yachts one sees in the south of France. In the Med, power boating is speed-focused, even speed obsessed.

We always felt culturally more at home with the sail boaters than the power boaters, for reasons I'll perhaps talk about in a later report.

Actually, I'm just making excuses for something I'm not very certain about. To jump to the point: When Sans Souci was in France, Roberta's and my perception was that we were working with great people, who were making an honest effort to maintain Sans Souci, but that it was outside of their core competency. We never had a major mechanical problem with Sans Souci, but I always had this sense that we needed to get back to the US sooner or later for some catch-up maintenance.

One of the benefits of this rally was the opportunity it presented to have Nordhavn directly involved with Sans Souci's maintenance. Over a six-month period we had the attention of Nordhavn's top people. I also took advantage of the opportunity to upgrade Sans Souci to as close as I could get to Nordhavn's current "state of the art." Nordhavn is constantly upgrading their boats, and Sans Souci represented their best effort, as it was six years ago. Since then, there have been innovations in many areas. The ones that interested me most were the electrical system upgrades and the improved cooling systems.

To make a long story short, between October of 2003 and May of 2004, Sans Souci became a very different, and greatly improved, boat. If I were to list everything that was done, I suspect there would be at least a hundred different entries on the list. Rip flew to Florida a week before Roberta and I arrived, for a test drive. His first words to me were something like "Ken – you won't believe it. It's like a completely different boat." He was a very happy camper.

As a software guy, I am intimately acquainted with a process called debugging. Whenever software is developed or modified, it needs to be tested for bugs. It has been my experience that there is not a straight-line correlation between the amount of code and the time it takes to debug it. There is an exponential relationship. Twice the amount of code means four times the debugging time.

Sans Souci had hundreds of upgrades, each of which needed debugging. I remember calling my contact at the shipyard to ask if he wasn't concerned that we were taking a boat that had had so much work done across an ocean, without a proper shakedown period. His response was that I was being overly nervous; that they had checked everything out, and would be prepared to meet the boat in Bermuda if problems showed up.

There have been issues that I suspect have their origin with the repairs that were made. The bolts coming loose on the steering may have happened because someone forgot to put lock nuts on when the rudder assembly was inspected. Dan Streech wrote this morning to say that he was 99% sure that when we study the alternator we will find that it is an enfant mortality issue. It was a new alternator, and perhaps a small percentage of them fail immediately.

Anyway, my only goal with the preceding paragraphs is to say that I see this differently than Rip. He sees what we are undergoing as "normal" maintenance, whereas I see it as being more issues than I'm accustomed to seeing, but that they are well below what I expected to see. I just do not believe you can have a boat in the shop for six months and expect everything to work on the first try.

Which brings us to the "issues" we've experienced today. Garret spent hours working on the large water maker to get it going. Apparently we had a badly leaking hose for the second time during the voyage. We were making water, but then pouring it into the back of our boat, rather than the water tank.

We also had an unscheduled main engine shutdown earlier today. We have a fuel transfer system aboard Sans Souci that helps us to move fuel from tank to tank. We have a total of six tanks, and are running the boat from one particular tank. We have the option to take fuel from any selected tank, or we can transfer the fuel to a particular tank and have the engine take it from there. I've always run by just taking fuel from whichever tank I wanted, and let the boats balance tell me which tank to pull from. If the boat felt heavy in the front, I pulled from the front tank, etc. Only one of the six tanks is physically higher in the boat than the main engine, the engine room starboard tank. We decided it would be nice to move the fuel into that tank, and keep life easy for the main engine, under the assumption that gravity fed fuel is simpler for the main engine to grab than fuel that has to be forcefully sucked from a tank 30 feet away. This also gives us the advantage of filtering the fuel one extra time, as the fuel transfer system has its own filter.

To move fuel into the engine room tank we need to run the fuel transfer system periodically. I've personally never used the fuel transfer system, but it isn't really complicated. You move some levers that tell the system where to get fuel, and where to

put fuel, and then you turn on the pump. Minutes later, you are done. Or, at least that's what it says in the book.

The fuel transfer system is being stubborn today. It's not a huge issue, as I ran the boat quite happily for six years without ever using it – however, it has been frustrating Rip, who would like to see it working. After a bit of discussion we decided that we should replace the fuel filter on the fuel transfer system to see if that would solve our problem.

Oops. We now know that if you are not careful, it is possible to suck air into the engine through the fuel transfer system. At about 1:00pm today, our main engine quit. That got everyone's attention. We suspected immediately what had happened, and that the fix was to bleed the lines.

Kirk White is a senior hauncho at Nordhavn, responsible for the final outfitting of the boats. He is also a crewmember here on Sans Souci. His reaction spoke volumes about his personality, and taught me a lesson. He never blinked. He saw this as a valuable opportunity to teach a lesson, and nothing more. He had no doubt that the engine would be going again in a few minutes. He simply challenged us to think about what happened, why it happened, and what the next step should be. He knew that if he ran down the stairs and fixed the problem, a valuable opportunity to advance our knowledge about engines and fuel systems would be lost.

Getting the main restarted only took a few minutes, but getting the fuel transfer system working correctly has proven a larger challenge. I'm sure it will be going by the time you read this, but for right now, we're still in the learning phase. Currently, our primary hypothesis is that the fuel transfer system has been working all the time. The operating manual for the boat says that it transfers 60 gallons of fuel per hour. The brand name on the pump doesn't match the manual, and the pump looks small. We think it is pumping just fine – but at only a small fraction of the rate we were expecting.

As I was typing these last couple of paragraphs, we were "attacked" by Goleen, who snuck up on us and then started hitting us with giant sling-shot launched bio-degradable water balloons. We defended ourselves well. I was involved long enough to make a decision as to what music we should blare through our ships hailer. I chose "Yellow Submarine" which seemed to be a hit with both boats. For a brief period, Sans Souci's front deck was consumed with "Pull, Launch, Duck and Boogey" (all of which are verbs that seemed to be acting upon our respective crews). I thought our crew was the most innovative when we launched a flying fish at Goleen that had washed up upon our deck. I took photos, but will not be uploading them. Been there, done that. We need a new outlet for our creative energy…

I'm now looking out the window at a sailboat. It refuses to answer calls via radio, and is the first small boat we've seen. We did get close enough to see its name, "Anna", and a French flag. It still won't answer on the radio, after repeated requests from our group and various horn honking. We got close enough to see a man in the back, and tried to communicate with him in both English and French, but he stubbornly refused to respond, or had no radio. A water balloon attack was briefly discussed, but we decided we had probably already frightened him

more than we should have. Can you imagine being approached out in the middle of the ocean by six boats that shouldn't realistically be there? We must have been quite a bizarre sight for him.

Everyone is settling into cruising. Time seems to be moving both fast and slow. Bermuda now seems a distant memory, yet we were there within the last 48 hours. Perhaps time is moving slowly because so much is happening. Days are filled with activities; twice daily roll calls, meals, watches, fishing, water fights, repairs, calculations, research, engine room checks, deciding what music to put on the iPod, etc. I've been finishing my days thinking: "Darn it, another day went by with no time to read, or to get work done," Boredom has not been a factor, which is nice. But, as strange as this sounds - if I didn't know better, I'd swear we have already been at sea for a month, and at this pace it feels like it will be years before we arrive.

P.S. - The weather outlook continues to be depressing (as compared to my dream of a totally flat ocean), whereas the reality continues to be near perfect. We have spent much of the day in fog, but it has otherwise been smooth sailing. For a while we ran within 50 feet or so of Emeritus. It was a very cool feeling...

Following is the current outlook:

For the Slow-Group, along the rhumb line to Horta expect:

Thursday/03: Variable to occ W-N 07-16kt. Swell NW 5=7ft. 6-8sec periods.
Friday/04: WSW-SSW freshen 10-20kt. NW-W 5-7ft.
Saturday/05: WSW-NW 15-25kt. NW 6-8ft with occ 10-11ft sets.
Sunday/06: NW 15-25kt. NW 6-8ft.
Monday/07: NW-WSW ease 10-18kt by noon. NW 5-7ft.
Tuesday/08: W'ly 20-30kt. West 8-10ft 8sec periods.
Wednesday/09: W'ly 20-30kt. West 6-10ft occ 11-12ft sets.

For the Fast-Group, along the 'apparent' rhumb line to Horta, expect:

Thursday/03: S-SW 11-21kt. Swell confused to West 4-6ft.
Friday/04: SW-WNW 12-22lkt. W-NE 6-7ft.
Saturday/05: NW 10-20kt. NW 6-8ft. 7-9sec.
Sunday/06: Freshen NW 15-25kt. NW 7-9ft.
Monday/07: NW-W 10-20kt. NW 5-7ft.
Tuesday/08: W'ly 20-30kt. NW-W 7-10ft.
Wednesday/09: W'ly 20-30kt. West 7-10ft.

Day 26 - 600 miles east of Bermuda

At noon today, I thought I would have nothing to say in today's report.

That's when a call came in from Goleen trying to suck us into another water balloon fight. I said yesterday that I was "beyond" water balloon fights, and wanted to find some new pass-time. Unfortunately, life doesn't work like that, and within minutes I was back in the action. Things got a bit more interesting when St. John and Garret dived into the water and swam to Goleen. We assumed they would be right back, but then Crosser called on the radio to announce that they were surrounded by whales, so everyone headed to Crosser.

The whales turned out to be a school of dolphins, but they were fun to see anyhow. As we were standing on the front deck admiring the dolphins, Kirk said: "Let's launch the tender and visit the other boats." Rip was in the engine room at the time working on the water maker. I was fairly certain he wouldn't support the idea, so I said: "Let's hurry."

We have the tender strapped down TIGHT on the front deck. We keep hearing that the waves can be big out here, and want to ensure that the tender doesn't get swept off the deck. But it wasn't so tight we couldn't get it in the water in 10 minutes, which we did do. Kirk and Phil took off in the tender to visit the other boats, collecting cookies and cigars. At this time an area of at least five miles of sea separated the boats.

It was also about this time that Rip came up the stairs to ask what was happening and where Kirk had went. Being a man of honor, I pretended to know nothing, and blamed it all on Kirk.

That's when Grey Pearl called (on the radio) to say they were going swimming. Roberta automatically started heading in that direction, and we noticed Que Linda turning back to join us. Goleen also joined in the fun. This kicked off a great swim time, with all of the boats emptying into the 16 thousand foot deep water. After the swim, we were able to lure St. John and Garret back to Sans Souci by promising them cigars and cookies.

Crews gather for an impromptu swim.

We were returning to Sans Souci when we had our first injury of the trip. Phil was jumping into the tender - which was being cast about by rough water - from Grey Pearl's swim platform, when he somehow caught his finger on something on Grey Pearl. We still don't know exactly how it happened, but the middle finger on his left hand was suddenly pouring a LOT of blood, and had a deep 2-inch long gash.

Quickly returning to Sans Souci, we alerted St. John, our EMT, that it was time for him to get to work. I must say that he took the matter very seriously. He grabbed an emergency kit the size of an average suitcase and started scrubbing, cleaning and bandaging Phil's finger. He also called the Doctor on Atlantic Escort. I doubt a cut finger has ever had so much attention. No stitches were needed, although Phil now has a large gauze-wrapped cylinder protruding from the center of his left hand, where his finger used to be (actually, I'm fairly sure the finger is still there hiding beneath the gauze).

Demonstrating how concerned we were, I heard several people asking St. John if he could hurry, because we were hungry and needed Phil to get back to work. Phil is sitting next to me now trying to type an email. It's hilarious watching him trying to work around his bandaged finger. He's smiling too, so I assume all is well.

Earlier this morning, I listened in on a radio conversation between Que Linda and a non-rally boat that is 10 or so miles ahead of us. It was just idle chit-chat amongst passing strangers, but was the kind of conversation that reminds me of why I bought a Nordhavn. They didn't know each other, but were swapping tales of where they had been and where they were going. Que Linda was talking about their run from Alaska to Florida and that they were now heading for somewhere in the Med, and maybe to the UK, but that they didn't know exactly where yet. The other boat, a 48' motor-sailor was talking about some of the places they had recently been, like cruising the east coast of the U.S., Trinidad, the Caribbean, and more. It was just a very cool feeling to think about boats wandering from country to country. While listening, I had to look at our own engine hours gauge to see how many miles San Souci had covered. It says "1535.2". That means Sans Souci has logged somewhere around 14,000 miles, and we still have a lifetime of cruising ahead of us.

Also this morning, Roberta and I were starting to tie down our plans for where we're going after Gibraltar. I hate being on a schedule, but some of the nicer marinas in the Med require reservations. We can always anchor and tender in, but I prefer having the boat in a marina. Our tentative plan has us going from Gibraltar to Puerto Banus in Spain, then to Cartajena (another port in Spain), and then Ibiza and on to Mallorca (Puerto Portales). That's as far ahead as we have planned. We know that ultimately we have to get the boat to France, but want to think only as far ahead as necessary.

A few days ago I mentioned that one of the passengers on Four Across, in the Division 2 boats, had a medical issue. We now have heard that all is well, and that the individual is back on their feet.

Here's an issue I'm tracking closely: Fuel. I am positive we have plenty of fuel, and will arrive with 500 gallons left over. However, knowing there isn't a problem has never stopped me from worrying. All I could think of as I was swimming was that Sans Souci was burning fuel and we weren't moving. We have five fuel gauges for six tanks, all of which have a certain amount of round-off error. Rip's calculations show us with 100 gallons more than my own. Under normal circumstances there is no need to know exactly how much fuel is on board, but this is not a normal trip. We had planned to run around 8 knots to minimize fuel consumption, but have been running between 9.5 and 10.5 knots all day. The sea is flat and it's a good time to move fast. We have a gauge here in the cockpit that shows actual consumption. It claims we are burning 12 gallons of fuel per hour. My goal was to use only about 8 gallons per hour. I was told before the trip that the gauge is wrong by 10-20%. I personally would be happier if my personal tank readings, and analysis of what the instruments say, weren't so inconsistent.

Speaking of fuel: The largest boat amongst us, Crosser, is actually a much faster boat than the rest of us. Whereas Sans Souci is happy at 9 knots, Crosser would be happier cruising at 13 knots. She wasn't really designed to be run for days on end at a slow speed. As I'm typing this, Crosser is on the radio saying that they were going to do a few laps around us, at full speed, just to give their engines a chance to run at full speed for a bit. When asked what their fuel consumption was at 13 knots they responded: 44 gallons per hour!

Following are excerpts from emails by St. John and Phil that I'm including for your perusal...

Everybody aboard may think I am funny or wish to correct me but I think the lingo that I choose around the boat is a perfect description of what this is, our temporary home. The front bow of the boat I have named our front yard. As that is where we lay out to read, tan, and have water balloon fights with our neighbors, the Goleens, water gun fights amongst ourselves, or just plain get out of the house (inside of the boat), to clear our heads with some fresh air. The door to the yard, or Portuguese bridge, if I have it correctly, is our picket fence keeping us safe at night inside our study, or pilot house where we get the work of running the boat done, and also our own work of writing emails, managing finances, etc. The aft deck I view as our porch, a place to sit and read quietly, by far the least bumpy place on the boat. Here you can sit on a nice comfortable seat and watch the sun rise, or set, read a book, take a quick snooze, do some exercising, or just get lost in the ocean. One could also transfer each of these areas into a little suburban house and no one would know the difference.

The crew, dressed as Pirates, stand behind the "picket fence".

I think it is safe to say family Sans Souci is really coming together. Our last name is really Sans Souci and not too much matters when you are in the middle of the Atlantic. Everyone else on the boat is here to help you, offer advice, play a game with, have a good laugh, a good chat, or just plainly be there to offer some company amongst this wide vastness of blue. This trip there has been a change amongst the crew as we all realize we are stuck together and after slowly testing the waters the first leg, we are all getting along great with one another. Joking around with each other at dinner, throwing water balloons at one another, even as far as asking little questions to get a better idea about who everyone is. Before we were owners, Captains, Chefs, medics, and guests, first mates, and representatives from PAE, now we are Ken and Roberta, Rip, Bill, St.

137

John, Garret and Kirk. Each of us providing their own little ingredient to the Sans Souci soup, which I think tastes delightful.

The seas are calm and the sun shines during the day. At night the moon spotlights us providing a nice light almost as if someone is saying, "Hey we know you are out there, and safe travels."

My first impression was that boredom would set in and everyone would be acting like the family on Seventh Heaven, with too many problems that not even a minister could handle. Luckily, I couldn't be more wrong as we each find something to do and someone else who by the end of the trip we can call our friend.

The sun sets as the fleet presses onwards.

=============== *From Chef Phil* ============================

11:50 pm, Thursday June 3, 2004

Tonight as I turned off the lights in my cabin I looked out of my porthole and I saw the full moon just above the horizon and it all hit me as to how amazing this experience is. Here I am about to fall asleep and I have left my safety and well being in the hands of two people who are standing watch in the pilot house while the boat moves forward through the darkness at about 9 knots via an automated system called an Auto-Pilot. I have no idea how it works, it just does. I simply cannot describe the sight right now as I look out my little porthole and see the moon reflecting off the water and watch the waves roll and move as we cut through the water at a steady speed.

I soon will fall asleep and all throughout the night this boat will continue moving forward. The engine will continue to run, the boat will continue to move in an easterly direction. I will awaken several hours from now and begin my task of feeding everyone on board. And then again tomorrow night this same pattern will repeat itself. I know this is not the way our ancestors crossed the ocean so many years ago. They did not have the luxury that I have right now as I sit comfortably in my cabin typing away on my laptop sending messages via a satellite up in the sky. But this is my experience none-the-less and it is nothing short of amazing. But I

138

can say that I do know how they felt as they looked up at the full moon reflecting off the ocean and were in awe of the vastness of the waters surrounding them. This planet is so amazing and I am just a spec in the middle of all this water. I am but a spec.

=============== *Chef Phil – Second Posting* =========================

Well guys, the first official injury that required Singen our EMT on board to jump into action happened today and it happened to yours truly. Before I go into the details of the injury let me backtrack to how it happened. It seems that so far, on a near daily basis, we all put our heads together and devise a plan to have fun with the other boats in our group. We were the first ones to launch a pirate attack complete with hurling (bio-degradable) water balloons at the first unsuspecting boat, Goleen. Today was no exception. Kirk and I launched the dinghy and headed out to visit all the other boats knowing we may meet with similar retaliation given the fact that we were an easy target. The first boat we reached was Grey Pearl and they attempted to launch water balloons at us but Kirk's quick maneuvering of the dinghy afforded us only near misses but no direct hits after 3 complete circles around the boat. The next boat we reached was Que Linda and as we made our first pass they opened their starboard boarding gate and to our surprise, they fired a cannon at us! Just a very loud bang and a lot of smoke, but I don't believe

it was really loaded. I think. Then it was off to the next boat. A special note: all these boats were anywhere from ¼ mile to 3 miles away and Kirk would put the petal to the metal in the dingy reaching speeds of up to 30 knots launching us over the waves with ease. It was better than any E-ticket ride at Disneyland. The next boat we reached after Que Linda was Crosser. Would we be met by friends or foe? Much to our surprise we were greeted with 2 bags of homemade cookies that were passed to us with beaming smiles. Then there was one last boat to visit, which was the farthest one from our original position - the Emeritus. To our great surprise they were happy and maybe a bit surprised to see us, even though our little adventure was being broadcasted over the VHF radio amongst all the boats. Much to our surprise and delight we were once again greeted with smiles. Although this time we were offered cigars and beer. We were very happy campers. As we made our way back we to the mother ship we found the Sans Souci, Goleen, Que Linda and Grey Pearl in a circle with most of the crew from all the boats out in the clear blue ocean swimming at a depth of 2797 fathoms or 16,782 feet (that's taller than Mt. Rainier!). For your info, our exact locations are latitude 34 degrees, 28 minutes north, and our longitude was 52 degrees, 56 minutes west. We all joined in with a game of more water balloon tossing and tons of laughter.

After a time of extreme laughter and fun it was time for all of us to go back to our respective boats and continue on the journey. Kirk was still driving the dingy and he delivered those who were just too tired from having too much fun back to their boats. I was on the rear platform (stern bustle) waiting for my ride back to the boat and it was at the moment that I boarded the dinghy that the tragic event happened. I still don't know what I cut my finger on but as I was jumping into the dingy, whatever I was holding onto with my left hand (and I still don't know what it was) sliced my middle finger open. I felt it as it happened and prayed when I looked at my finger that it was nothing more than a scratch, but unfortunately that was not the case. I had a two-inch rather deep gash, on the inside of my middle finger, from the tip right down to the middle. I knew the best thing I could do was to hang my hand in the healing salt water and I told Kirk to make a b-line for the Sans Souci.

As I boarded the boat I said to Singen, "Grab your medical bag, I've got a job for you" and showed him my bloody hand. Singen went immediately into EMT mode and after a sterile saline wash he applied 4 or 5 butterfly steri-strips and wrapped me up. His assessment was that no stitches were needed. So all is well, just ask the crew. I was up making hamburgers for lunch with an hour. So you see, if we aren't gazing at the seas on a moon lit night we are having a blast in the ocean and rolling with the punches. This won't stop me from experiencing everything I can everyday of this trip. Besides, I'm right handed and I injured my let hand.

Best regards to all,

Chef Phil

Day 27 - 800 miles from Bermuda

We said we would swim in the middle of the ocean, and today we did it. We looked at the map and guessed at the halfway point between Ft. Lauderdale and Gibraltar, and decided it was time for a swim. We did have a few of the boats together yesterday for a brief swim, but today's swim was a much bigger event, with everyone included.

There were some tricky logistical issues. The sea and the wind were refusing to cooperate, as we attempted to get all six boats close enough to make it a party. Dropping anchors was not an option, although Hal on Que Linda did point out that we were sitting on top of a HUGE undersea mountain, and that whereas yesterday we were in 16,000 feet of water, today it's a measly 2,200 feet deep. That's better, but still a little more than I have anchor chain for. We stopped all six boats within about a 100 yard radius and jumped in. Sans Souci contributed the music with the Beach Boys at maximum volume. Crosser provided the primary swim platform. Que Linda had the hot tub going. I'm happy to report that all went perfectly and we have no injuries to report.

On other topics…

Last night on Roberta's and my 8:00pm to midnight shift, we observed a huge blip on the radar about 8 miles behind us. By tracking it on the radar, we decided that it was going to pass right through the center of our fleet. We were moving at 8 knots, and the cargo vessel at 15 knots. I called them on VHS to ask whether or not they saw our fleet, and they reported that they did. They also reported that they were a bulk transport vessel (which I assume means container ship), and that they were en route to Turkey.

Then the part of the conversation I found memorable occurred.

> Golant (the mega-Freighter): "Are you sailboats?"
> Sans Souci: "No, We are power boats."
> Golant: "Could you repeat that?"

Sans Souci: "Power Boats."

Golant: "How large?"

Sans Souci: "We range from roughly 50 feet to 90 feet"

Golant: "Oh... You are military?"

Sans Souci: "No. Pleasure Craft."

(Pause)

Golant: "Pleasure Craft?"

Sans Souci: "Yes."

Golant: "OK, we will pass you on the port side."

I was imagining the confusion on the deck of the freighter. They had probably made MANY crossings, but never run into a pack of small powerboats traveling together this far from shore before. No one ever has. They must have thought they had discovered some invading force sneaking its way across the Atlantic. Que Linda has a cannon, loaded with blanks that they fire from time to time. I'm very happy they did not fire it at that particular moment...

Crosser called them, to pump them for a bit more information, and after a brief interrogation said: "OK. We will permit you to pass us" This also struck me as funny. The freighter was huge, and we were granting it permission to pass us.

The freighter had its own interpretation of the words "we will pass you on the port side." Our entire fleet was tracking them closely on the radar, waiting for them to turn to port. The port-most (most northern) of our ships was Crosser. We were immediately to their starboard side, about 1 mile off. The balance of our fleet was to our starboard side, or in front of us. The freighter did not turn as they said they would. As it came closer, Crosser called the freighter to ask if they wanted Crosser to move aside to starboard. The word came back from the freighter that our fleet should change nothing. The freighter had everything under control.

And, they did. After a few more minutes their intentions came clear. They were going to pass between us and Crosser! We were separated by a mile, so there was plenty of room, but it was still very strange looking out on the port side seeing a city-sized ship fill our view, and to see Crosser disappear completely on the radar.

We had a bit of an issue at the 8:00pm roll call yesterday. Sans Souci received the slip assignments in Horta from our advance person there, Milt Baker. Each of us had a slip, with one exception - Goleen. They have 17 slips to be shared amongst our 18 boats. Their suggestion for Goleen was to raft alongside of Atlantic Escort. The only explanation offered was that they ran out of slips, and that the simplest would be to raft together two Nordhavn 57s. Chris (owner of Goleen) took the news well, but then as he thought about it, got a little more upset by the minute, with good cause. Horta has known for a year that we are coming, and we are arriving with fewer boats than we had planned. Fortunately Sonaia on Goleen speaks Portuguese, and can argue with the marina much better than any of the rest of us could have. Chris assured us that he would not be rafting, and I believe him. I would not want to be the person in charge at the marina in Horta, as I am confident that Chris will be informing them loudly of his discontent.

I understand how he feels. It would be difficult for a variety of reasons. You can't get off your boat without passing through another boat. Your power cables don't reach the dock, or if they do, there is no place to plug them in, as Atlantic Escort would already have their power cord plugged in. After 10 days at sea, we are all going to want things to be "right" when we finally reach land. I hope he is able to get somewhere with the marina.

Fuel burn here on Sans Souci continues to be an issue. We are running about .85 miles per gallon. This morning at 8:00am we had 1635 gallons of fuel remaining with 1070 miles to go. Our range on the fuel we have remaining is around 1400 miles. This mileage is worse than what we ran on the first leg. Perhaps the prop picked up some crud while we were in Bermuda. Goleen offered to send down a diver to look at our prop, but the wind and waves were too high when we stopped for our swim.

We spoke with Division 2 this morning, who are doing fine. No medical issues, and no mechanical problems. Interestingly, they stopped to transfer fuel to Uno Mas, the  smallest ship on the rally. 100 gallons of fuel was transferred in an hour and a half. I'm surprised that they were transferring fuel now, long before it is needed, but perhaps they decided the transfer would be needed sooner or later and wanted to do it before bad weather creeps in. Our weather report is predicting possible gale force winds as we approach Horta. That's still six days away, so who knows how accurate the weather forecast is. We're not worried about it (at least for now). Uno Mas is a Nordhavn 40. Last year, a Nordhavn 40 navigated the world in 28 weeks, including making a passage of 2,600 miles to Hawaii. This raised the question of how they did it. The answer: very slowly. The slower you run these boats the farther they go. The 40 that made the circumnavigation ran the passage at 5 knots. Division 2 is cruising this leg at 7 to 7.5 knots, which shortens the range of the 40 greatly. We have the same issue here on Sans Souci. If I ever get seriously worried about fuel, I always have the option to drop my speed a knot or two and significantly raise our range.

No dolphins or whales today, but we've seen sea turtles and flying fish...

Day 28 - 875 miles to Horta (Azores)

You may have noticed that the title of this chapter gives our distance from Horta (in the Azores) rather than our distance from Bermuda. That's because we have passed the mid point! Conversation is now focused on arrival in Horta.

Chris, on Goleen, has been speaking with the marina in Horta, and has been able to procure slips for all of us, and also get agreement that we can arrive on Thursday, a day early. I'm sure this will not excite Nordhavn, who would prefer an organized arrival in order for us to be greeted by the press. After 10 days at sea, arriving at the perfect time to make the press happy will NOT be foremost in our minds. To do this we need to pick up the pace. Our fuel report this morning looked much better than yesterday's, so I'm fine with it, subject to watching our fuel closely. Kirk suggested that as an alternative to speeding up, we could shift to a course that would allow us to join the slower boats, and all arrive together in Horta at the previously agreed time. Chris' answer demonstrated how eager everyone is to once again see land. His response "Well, that would be a big negative on that one. We will not be slowing down"

As I mentioned in an earlier daily update, we are running the boat from one fuel tank, and transferring fuel into it from the other five tanks. Sans Souci has a fuel transfer system that allows us to easily transfer fuel from tank to tank. Unfortunately it has been running slower and slower. Garret replaced the fuel filter on the transfer system a couple of days ago, and that didn't help at all. It has been taking us 3 to 4 hours to transfer 50 gallons of fuel. Rip spent much of yesterday trying to determine why. Finally, we realized that the fuel transfer system needed bled. This was a bit complicated, and involved somehow pumping fuel backward through the fuel transfer system. I'll have Rip and Kirk walk me through how this is done, in case I ever need to do it. We are now transferring fuel at a pace that is still slower than we like, but acceptable.

I overheard a fun conversation between the fleet yesterday. I shall not reveal the names of those parties involved, but some of the boats were explaining to the other boats that there is a mailbox in the exact middle of the Atlantic. The idea is that you can write letters, put them into the mailbox, and once a month the military collects the letters from the mailbox and posts them. The mailbox was described as being like a floating jug, with a huge cork in the top. You pull the cork, pop in your letters, and continue on. The exact latitude and longitude of the mailbox were being shared, and the writing of letters was being encouraged. I asked Rip if it was for real, and he said: "It's an old sailor's myth that has been going around forever." No one has ever found the mailbox. Too bad, it seemed like a cool idea.

The only excitement during Roberta's and my 8:00pm to midnight watch shift last night was watching an approaching storm come in. It first appeared as a few specs on the radar, then, within a few minutes the entire left side of the radar went bright white. It didn't look like a squall, but it did look like it could be a hard rain. At the time all six boats were running very close to each other (all within a two mile radius). I wasn't sure if the radar would work once the rain hit, so we started immediately maneuvering ourselves away from the other boats. I was reasonably certain, but not positive, that there wouldn't be much wind, but thought it wiser to get away from the rest of the boats, in case we might need to fly blind for a while. The radar does have a setting to minimize rain and to adjust for bumpy seas, but neither works perfectly. On several prior occasions we have been through squalls with high winds and had zero radar visibility. This turned out to be nothing more than a long hard rain, with only 13 knots of wind. We were thankful for the free fresh water wash down. If you were here, barefooted, sharing decks with Shelby, you too would be happy to see rain.

I missed sunrise this morning, but apparently it was incredible. St. John got some great pictures of the sunrise, one of which I put on the website. Bob Rothman on Emeritus announced the first glimmer of sunlight on the VHS by saying, in his deep booming radio voice – "Ladies and Gentleman, I give you the sun!" Sans Souci responded in our own way by finding the Beatles tune "Here comes the sun" and playing the entire tune on the VHS radio as the various crews admired the sunrise. Sorry I missed it.

At the 8:00am roll call this morning we spoke with Division 2. All was peaceful at their end. No medical problems and only one mechanical problem. Envoy's stabilizers have failed. Braun, on Grey Pearl, mentioned that he also had a minor stabilizer problem. Apparently the tank that holds the reserve of hydraulic fluid had fallen off the wall. A bolt had sheared itself off. He patched it back in place. He spoke with Naiad (the makers of the stabilizers) and has them sending a technician to Horta with spare parts.

The group had a long discussion about the weather. We are getting weather information from more than one source, as well as our own interpretation and forecasting. I subscribe to the Ocens service (www.ocens.com) and have been studying the weather reports from them. Thus far, the weather has been far calmer than anyone has predicted. We still haven't had a really calm day (on this leg), but we haven't had any rough days either. Our primary weather forecaster (Walt Hack) is cautioning us that we may see near Gale Force conditions on our final approach to Horta. From looking at the maps of Horta, it appears to be an easy approach and we should be able to get in under high winds without much trouble. The high winds aren't supposed to arrive until Friday, further reinforcing why a Thursday arrival in Horta would be a good idea.

I just looked out at the front deck. The 62 has a huge front deck. Even with the tender, we have a ton of space. Phil has set up a lawn chair, and is wearing just shorts, headphones and sunglasses. He has been there for the past couple of hours. Yesterday, we had most of the crew on the front deck stretched out reading. A few days ago St. John wrote a little essay in which he compared the boat to a house, with the front deck as the front yard. It certainly seems an appropriate comparison today. Phil looks like he is loving life. I'd go out there, but my days of lying in the sun are over. I'm a "hide in the shade" guy these days. I know too many people who have had skin cancer, so I avoid laying in the sun for hours. Phil is looking pretty red…

When we get to Horta we will be meeting Roberta's parents – John and Nova. They have traveled most of the world with us, and will be fun to have on board. They will do the last leg of the trip with us, and then help Roberta and I will run the boat to France. Our plan is to run for another couple of weeks after Gibraltar, but we have no firm schedule. Roberta's parents are great people, and far younger than their age might imply. They love to dance, and I'm betting we'll have dances going on the front deck within 24 hours of their arrival. At first I opposed to having them on board for our final leg, but Roberta persuaded me. Our last leg is likely to be the roughest. My thinking was that they should meet us in Gibraltar, as the cruising from that point on will be reasonably short day runs. A five-day run in bumpy seas will be rough physically and mentally. Roberta explained all of this to them, and they're excited about coming on board. I have no doubt they would have happily done the whole trip from Florida if we had asked. It is always fun watching Roberta and her Dad interact. Both of them love to argue politics, and they get into heated debates that last for hours. Once in a while I need to intercede, to calm things down, but 99% of the time it's just fun watching them stubbornly argue their positions for hours and hours.

This morning we were surrounded by dolphins. We've had them before, and they are always welcome to come visiting. They like to play in the wake at the front of the boat, and will stay with you for hours. I uploaded pictures of the dolphins, and of our swim yesterday to the website. The pictures are in the

section called "Photos – Part II" at http://www.trawlerweb.com. St. John said that if we stop the boat next time he will dive in to swim with them. He seemed serious, and I don't think that dolphins bite. Perhaps it isn't a totally crazy idea.

While everyone else was relaxing, I worked on paying our bills. Roberta and I travel nearly non-stop. We claim Seattle as home, but I doubt we were there more than about six weeks over the past year. I suspect most retired boaters have the same problem we do paying bills. People mail you things and assume that you open your mail regularly. We have had important bills sit for months unopened. I still haven't found a perfect solution, but will share what we do now. I use an online bill payment service - www.paytrust.com. All of our bills go to them. For $12 per month they scan all of our bills, and send us an email when a bill comes in. I go to their website and authorize payment, and they mail the check. I can define rules that cause bills to be paid automatically as long as they fall within certain parameters. This works most the time, but there are some of our venders who stubbornly refuse to send their bills to the bill payment service. For instance, I still cannot convince the electric company to send our bill to Paytrust. They say it's against their policy. I get around this by estimating our electric bill and automatically sending them a check for slightly more than I think the bill is each month. Whenever I finally see the bill, we are always slightly overpaid. I've got things as under control as they can be – but like I said, it's still a bit messy. It is amazing though that I just issued a check for a fence repair at our house in Seattle from a boat in the middle of the Atlantic.

I'm not sure if I mentioned it in an earlier update, but we are accessing the internet through a Fleet 77 system. This is my first trip using it, and I'm really impressed. It isn't DSL, cable modem or even dial-up, but it is acceptable speed for most things, and has been solid thus far. After I had the Fleet 77 installed, they released a 55 that does the same thing and costs less. When I get the boat back to the US I want to try one of the high-speed internet systems. I think KVH makes one. I've heard they are unreliable. I am definitely internet-centric, which I think is driving some of my fellow crewmembers crazy. Kirk and Roberta have conspired at times on how to lure me away from the computer. I'm playing chess with my dad, who is in southern California, even now while I am typing this.

Lastly, St. John just surprised us all by saying that he received some funding for this trip from his college. He convinced them that this was a research project. At first I thought it was strange but then when he described the research he was doing it got more interesting. His topics (as best I remember them): "How do people react when a younger person seizes control of a situation" (he is the youngest on board, but will be calling the shots if someone gets hurt – he's an EMT). "Issues associated with strangers living in confined places" and his third topic: "How someone who has never been on a boat adapts to a long sea passage." (both St. John and Phil are new to boating). It's a little weird to think that we have been studied all this time. Had I known, I would have worn shoes and perhaps combed my hair. It will be very interesting to see what's in his report!

That's it for today!

Day 29 - 650 miles to Horta (Azores)

Roberta summarized our current weather on the morning roll call with the other boats by saying: "When I first looked out the window this morning, I was positive that we were back in Seattle". We have been working our way Northeast, and are now near the same latitude as North Carolina. Today is grey and dinghy.

Morale seems to shift with the weather. When we have blue skies and flat water, no one looks to see how much further we have to go. Whereas today, with the boat being slapped from side to side by the waves (a steady 15 knot wind on our port beam), everyone is focused on getting off the boat as quickly as possible. Everyone is smiling on the  outside, but you can hear in their voices that tempers could flare on a moments notice, should anything not be as they planned.

The weather conditions around us are not all that bad. We shouldn't be getting pushed around as much as we are. We have a few different theories as to what is going on.

> The boat is light, and we're bobbing like a cork. This is Rips theory. We have burnt off about 1,100 gallons of fuel. My recollection is that diesel weighs around 8 pounds per gallon. This means we have lightened our load by over four tons, not counting our food supply, which seems to be vanishing at the same rate as the fuel. I am not putting a lot of stock in this theory. Sans Souci weighs somewhere around 60 tons, and a difference of 4 tons shouldn't make a huge difference in the ride.

➤ My personal theory is that we're bobbing the correct amount, given the fact that it's a beam sea, with high waves (around eight feet). Since the waves are coming from our port side, we are just riding wave after wave to the top, only to surf down the other side. We have stabilizers that are supposed to handle this, as indeed they are. I am confident that if I were to turn off the stabilizers, Sans Souci would have seven sick crewmembers leaning over the rail within minutes.

Prior to the trip, I was contacted by Naiad to solicit my interest in upgrading my stabilizers. The technology has changed radically over the past six years, and they were willing to sell me the "latest and greatest" technology at a heavy discount. They wanted a chance to showcase their newest technology. I considered making the upgrade, but even a deep discount is not free, and this is an area where I didn't think the investment made sense.

Stabilizer can be seen just below the surface.

Roberta and I are not normally the type of people to do long passages. We see this voyage as something that every serious boater should do at least once, but not something I'd like to repeat if I can find a way around it. I responded to Naiad's proposal as honestly as I could. I consider myself more an "anchorer" than a "boater". I'm in boating for the days when the water is flat and the days are warm. My favorite trip involves anchoring off a desolate island, spending the day (or days) swimming from the back deck, followed by a barbecue on the back of the boat, and a nice bottle of wine. When weather comes, we either head to the nearest marina, or find a calm bay to hide out in. My focus is on picking days to go to sea that don't require stabilizers. The stabilizer system on Sans Souci may not be the "latest and greatest" but it performs well, and meets or exceeds my expectations. Having said that, if the stabilizer salesman were standing before me as I type this, I'd happily buy anything that would stop us from being slammed around right now! It would be nice to stand up again someday without having to hold on to everything in sight.

You may have noticed that in the above paragraph I said that I like to be surrounded by warm water, which is inconsistent with us bringing the boat back to Seattle in January 2005. Sans Souci is going to Alaska next year. This apparent incongruity is explained very simply: Sometimes Roberta gets to pick where we go. Sometimes I get to. Next year it will be her turn.

Returning to our current trip:

➤ The Division Two boats are only slightly ahead of us now. By this evening, both groups will be exactly the same distance from Horta. However, we will not see each other, darn it. We are following the "rhumb line" approach to Horta, whereas the Division 2 boats are on a more southerly track. I checked this morning, and compared their mileage to Horta with ours. Each of us has roughly 650 miles to go, whereas our distance to each other is roughly 110 miles. Not only will we pass by them without ever being in radio range, but we'll tie up in Horta nearly 24 hours before them.

➤ Neither group has any major mechanical or medical problems.

- Sans Souci's water maker has died (at least until we get it repaired). Luckily we have a backup. We have a 500 gallon water tank, which would last us for several days were it not for the washing machine. Everyday seems to be laundry day here aboard ship.

- Boredom and trip fatigue is finally settling in. Kirk has been trying to pump energy back into the group by thinking of things to keep us busy. Trivia games that span all the Division 1 boats have become common. Kirk caught me reading the news online and talked me into reading the headlines to the entire NAR fleet. I announced that I would research any story that caught their interest and get back to them with added info. To make sure everyone was happy, I sought headlines from both the conservative and liberal press, the financial press, the entertainment press and even the sports press. At the end of my 20 minute "speech", I asked if anyone wanted more info on any particular story. The only response: Who is J-Lo marrying? And, was her wedding dress white?

Talk to you tomorrow!

Day 30 - 470 miles to Horta

The Division 1 (faster boats) are now officially in front of the Division 2 boats. They are taking a more southerly route than we are, and we never came within 40 miles of each other. At the current speed, we will be arriving in Horta at 6:30pm on Thursday, and they will arrive on Friday morning at around 7:00am.

Our latest weather report:

"...SUPPORTING GUIDANCE STILL SUGGESTS THAT SEA CONDITIONS WILL DETERIORATE DURING THE COMING 3-4 DAYS. WE SUGGEST PREPARING FOR POSSIBLE WAVES OF 9-12FT, COMBINED SEA/SWELL AS EARLY AS TUE/08TH-NIGHT FOR THE FAST GROUP, AND FOR BOTH GROUPS WED/09TH THROUGH THU/10TH...."

This morning's roll call was dominated by weather discussions. We are receiving conflicting weather reports from multiple analysts, plus we have several people who are doing their own interpretation of the weather charts. The prognosis for the next two days ranges from relative calm to 10-foot seas. I'm cheering for those who predict calm seas! Unfortunately, everyone is in agreement that our arrival on Thursday will be rough. Let me rephrase that, and say "bumpy". These are sturdy boats. There is nothing in the forecast that represents a real safety challenge. It will just be bumpier than I would like it for our arrival in a strange marina.

To some extent it is irrelevant what the weather report says. We're 500 miles from the nearest land. Whatever it will be, it will be, and there isn't a darn thing we can do about it. Ordinarily I'd be studying the charts for places to hide from bad weather. There is no such concept on this passage. Our plans are not likely to change, whether the winds are at 10 knots or 40 knots.

My fuel concerns are evaporating. We have a thousand gallons of fuel on board, and only 461 miles to go. Thus far we've been averaging around .93 miles per gallon, giving us a range of 930 miles. In other words we can easily make it to Horta.

Life aboard ship has become quite boring. We're all just putting in time. Trivia games and reading help pass the time, however, the trip seems longer and longer. In one conversation today, we started referring to sleep as a time machine. We know that if we go to sleep, the distance will drop dramatically before we wake. It's like being able to leap forward in time. I reminded people that Steve Jobs wrote a book called "The

Journey is the Reward". We need to stop thinking about land, and enjoy what we are doing. That didn't make anyone feel better, including me. We want land, and sooner is better. In another indication of everyone's mood, this morning Roberta noticed we had dolphins on our bow again, and no one expended the effort to look at them.

Roberta and I are starting to disagree over what comes next. After over a month on the boat, I know that I will be in the mood to stay on land for a while. Roberta says that our "boating experience" won't really begin until we finish the rally, slim the crew down to just her parents and us, and start wandering the Spanish coast. We are under no time pressure to return to the U.S., beyond some commitments at the beginning of August that could be moved.

We DO need to get the boat back to France before we leave for the U.S., so that it is positioned for its eventual trip across the Atlantic this winter. I've made arrangements for a boat slip near Monaco (on the French Italian border). My math shows this trip at roughly a thousand miles from Gibraltar. I would like to do a relaxed couple of weeks cruising after we arrive in the Med, but I don't know that I want to span any great distances. I'd like to move at a mellower pace and use our time to see new places and meet new people.

This brings up lots of issues about where we cruise and how we get the boat to its slip in France. In some ways, it is too early to make this decision. It is the wrong time to be making decisions about future passages. The urge for land is biasing my judgment. The outcome from this morning's discussion with Roberta seems to be that we'll cruise for two or three weeks after Gibraltar, and then have a delivery crew move the boat to its temporary slip in France.

Reality is setting in as I think about what is in front of us. Whereas it feels like we're on the downhill slide, we still have 450 miles to Horta, followed by 1,200 miles to Gibraltar, and then the 1,000 plus mile run to Monaco. All of this is being done at roughly the speed of an ordinary jogger. I am not complaining. We have been extremely lucky on

Sans Souci. No major mechanical problems. No crew conflict. Awesome people and awesome food. 10 minutes after we reach shore I will remember how great this trip was.

Before I forget, I should comment on last night's dinner, which was exceptional as usual. Phil made a chicken stir-fry that was a huge hit. How he was able to chop vegetables while hanging onto rails with one hand, and a still-bandaged finger on the other, I don't know. On another Phil-related topic, he dropped a bottle last night with a message in it. It will be fun to see if he ever gets a response.

After last nights weather discussion, Crosser announced that they would prefer to get into port as soon as possible, to avoid the coming bad weather. They upped their speed to 11 knots and are now 15 miles ahead of the group. We too have accelerated a bit, and are now showing speeds between 8.5 and 9.5 knots. My plan is to stay at this speed unless we get a nasty surprise on fuel consumption, which I'm not expecting.

I am constantly amazed at how many people are reading my daily updates. When I posted the pictures of the swim party on Crosser, I received a radio call from Crosser within minutes reporting that they were getting calls from home saying they had seen the pictures. In another example, I commented yesterday that I had passed on a stabilizer upgrade prior to this trip, and am now wishing I hadn't. That also has resulted in a series of emails and calls from other rally boats, all trying to help. I've now spoken with both Que Linda and Grey Pearl who say they are running straight, whereas Sans Souci is lurching from left to right as we go. I'm now convinced – a stabilizer upgrade is very likely to be part of our future.

Talk to you tomorrow!

P.S. - Following is an email I received talking about Sea Fox, and also an email I received that gives more information on the "mailbox in the middle" that I discussed a couple of days ago.

Ken,

As a crew member aboard the Krogen 58' Sea Fox during the first leg of the NAR and being in communication with owner/captain Dennis Fox during Leg 2, I offer the following insight into some of the information having been reported on this site:

First, I'd like to clarify some of the comments regarding the inability of Sea Fox to keep up with the bigger boats during the first leg of the rally resulting in a decision to run with the smaller boats in leg 2. Dennis, as a competent and conservative captain, usually runs Sea Fox in a "dogged down" environment at sea whereby all hatches, ports, and doors are closed for safety, with the generator and air conditioning providing a comfortable climate controlled environment for the crew. A comfortable crew is a rested crew should things go wrong at sea. With the larger boats running faster than the previously agreed upon speed during leg 1, Dennis elected to reduce speed for a 12 hour period as the fleet neared Bermuda. He did this in order to obtain current data for fuel/range calculations in the fully climate controlled environment so as to be able to plan appropriately for the 1800 mile second leg. At the conclusion of the 12-hour test, and with pleasing results, Dennis increased speed arriving into Bermuda between the two fleets.

Dennis' decision to run with the smaller boats for the second leg is yet another example of his prudent seamanship. Approximately one-third of the way across on leg 2, he reported a remaining range of over 2500 miles in his climate controlled environment (generator running, A/C on and hot showers). I'm sure Dennis and crew are comforted by having more than ample reserves in case heavy head seas were encountered during the trip.

Dennis Fox's Sea Fox.

With the exception of a nagging problem with the stabilizers, Sea Fox continues to run like a Swiss watch. Now on his fourth Krogen, Dennis has run Krogen designed hulls thousands of miles and captain and crew continue to be safe and comfortable aboard the form stabilized hull even without the additional motion dampening provided by active fin stabilizers. Dennis has previously run 650 miles from Puerto Rico to the Bahamas in 10 foot seas without them and had a great ride.

On another note, I'd like to take this opportunity to thank all those at PAE for the coordination of this event and making the Krogen team feel so welcome. I met many wonderful people in both Fort Lauderdale and Bermuda and wish a continued safe journey to all.

Many thanks,

Kurt M. Krogen

And regarding the "Mailbox in the middle of the Atlantic…"

We always pulled that one on the new guys when I was in the Navy. We called it the sea buoy and would have guys staring off the bow for hours looking for it.

As we approached the International Date Line, we'd set up one of the variable cursors on the radar scope to a north-south orientation well off the west of us and announce on the intercom that this strange electronic phenomenon associated with it was now on radar. Somebody would surreptitiously advance the cursor to close us, and before the distance was at our visible horizon, we'd tell the suckers to go forward on the bow to watch for it.

Another trick was the sea bat. We'd announce the capture of one on the fantail about the time "sweepers" was called - thus people standing around with brooms were not suspect. As the unwitting were lead to an overturned box with a small viewing hole in it, they had to get down on hands and knees to see. And then the "sweeper" pounced smacking them in the butt with their brooms.

Rich Gano
CALYPSO (GB-42-295)
Southport, FL (Panama City area)

Day 31 - 266 miles to Horta

We're almost there! As I write this, it is 9:45am here, and we are planning our arrival for tomorrow, sometime in the late afternoon.

Our ability to beat the weather predictions continues. I am looking out at a calm sea. There is an 8 to 10 foot swell going, but the waves are so spaced out that it's really not an issue. We're proceeding east into a 10-knot headwind, being carried forward by a strong sea current. Throughout the night, the current was slowing us to 8 knots, and now with exactly the same engine RPMs (1700) we are running 10 knots plus.

Both divisions have boats that decided to scoot ahead, to get into port before the predicted storm on Friday. Crosser split off from our division and is now anticipating arrival at 11:00pm tonight. Strickly for Fun, Sea Fox and Four Across split off from the slower division, and are targeting an early (7:00am) arrival on Friday. Division 1 (our division) is forecasting an arrival of late afternoon tomorrow.

As I am typing this, Bob on Emeritus, has come on the radio to announce that he has just spoken with the Horta marina and they informed him that they will be closed all day tomorrow for re-modeling and to swap out the water. If he hadn't added the bit about swapping the water, I may have fallen for it.

One of the items I have added to my post-voyage checklist is to have our radios checked. Emeritus and Que Linda clearly have the best-tweaked radios in our group. Sans Souci's radios are working fine, but our range is much more limited. Twice per day, we have been doing an SSB talk with the other division. Emeritus has taken over this duty, because Sans Souci's radios won't reach. We can hear Atlantic Escort in the other division, but they can't hear our transmissions. I think it's nothing more than having someone who knows what they are doing help us refine the antennas.

I've enjoyed hearing Bob from Emeritus on the radio. Someone said that he's a retired pilot. You can hear the years of experience in radio communications in his voice. I can't explain it, and I sure as heck can't emulate it, but his style on the radio is both light-hearted and professional. He has done a masterful job of handling the inter-divisional communications.

Yesterday was ultra-quiet. Our team has taken to reading, or watching DVDs on their laptops. There was almost no discussion on the radio, and not even much discussion amongst Sans Souci's crew.

The few highlights from the day:

➤ Garret removed our small water maker from the engine room. We have two water makers, a small 12-volt one that only makes about seven gallons per hour, but runs off the engine alternators just fine, and, another larger one that generates approximately 50 gallons per hour, but requires that we run a generator. To conserve fuel, I have been reluctant to run the generators more than I need to, so we've been running the small water maker non-stop. After thousands of miles of flawless operation, it wants some care and attention, which Garret is in the process of administering. Now that we have Horta comfortably in range with a predicted 550 gallons of excess fuel, we can run the generators and large water maker all we want.

➤ Yesterday afternoon, Goleen called us to look at our GPS. At first we thought something had gone wrong, as it read: 37'07, 37'07. The latitude and longitude were exactly the same! There was nothing magic about it – it was just a cool coincidence. Goleen decided to exploit the situation by dropping 16 bottles with notes in them.

- Roll call this morning was a non-event. At the start of our trip, roll calls were one hour plus affairs, but now people respond "Plenty of Water, Plenty of Fuel, No Mechanicals, No Medical problems." There is still an occasional burst of humor, but it's clear that the calls are getting shorter. The call lasted perhaps 10 minutes.

- Looking around, I notice that everyone is wearing jackets, and Phil just mentioned that he is off to change into long pants. Hopefully it will warm up later this afternoon.

- Shelby, our dog, doesn't seem to be reacting well to the trip. She has slept the vast majority of the trip. Her paws can't get traction on the wood floors, so when she tries to walk she winds up sliding from one end of the room to the other as the boat tilts. I'm sure she's happy just to be with us, but I don't  blame her for trying to sleep all she can, in the hopes that land will appear when she wakes.

Roberta and I spent last night plotting various routes for our trip beyond Gibraltar. We've both decided that an additional 1,000 miles is too much. We would like to do three weeks of cruising, but want it to be "fun" cruising, not macho passage making. This means we need to find someone to run the boat to its moorage near Monaco. Roberta's preference is that we run the boat ourselves from Gibraltar to Mallorca, and then have a delivery crew meet us there. Her thinking is that we have never run the southern Spanish coast. I prefer the cruising past Mallorca, which is the southern coast of France. I want to see all my favorite places in the Med once more before we ship the boat back to the U.S. My guess is that the decision will be made for us as we seek someone to do the delivery.

Looking at the calendar, we will have nine days in Horta. I know nothing about Horta beyond a few emails that I've received. I'm envisioning a VERY small town, and that we will be bored an hour after arrival. I'm hoping it's warm. If so, it would be fun to take the boat out and seek a quiet bay to anchor in for a few nights. We'll see...

P.S. - Here's another email I received regarding the ongoing topic of waste disposal at sea.

Dear Dan,

Your response to Henry's e-mail regarding the kinds of materials one may with clear conscience discard at sea, was right along the lines of my thinking when I was part of a crew of four who delivered a sailboat across the Atlantic during December, 2003.

In spite of my waning interest in sailing and growing passion for the Nordhavn 43, I was asked by lifelong boating friends to help crew on the delivery of their new Lagoon 410-S2 Sailing Catamaran Moonshine from her birthplace near La Rochelle, France to the British Virgin Islands via Tenerife, Canary Islands and St. Barths, FWI. The voyage from France across the Bay of Biscay and down the coasts of Spain and Portugal allowed plenty of stopovers and water was never an issue, so we ate every meal off real plates and washed them. Ditto for the jaunt from Gibraltar to Tenerife, which took only 5 days in flat calm conditions.

The 2,940 NM trip from Tenerife to St. Barths was a different story, because we were contemplating a sailing voyage of three plus weeks with a finite supply of water (220 gallons, plus about 70 gallons of drinking water in 5 liter containers) and no means of replenishing that supply at sea. Fresh water showers came only every four or five days at first and we provisioned lots of paper plates so that we could avoid or minimize the use of fresh water for washing dishes at least once or twice a day.

Prior to our departure from Tenerife, we discussed among the four of us what we would jettison and what we would keep. It was decided unanimously that once we were well out to sea, paper of every kind would be discarded as long as it did not appear to be plasticised or printed with inks or dyes. Food scraps and any unwanted leftovers would be thrown overboard as well. We would keep everything else.

Because we were sailing and had limited fuel, we were advised by our weather forecaster Walt Hack (thanks to Jim Leishman for that recommendation...Walt's forecasts were flawless) to continue south to the vicinity of the Cape Verde Islands before turning west, which added about seven days to what would have been, in a Nordhavn, a rhumb line course direct from Tenerife to

St. Barths. 21 days, 9 hours and 22 minutes after we left Tenerife, we reached St. Barths with 14 large bags of garbage in our forward hold.

I believe that on that voyage we were as good to the environment as we could have and should have been. We knew that our garbage and recycling would be something of a burden and in fact, by the end of the trip it had nearly filled the available space in our port bow storage area. We saved and recycled all of our aluminum cans, steel cans, printed can labels and every bit of plastic. We committed the accumulated contents of the wastebaskets in the heads to the landfill in St. Martin. We intentionally did not use one of the packages of paper plates we had bought because we discovered the plates were coated with what appeared to be a plastic compound. We had looked for biodegradable toilet paper in Tenerife, but finding none we bought toilet paper without coloring or scent, as we knew that dyes and scenting compounds could be poisonous to marine life. In short we took the preservation of the marine environment very seriously. And after sighting literally hundreds of floating, mostly plastic and Styrofoam objects at sea, we were convinced that our mindset and our hold full of recycling and garbage was a really good thing.

And until this afternoon, I thought that we had made the appropriate choice regarding our paper plates.

Before e-mailing the above to you to enthusiastically support your position, I phoned my mother-in-law, Dr. Isabella A. Abbott, who was a Stanford University Professor of Biology at Hopkins Marine Lab in Pacific Grove, California for 31 years and is currently Wilder Professor of Botany Emerita at the University of Hawaii, Manoa. She has, for more than 60 years, studied the oceans as a distinguished marine biologist and written countless books and papers on the marine environment. I thought that she might have an opinion on the subject, and she did.

She told me that most paper products are, as you suggested in your letter to Henry, quickly and effectively absorbed by the oceans. She said that newspaper and most toilet papers and even most paper towels and facial tissues are readily converted back to cellulose fibers by water, as their fibers are only loosely bound. According to Dr. Abbott ("Izzie" to her friends, colleagues and favorite son-in-law) those kinds of paper products as well as discarded food products are likely to be ingested long before they hit bottom, by any number of marine organisms.

However, on the subject of paper plates, Izzie said that even if they are not coated with visible plastic compounds, paper plates usually contain chemical binders designed to prevent liquids from penetrating their fibers. She added that in general, more expensive paper plates which tend to be thicker and more dense, contain more binders and are worse for the environment than the cheaper thin varieties, which she chortled, "is why the cheap ones leak all over your lap and the expensive ones don't."

While Dr. Abbott applauded your and my thoughtful efforts on behalf of the environment on our respective voyages and agreed that only minimal environmental damage was done by our mutual attempts at "Downwind Paper Plate Frisbee Toss With Food", she ultimately sided with Henry and suggested we both should have kept the paper plates aboard. I promised Izzie I would take advantage of a Spectra watermaker on my next offshore adventure, which will be aboard a Nordhavn 40, and serve every meal on FINE CHINA! How decadent!

Thanks for the stimulating discussion thus far. Hope to hear opinions from other concerned bluewater cruisers.

Sincerely,

Paul Foerster

Day 32 - 32 miles to Horta

We're almost there! Within a few minutes, I expect to hear someone shout on the radio LAND HO!

Once we have arrived, I'll upload pictures from our arrival to the website.

The arrival itself will be a bit of a challenge. I just spoke with our advance team in Horta who said that they have 25-knot winds at the marina. The weather report calls for this to increase to 30 knots. I'm confident we'll make it in fine, but it will be interesting.

Last night was miserable. We've gone through 12 hours of sustained 20+ knot winds, with gusts to 30 knots. The wind, which was supposed to be behind us, was instead on our starboard beam. The waves were running 15-20 feet. Movement aboard the boat was impossible. I was very impressed with how Sans Souci handled it. There was never a time when we were scared, nor did the autopilot ever quit. My greatest fear was that someone would get injured trying to move around on the boat. Even simple tasks like standing up had to be timed to the movement of the boat. It was like being on an elevator. One second you would look out the window and see only a vertical wall of water, and then a few seconds later, find yourself raised to the top of the wave, staring down into the trough, only to fall back down a few seconds later. Normally we rose straight up, only to fall straight down, but about every 10-15 minutes we'd hit a nasty wave that would turn us sideways on the way down. With each fall, the prop would cavitate for a few seconds, with an accompanying ugly growl.

On the morning roll call, several of the other boats reported sick passengers. A reporter on one of the other boats was described as having not moved for over 24 hours, and looking an interesting shade of white.

Here's a quote from the normally unflappable Bob Rothman on Emeritus – "When the bow goes down, it makes that cracking sound, and that's a little unnerving."

About 11:00pm, during Roberta's and my watch shift, Que Linda reported that they had suddenly dropped in speed to 5 knots, without explanation. They thought that perhaps we had hit an adverse current. After being advised that the rest of the fleet was running fine, Que Linda slowed the boat, put it in neutral, put it back into gear, throttled up, and the problem disappeared. I'm sure they'll be digging hard to determine what happened after we reach Horta.

We have now confirmed that Crosser arrived safely into Horta last night. We arrive at 4:00pm today. Strickly for Fun, Four Across and Sea Fox should arrive at daybreak tomorrow morning, and the balance of Division 2 should be in by noon tomorrow.

I've been doing a bit of research on Horta and the Azores. I've just realized that we will have nine days on an island that doesn't have much to do. In all of my research, I've only been able to find reference to one restaurant. I'm predicting that within a few days, momentum will build for "going some place". I will be very surprised to see the whole group sit still for nine days. Whether this means leaving early for Gibraltar or leaving port to go anchor somewhere, I don't know. It's also possible that we'll fall in love with Horta and never want to leave. It's too soon to say. It surprises me that I'm already thinking about heading to sea again when we haven't even got land in site. Strange…

Horta has one fun custom I'm looking forward to. Tradition dictates that all arriving boats paint their logo on the sidewalk at the marina. It's bad luck to leave Horta without having done so. I've already received emails from people who visited Horta in past years, wanting me to look for their logo to verify if it is still there. I'm looking forward to walking the quay reading the inscriptions from past mariners who have made this journey.

More later from on shore!

Day 33 - We're in Horta!!!

A view of Horta's Marina.

Sans Souci is safely in the marina here at Horta, after traversing 1880 miles of ocean non-stop, as are most of the boats from the rally, with two exceptions.

Before I tell you what I've heard, I'd like to make the following statement. I have heard conflicting reports about what follows. I have done what I can to collect accurate information, but a lot of different stories seem to be floating around the dock. Hopefully, I will be able to give an update tomorrow with better information.

Shelby was thrilled to be on solid ground!

Autumn Wind, a Nordhavn 62 that was escorting Division 2, is still not into port. Sometime yesterday, 150 miles out, their main propeller became tangled in a fishing net. Details are sketchy, but apparently Atlantic Escort went back 50 miles to help them. Autumn Wind had to run overnight, at 2.7 knots on the wing engine, waiting for calm enough seas that a diver could go under the boat to cut away whatever was stuck in the prop. I asked who had done the diving, and was told Eric Leishman from Atlantic Escort. Apparently he was successful, as Autumn Wind is now running at 9 knots and will arrive tonight. I can't imagine what it must have been like to be beneath Autumn Wind, as a solo diver, trying to cut away a net, in open ocean. The winds have subsided a bit, but I doubt it was anything that could be called a calm sea.

Had Atlantic Escort not been around, Autumn Wind would still have reached Horta, although it would have taken a while, thanks to their wing engine. I don't remember if I have already explained what a wing engine is, but a wing engine, as defined by Nordhavn, is a completely redundant engine and prop. The prop for the wing engine is small, with roughly a one-foot diameter. It is located about midway between the main prop and the starboard side of the boat, and is a feathering propeller, which means that when it isn't being used, it folds up neatly so that it does not create excess drag, which would slow the boat down and reduce fuel efficiency. It does not spin at all unless the wing engine is being used to power the boat. The wing engine itself is reasonably small - only 75 horsepower on Sans Souci. I am constantly amazed that such a small motor and propeller can move a 65-ton boat! Roberta and I once used our wing engine to get into port, while nearly 100 miles from shore. I remember being VERY happy I had the wing engine.

Not all of the boats on the rally have a wing engine. There is some debate amongst boaters as to the best way to implement "get home" capability. An alternate solution being employed by some of the boats is to have an alternate power source, such as a generator, that can also power the main shaft (prop). I would never consider a solution that did not employ a redundant propeller. What would they do in a situation such as occurred with Autumn Wind? There are rare situations where the main shaft can freeze, or the main propeller gets damaged, such that repairs can't be made at sea. What would these boats do in such a situation? Float and hope for help? Maybe there is a solution I'm not thinking of....

Here, the Wing Engine prop is displayed in its "feathered" position.

I was confused when I heard this story because I didn't understand why Atlantic Escort would have been running 50 miles in front of Autumn Wind, and the explanation raised more unanswered questions. I was told that Autumn Wind had been lagging the balance of the fleet in order to provide assistance to Uno Mas. In the version of the story I heard, Uno Mas had both their main engine and the wing engine fail, which sounds unlikely. My apologies, but the only thing I know for certain is that Uno Mas is not here in port. Someone else told me that there never was a problem with Uno Mas, and that it will arrive here later tonight.

I also heard that Satchmo, which IS here at the docks, had a problem with their stabilizer cooling system that had to be repaired at sea. The waves were too high to launch a tender, so one of the young men aboard Atlantic Escort, Justin, decided to swim to Satchmo. This is unconceivable to me. Prior to the trip, Dr. Kevin Hare spoke to the group about triage. His rule: you do not put a second boat into danger in order to rescue a boat in trouble. Justin must not have attended that lecture, and based on the seas I witnessed yesterday, is a true hero. When his swim was described to me, the words used were "He had to be fished from the sea both when he got to Satchmo, and when he returned to Atlantic Escort."

Stabilizers seem to have been a major failure point throughout the fleet. Within our own group, 10 miles before arrival, a call came on the radio from Emeritus, who had just lost their stabilizers. We don't know what is wrong yet, but assume that they snagged a rope or fishing net. I was just on the docks, and Garret, from Sans Souci, was about to dive under Emeritus to see whether or not, as we suspect, something had become tangled in the stabilizers.

As lumpy as the seas were, I was surprised to hear how much seasickness was a major issue on this last leg. On Sans Souci, we had no one who was seasick, but we were an exception. I do not know the exact count, but there are several people who will not be going on the next leg. One reporter from a major boating magazine is said to have spent the entire trip in a fetal position, crying sometimes for hours. I spoke to another person who was horribly sick throughout this last leg, even though she had come from Seattle to Bermuda without a problem. We are now 12 hours beyond arrival and she said she is still having trouble breathing, and will be flying to Gibraltar.

As Roberta and I arrived yesterday, we were greeted at the docks by Roberta's parents, John and Nova. They had flown in just hours before, and will be joining us on the next leg. I've mentioned before that I am worried about them. Our third leg will be "the rough one," as the run from here to Gibraltar is known for high seas and wind. Sans Souci's pilothouse is upstairs, and we go up and down the stairs dozens of times each day. I'm thinking ahead to Nova climbing those stairs as we are being slammed by waves, and don't like the thought. Nor do I like the thought that her or John might become seriously seasick. That said, a couple of the captains on this rally are in their seventies, and are having no trouble whatsoever. John and Nova are extremely athletic and have traveled the world with Roberta and I, so I'm sure it won't be an issue – I hope.

Most of the activity this morning on the docks revolved around the quest for shore-power. I've gone through this before in other marinas in Europe. Each marina has their own system, and connectors. There is no standard, and there is no documentation. As someone said to me on the docks this morning, "I've just wired up a cable and plugged it in, now I need to go aboard ship and see if I've blown anything up." He was not smiling as he said it.

We moved into a hotel, leaving the crew behind with the boat. It appears that we are the only ones to have done this, and it seems to bother both our crew and the other owners. It is making us outsiders in the group. Hopefully everyone understands that this is not our intention. We just think its better to provide everyone a little space when possible. One owner I spoke with this morning asked if I thought there were additional hotel rooms available for his crew. His tone hinted that his was not a crew that had bound together well. He wanted some time away from the crew, and I understand how he feels. Our boat has had no dissent. Everyone is getting along amazingly well, and I'm hoping that we maintain our relationship with these people for many years to come. That said, Roberta and I are looking forward to "when we get our boat back."

Our first evening in Horta was strange. EVERYTHING was closed. We hadn't realized it was a holiday and had thought at first that we were in an episode of the twilight zone. We hiked for an hour around town, in the rain, without seeing anything that was open. Finally, we had dinner in our hotel, which was a mistake. I've never been a fan of hotel food, and last night's dinner was no exception.

We have been told that "the place to be" in Horta is Peter's Sport Café, a local pub, frequented by boaters. We went there at around 6:00pm and discovered it was absolutely packed. There was no hope of finding a place to sit and we were too tired to stand. None of the rally group was there, although apparently our group did successfully

arrive there later in the evening. Most boats have a no alcohol policy at sea, including our own, so you can imagine that Peter's was a very welcome sight. Our group apparently had quite a successful evening at Peter's. I was warned that Peter's packs in an international crowd, and confirmed this during my brief visit. I heard French, German, Portuguese, Spanish, and other languages I didn't recognize. It had the feel of a great place, and my prediction is that we will become well acquainted with it.

It's perhaps good that I couldn't understand our fellow mariners at Peter's, as I believe we may have been a popular discussion topic. Nordhavn must have pulled a lot of strings to get all of us berths in the marina. Horta is a popular stop for boaters crossing the Atlantic. They do not normally have 18 open slips at this time of the year. In order to accommodate us, they had to move other boats out of the way. Sailboats were rafted four deep along the outer quay. I don't know, and don't want to know, how they explained to these people that they had to raft up to make room for our powerboats. I feel a little guilty each time I walk past them.

Horta has exceeded all our expectations. Prior to our arrival, Horta was described to me as "somewhat third world." I'm not sure I know what this means, but it isn't an accurate depiction of Horta. We live most of the year in Mexico, so we are acquainted with life in "out of the way" places, which is not what we found. Horta is a very modern city.

Thus far we have been impressed with all we have seen. It is amazingly clean, modern and the people have been very nice to us. Our only frustration has been with trying to communicate. Roberta speaks Spanish, and I speak French. Between us we usually get by well in Europe, but here, we seem to get nowhere. Today at lunch was comical as Roberta's mom tried to explain that she wanted her hamburger well done. We tried every word we could think of, but nothing worked. Somehow whatever we said translated into "warm milk" which she liked, so at least the story had a happy ending.

Tomorrow I want to spend more time around the port. Our friends sometimes think we are crazy, and I can't explain it, but both Roberta and I love being in marinas. We've spent many months of our life living aboard Sans Souci in one marina or another, and feel at home with boaters. There is a common bond that links boaters, regardless of their nationality or background. The people we've met in marinas are fun to hang out with, and interesting almost without exception. I also want to learn more facts about what happened with Autumn Wind, Satchmo and Uno Mas. I try to learn what I can from other's problems, as I know that sooner or later it will be my turn, and I'd like to deal with whatever comes my way as well as I possibly can.

One cool thing from yesterday... We are parked beside another Nordhavn 62, called Karma! It was purely a coincidence. They are circumnavigating the world going "the other way." I'm looking forward to speaking with the owner to hear about their voyage.

Lastly, I received an email asking whether Roberta and I would now be willing to make this trip again, without the rally. The answer is: Yes – to the extent that we had someone along who was a skilled mechanic. I am not at the same level as most of the owners here. I can handle filter changes, and oil changes, and perhaps even bleeding the lines – but, diagnosing any type of serious electrical problem, or fixing a leaking hydraulic system, is over my head. Even with the wing engine as a backup device, I wouldn't feel comfortable. However, this trip has definitely expanded what I would feel comfortable doing. I remember worrying about 10 hour runs in 15-knot winds. This now sounds like a milk run. Roberta and I wouldn't hesitate to undertake a 24 or 48 hour run.

Although I would be nervous to cross an ocean alone, I suspect that mine is a minority opinion. I haven't spoken with everyone about their plans, but most of whom I have spoken to are in no hurry to go home. Some see this as the first leg of a circumnavigation. Others plan on cruising the Med for a few years before deciding where to go next. Sooner or later, most of the other boats on the rally WILL be making the trip back to the U.S., and I assume that most will make the trip alone. Sans Souci is the only boat I'm aware of that is being shipped back to the U.S. I am SO jealous of the other boats, who are just beginning their time in the Med. We've already spent four years there and are ready for something new, but I will be very sad when Sans Souci begins its journey home.

P.S. - Several of you have written asking that I try to find their logo, which has been painted on the dock here in Horta. We didn't have time today, but I haven't forgotten. We will search the docks within the next couple of days.

P.P.S. - We're just going out the door to dinner. I have more pictures that I will post later tonight...

Day 34 - the rest of the story

I am happy to report that all rally crews and vessels are now safely here in Horta.

My email yesterday contained several inaccuracies. At the time it was sent, a few boats had not yet arrived in port, and information was sketchy. Since that time, I have spoken with the crewmembers from Uno Mas and Autumn Wind, and know a bit more about what occurred. I'm sure that I still do not have the full story, as when I saw the crews, they were just in from 12 long days at sea, and talking to me was NOT the foremost thought on their minds.

Autumn Wind, as I had reported, did foul their main prop with a fishing net. After running for some time on the wing engine, two young men from Atlantic Escort, Justin and James, dove beneath the boat to see if they could free the propeller. As calm seas were still days away, they dove under the boat wearing only face masks, in 10 foot seas. I will ask when I see them why they did not wear tanks. My assumption is that they felt safer without the tanks. After many attempts, they were finally able to cut through a couple of the lines. Autumn Wind's propeller was impossible to clear completely, but they were able to get it turning with most of the mass still attached. Brad, who was on Autumn Wind, reported that they found that at 1700 rpm the vibration wasn't too bad and were able to make it into port.

I incorrectly reported that Satchmo had stabilizer problems. I had their story crossed with that of Uno Mas. I still have not spoken with anyone from Satchmo, but am told that their main engine AND their wing engine quit. The problem was fuel related, and was solved reasonably quickly.

The Uno Mas story amazes me, both their story from yesterday, and their overall story. Uno Mas, a Nordhavn 40, is the smallest boat in the rally. I do not know whether or not its size was a factor, but yesterday Uno Mas was "knocked over" by a wave. They were running in beam seas (meaning the waves were coming at the boats from the side) and got caught in a squall, with winds gusting to 50 knots. According to the Uno Mas crew, a wave rolled them over to at least a 45-degree angle. On Uno Mas, the electric inverter is located in the lazerette, in the cockpit of the boat. The lazerette is a space beneath the floor, in the open portion of the back deck of the boat. When the back of the boat was partially submerged, water leaked into the lazerette and fried the inverter. The inverter is responsible for generating 110 volt current from 12-volt batteries. Alarms immediately started sounding. As it was described to me – "I couldn't tell if we were on fire, or if we were sinking. The high water alarms were sounding, and smoke was pouring from the lazerette."

Once Uno Mas had righted itself, the crew cut power to the inverter. I did not ask whether or not the main engine quit, but assume that it continued running. Uno Mas' crew was able to get moving again, but found that without 110 volt current, the cooler for their stabilizers would not work. Without stabilizers, Uno Mas was being tossed about by the waves in an unacceptable, and dangerous, manner. They were able to run a generator, to make 110-volt electricity, but unfortunately, the electricity from the generator had to pass through the inverter before reaching the stabilizer cooler, and the inverter was hopelessly fried. Atlantic Escort gave radio guidance on rerouting the power around the inverter, but Uno Mas' crew had difficulty knowing which wires to cut or reroute. Justin, from Atlantic Escort, provided assistance by SWIMMING to their boat in the high seas! After a bit of rewiring, they were underway with the generator providing the electricity needed to cool the stabilizers.

I asked how many crewmembers were aboard Uno Mas, and was surprised to learn that the entire crew of three persons was standing before me. (Note: they gave me their names, but as we were shouting at each other while packed elbow to elbow at Peter's Café, I seem to have forgotten them, if I ever clearly heard them). When I remarked on how impressed I was that they were able to make the passage with only three crewmembers, they said that three was a luxury! Two of them, a couple, had brought the boat to Florida from Alaska alone, with the two of them alternating three hour shifts on the long passages. There are some amazing people on this trip!

One last comment on Uno Mas - those of you who have been reading my updates for a while will remember that they were transferred 100 gallons of fuel about half way across the Atlantic. I had to ask how much fuel they had at arrival. The answer - 101 gallons!

Jim Leishman of Nordhavn, and David Shuler, a photographer who was aboard Atlantic Escort, have promised me pictures from their voyage. My goal is to get some photos onto the website later today or tomorrow.

P.S. - Many of you received yesterday's email multiple times. My apologies for this. It was a computer error, which I believe I have under control (crossing my fingers).

P.P.S. - I received an email asking why I had been using such a large font. When we were at sea, I was having trouble reading my laptop screen as we bounced around. The larger the font, the higher the waves (grin). Now that I am in port, I can return to a more reasonable font size...

Jim Leishman, one of the founding partners of P.A.E., builders of the Nordhavn Trawlers that took part in the rally, stands proudly on the bow of Atlantic Escort.

Day 35 - Life in Horta

I spent most of today trying to solve the problem that caused many of you to receive dozens of emails that were not supposed to have been sent. This would have been easy to fix if I had a decent internet connection, but from here in Horta, with only a poor and expensive dial-up connection, it hasn't been so easy. If you receive this email, then hopefully that is good news. If you receive it more than once, then please rest assured that I am working on the problem.

Now back to the rally....

I do not have much new to report. Yesterday Roberta, her parents and I spent the day sightseeing. We drove completely around the island, to the top of the island and just about every road on the island. I really don't want to sidetrack this mailing list into becoming a travel log, so I won't bore you with the details. Suffice it to say that this is a very beautiful place, and we had a great time.

Faial has some beautiful scenery.

Yesterday afternoon was spent wandering the docks. My primary goal was to talk several other people out of CDs full of pictures. I now have hundreds and hundreds of new pictures to upload. The website has been light on pictures from Division 2, and I can now resolve this inequity. I was a little frustrated though, in that I wanted pictures of the heroic efforts made to get Autumn Wind and Uno Mas rolling again, and struck out. I have a lead on the pictures I'm seeking and will upload them as soon as I can get them. My current challenge is that it would take a lifetime to upload all the pictures I have on a dial-up internet connection. There is an internet café here that allegedly has reasonable speed, but is closed today. For this reason, I may wait to upload new pictures until tomorrow.

One interesting rumor I heard on the docks - several boats are considering the possibility of leaving early. According to the schedule, we are to be here in Horta for another week. Plenty of time was left in the schedule so that we would have a buffer to provide for repairs or weather delays. It is now apparent that most of us do not need this time, and many of us are itching to go.

The Azores islands are very spread out. It is nearly 400 miles from one end to the other! The major island in the group is St. Miguel, and we are on the island called Faial (the city is Horta). I've been interested in going to St. Miguel because it has the largest population, golf courses, restaurants, etc. Horta is a bit more of a small town. I went to the airport yesterday to ask about flights to St. Miguel, and even asked one flight attendant if it was worthwhile to go. Her response, "If you haven't been to St. Miguel, you haven't been to the Azores."

It was a coincidence that I had been thinking about flying to St. Miguel, because that is exactly where the others boaters who wanted to get moving were thinking to go. We would go to St. Miguel and anchor out for a few days. I immediately agreed. The good luck is that St. Miguel is 200 miles in the same direction as Gibraltar - East. Instead of leaving a week from now, we could be rolling within a couple of days! As much as I wanted to be on land, I'm impatient to get back on the water. I am also looking forward to being at anchor, with a big city only a tender ride away. I should know later tonight whether or not this is just talk, or something we are going to do.

I was blindsided by one piece of bad news. We are losing Garret and St. John from Sans Souci. As I hinted in a prior update, several boats have had crew issues. Aboard

Sans Souci, we've been fortunate to have a crew that has gotten along well. This is not true of all boats. On some boats, the tensions have reached the point that change is necessary. I have made no effort to find out what boats have had problems, or what the problems were. The rally organizers decided that the easiest way to resolve the issue was to mix up the crews where possible. I do not know what process was used to decide who was moving, but learned through the grapevine yesterday that two of our crew are being replaced. We shall miss them.

The positive side of this is that we are gaining two new crewmembers, both of whom I've met and both of whom seem like they will be great crew members. They are Eric Leishman, and Michael Ronquillo. Other than that Eric is Jim Leishman's son (a Nordhavn hauncho) and Michael is an EMT, and that they both seem nice, I know nothing about them. I'll relay more as I learn it.

Eric Leishman   Michael Ronquillo

Other news…

I have a little more information on how the Division 2 boats fared on this last leg. Roberta spoke with the crew from Stargazer. They were happy to report that they had NO problems. She asked about their stabilizers, and they explained to her that they use paravanes rather than stabilizers, and that they worked perfectly. My guess is that at least half the people on this list are scratching their heads as to what paravanes are. I don't have time to explain them today (because of a rally event that starts in a few minutes) but I'll do my best to describe them tomorrow. I was on another boat briefly (either Egret or Envoy – I confuse them) and noticed that they were replacing the hydraulic pump for their stabilizers. I asked how they were able to get a new pump and they said that a Naiad representative hand carried it here. I didn't make it by Uno Mas, but I'm very curious to find if they will be able to get a new inverter in time to make the next leg. They can run the leg fine without the inverter, but would need to run their generator non-stop. This would have an adverse effect on their fuel consumption, and could be a major problem. When last I spoke with them they weren't sure what would happen.

Talk to you tomorrow!

Day 36 - Still in Horta

We now have a new plan for leaving Horta.

Our original plan called for us to be here through Sunday, another six days, and then to go non-stop the 1,200 miles to Gibraltar. Now, we are planning for a few of the boats to leave early Thursday morning, to go to an island called Terceira. We will anchor out for the day, swim, picnic, and then run overnight to St. Miguel. The total distance is around 200 miles. We'll rest there for a couple of days, and then have "only" a thousand mile run to Gibraltar.

I'm still not 100% certain that the trip is on. Sans Souci is the escort vessel, so I feel an obligation to stay with the group. Having said that, my division, Division 1, is only five boats. One of these boats, Emeritus, will not be ready in time for an early departure. A technician is arriving on Wednesday to work on Emeritus' stabilizer problems. Their stabilizers froze during the last hour of our trip from Bermuda. Originally we thought something had tangled in them, but then found that there was a far more serious problem. That leaves only Grey Pearl, Que Linda, Goleen and us.

I had a noteworthy conversation last night with Bob Rothman of Emeritus. Those who have been reading my updates for a while will remember that Bob has an independent spirit. On the run to Bermuda he ditched us to run alone, with no warning. He announced again on the second leg that he was leaving us to take a short cut. We didn't want to lose him, so we also took the short cut. He was a good sport about it. His sense of humor surprised us all as we got to know him better. One time when we called him for roll call he did a perfect imitation of an answering machine, explaining that "Emeritus is not here now, but you may leave a message after the beep." It had all of us rolling with laughter.

Since St. Miguel is on the way to Gibraltar, Bob could easily join up with us after his repairs. I was certain that Bob wouldn't object to us departing four days ahead of him.

All that would be required would be for him to run the 200 miles alone. Having said that, I felt I needed to get his permission. What I was feeling bad about was that if he experienced a problem en route to St. Miguel, he would not have anyone to provide assistance. When I raised this issue with Bob, he looked at me like I was a total idiot and said - "Ken, I've run 25,000 miles alone. I think I can handle getting to Gibraltar by myself." I explained to him I was talking only about having him meet us in St. Miguel – not Gibraltar. It will be interesting to see if he joins up with us or does the entire Gibraltar run alone. I'm hoping he joins us. As much as he likes his independence, my sense is that he enjoyed running with us as much as we enjoyed his company on this last leg.

Today was mostly spent on my computer. Yuck. Several people have asked me to upload pictures, which I've been slow to do because I have been bandwidth challenged. It took a while, but I just uploaded a LOT of new pictures, including some cool pictures of Justin and James swimming to Autumn Wind to clear its prop, and a great picture of Uno Mas trying to run with broken stabilizers.

Justin and James swim out to assist Uno Mas.

Uno Mas suffers stabilizer problems.

On the dock today:

Autumn Wind was displaying the clump of rope that was removed from their propeller yesterday. I am speaking of the rope that was left on their propeller AFTER enough was

cut off at sea to allow them to run the last 150 miles into Horta. It was a huge mass of rope, perhaps two feet across. To display the mass, Autumn Wind was dangling it a few feet off the ground from the pole of one of their flopper-stoppers (I'll explain what these are later). It is inconceivable to me that

Autumn Wind was able to run with all this rope wrapped around their main shaft and propeller. I had thought that they had run over a net, but it looked to me like a collection of old rope that somehow was washed off the deck of a boat. Bill Smith, Autumn Wind's owner/captain, said that when it first occurred, he had no idea what had happened. He had been running fine, in the middle of the night, when the engine started lugging, and then just quit. It could have happened to any of us. Scary…

I spoke with a crewmember from Four Across who told me an interesting story. A couple of days out of Bermuda, their water maker completely died and could not be repaired. I asked her "How were they able to continue without water?" Actually, I first made the mistake of asking her if they had a backup water maker? She thought I was joking. We are spoiled aboard Sans Souci, in having a backup for most major components. Four Across had no such luxury. She said that they continued because they felt that if they stopped taking showers, did no laundry, minimized flushing toilets (I didn't ask), and didn't wash dishes, they could get by. This is not the way it turned out though, and explains a picture I saw and was confused about. In the picture, there is a rope stretched between two boats, and a young man hanging from the rope. If you look closely, there is both a rope and a garden hose spanning the two boats. I didn't upload the picture to my website because I didn't know what it was. Now I do. Atlantic Escort heard about the problem, and decided to transfer water, using the same technique they had used to transfer fuel to Uno Mas. According to the young lady I spoke with, this worked perfectly, and Four Across arrived in Horta with a nearly full water tank.

In an earlier update I mentioned that we were parked next to another Nordhavn 62, Karma, which is not part of the rally. I was able to spend a few minutes with her owners, Marty and Marge Wilson. Marty mentioned that he sold his company nine years ago (the same year I sold mine!) and has been circumnavigating ever since. I asked if he had ever been to Horta before, and he said "Sure - on our first circumnavigation." When people say things like that I am at a loss for words. I asked what he was doing for crew, and he said that he was running with just himself, his wife and another couple, their friends. I asked where he was going next. "Newfoundland" was his response. He had a fun story. He said he remembered being in port in Dana Point a couple of years ago, and overhearing a boater talk about his plans to circumnavigate, and that the gentleman was leaving "soon." He said the next time he was in Dana Point was a couple of years later, and that the same gentleman was sitting at the same bar stool, still talking about circumnavigating. Marty, had just finished his first lap, and was leaving for his second. He said that the moral of the story is that you can't just talk about it, you have to get out there and just do it.

Lastly, I promised yesterday I would explain what paravanes are. Before I explain paravanes, I will give a brief overview of stabilizers, for those who might not be familiar. Stabilizers look like stubby airplane wings that poke out from the side of the boat a few feet below the surface. The stabilizers are hinged at the front, and can rotate up or down. As they move, they lean the boat left or right, with the goal of keeping the boat level. They are analogous to the elevators on an airplane wing. As you can tell from the number of stabilizer problems the rally boats have experienced, stabilizers are complex and take a beating when in rough seas. They are in constant motion, as they attempt to stabilize a 125,000 pound boat, in seas that are slamming it from side to side randomly. To add stabilizers to a boat is an approximate $25,000 investment, but for crossing oceans, they are indispensable.

Having said that, there is a cheaper solution to the problem. I believe that of all the boats on the rally, only the Nordhavn 46's have paravanes. My recollection is that two 46's have paravanes, two have stabilizers, and one 46 has both stabilizers and paravanes. Paravanes fulfill the same need as the stabilizers, but using a different technique. With a paravane system, large poles extend on each side of the boat. They look somewhat like giant fishing poles. At the end of each pole there is a line that hangs into the water. At the end of that line there is a metal object that somewhat resembles a cross between a paper airplane and an anchor. I call it a fish, and I believe that's what others call it, but I am not certain. Did you see the movie "The Perfect Storm?" Paravanes figure prominently in the movie, as the waves get rough enough that the fish become flying fish, and one of them goes wild flinging itself into the pilothouse. One of the characters in the film (I think Mark Wahlberg) has to climb out on one of the poles to cut the fish loose before it kills someone. Perhaps this could occur during a perfect storm, but is unlikely in "normal" bad weather. Typically the fish fly along about 15 or so feet beneath the surface, each about 15 feet outward from the boat. As the boat moves though the water the fish fly under the water. Any attempt by the boat to lean to the left or right requires a similar motion by the fish. In any attempt by the boat to roll, one side must rise and the other lower. The side of the boat that wants to rise must "pull" the fish higher. The fish is happily moving forward under the water, and pulling it upward takes energy. The effort to pull the fish upward dampens the boats temptation to lean. Hmm… without a picture, this is harder to explain than I thought. All I can say is that if after reading this, if you are still curious, look at the pictures on the website, and go see Perfect Storm. You'll get it.

Earlier I mentioned Flopper Stoppers. I remember looking at my first Nordhavn 62, and seeing what I thought were paravanes. I think I even took pride in explaining to Roberta how the paravanes worked, and then hearing the word Flopper Stopper and being totally confused. Here's what they are - Flopper Stoppers are a special form of paravanes that are used for anchoring. They are identical to paravanes, except that the fish work when the boat is standing still instead of moving. Normal paravanes are useless when the boat isn't moving. Imagine a paper plane that isn't moving through the air. Nothing happens. It won't fly. Flopper Stoppers function like an upside down parachute, creating tension on the side of the boat that is trying to lift. Roberta and I have used the Flopper Stoppers several times when we've anchored in places that weren't as protected as one could hope. For instance, we anchored one night off of Ibiza, and were being tossed around so much we knew that sleep would be impossible. We dropped the Flopper Stoppers, and immediately, life was good again.

Talk to you tomorrow!

Day 37 - Going Nowhere in Horta

I've had a busy 24 hours, but feel frustrated, because I did a lot, but accomplished nothing. Roberta said I was grouchy today, and it's possible she is right...

I get uncomfortable when things seem disorganized. As I mentioned yesterday, many of the boats are planning to leave on Thursday to go to another island here in the Azores. We're staying in a hotel, so I'm a little out of the information flow. Today I spent several hours on the docks to see if I could confirm the plans for our departure. I felt a little bad trying to talk to people, when everywhere I went people were hard at work on their boats. At each boat, as I found the owner, I would say "Is Thursday still on?" The response was always something like, "Are you planning on going?" To which I would respond "Absolutely." And they would say: "Great, let's do it!" Then I would dig in a bit deeper and say: "When are we leaving?" only to be told, "I don't know." Or, sometimes, just to verify that everyone was on the same page I would ask: "Where are we going?" To which I would be asked: "Where would you like to go?" One person I spoke with mentioned several Division 2 boats that were going that I hadn't known were going.

Nordhavn has spoiled us. My experience today highlights how valuable Nordhavn has been on this rally. For our departure from Bermuda, they scheduled a captains meeting, where all the details were sorted out. For our landing in Horta, they had an advance team who made sure everything was organized. Prior to the trip, they put together a book that was hundreds of pages thick with every imaginable detail, and many I would never have imagined, thought out for us. The people at Nordhavn have been awesome, as usual, and I cannot thank them enough.

One of the things I like about boating is that it is a generally laid back lifestyle. There are days you hang out in port, and days you anchor, and days you don't know what you are going to do until something motivates you to get moving. If I were traveling alone, that's exactly how boating life should be, but in this case, there are 18 boats involved, and some percentage of them are going to move en mass to another island, and some of them aren't. Some of them are looking to me to be their escort vessel. As I write this email, I am not sure when we are leaving, or exactly where we are going, or by what route. Perhaps there is a precise plan, and I just haven't unearthed it yet.

The actual run to Terceira and St. Miguel appears simple. It's only 150 to 200 miles in what appears to be okay (not bad, not good) weather. The tricky part is that a lot of logistics need to get sorted out. How or where will we reunite with Emeritus, the Division 1 boat that isn't departing Horta until Sunday? Do we have reservations at the marina? How will the Division 2 boats reunite? When? Does my new crew know we are leaving? If we are leaving early, should I move aboard the boat tomorrow night? Etc. Etc.

It was sooooo much easier when Nordhavn was orchestrating everything, but in this particular case, we are "off the planned agenda." The Nordhavn staff I've spoken to about this all agree that it's a great idea (going to Terceira and St. Miguel), but they correctly see the organizing of this side trip as our responsibility, not theirs. There's a cocktail party kicking off an hour from now. Hopefully all my questions will be answered and I will be kicking myself for spending the day agonizing over the details...

On a happier, but also "nothing accomplished" note, Roberta and I spent a lot of the last 24 hours thinking about "Should we consider ordering a new boat from Nordhavn?" We love Sans Souci, but there are some compelling reasons why this is the right time to ask ourselves this question. Nordhavn has several new models coming out that we have thought about: the 55, 64 and 72. We've ruled out the 72 as too large for us. Roberta and I want a boat we can run alone. We are very private people, and like the feeling of running the boat ourselves. Even as much as we love Sans Souci, there are days when we think it is more boat than the two of us can handle alone. We looked at the plans for the 64 last night and were blown away. It's one heck of a boat! But, we also decided it was more boat than we need. Roberta is looking at the plans for the 55 now, and it looks perfect, but as we study the plans we keep noticing ways in which it is different from Sans Souci. The 62 is tough to beat, and we have Sans Souci set up exactly as we like it – with one exception, and that is what has us looking at plans. We currently have four staterooms: a very nice master stateroom, and three relatively small staterooms, each with their own also small head. For this voyage, that is perfect, but this is not normal cruising for us. Our normal trip is really just Roberta and I, and on rare occasions another couple. What we really want is two deluxe staterooms with equally nice heads. I'm not sure how serious we are. The probable outcome is that we will do an interior remodel on Sans Souci, after shipping it back to the U.S. as originally planned. One of the factors causing us to think about this is that it is expensive to move the boat from Europe back to Seattle. Plus, Nordhavn is opening a new sales office in the U.K., and it would be SO simple to just have them sell Sans Souci in the U.K. and deliver us a new boat to Seattle. Another possibility is to just order a new 62 outfitted exactly the way we want it.

And, continuing in the vein of "not accomplishing anything," I spent some time on the boat today trying to get the television working. Sans Souci is unusual in that we are already set up for European television. We have a Sea-Tel system that receives satellite television, and two different receivers, one for French television and one for British television. A quick side note: We added the French satellite receiver so that I could practice my French. What I didn't anticipate was how boring French television is, and how much fun British television is. As serious as I am about my studies, I find it impossible to force myself to watch French television. My challenge today was to get ANY television working. It may be that we are still too far from Europe, or it may be that the system isn't working. After hours of effort, I am no closer to knowing whether or not I have a problem.

And to top off my day:

As I am finishing writing my daily update, my internet connection has stopped working. I am using a dial-up service that has worked great the last few days. It is slow (standard dial-up modem speed), but has been working reliably – until today. Argh!

I want to go back to sea. Life is so much simpler...

Day 38 - We're going to sea!

Tomorrow at this time, unless something VERY surprising happens, we will be at sea.

I was worried that our voyage would never come together, but finally, at 5:00pm today, we had a meeting to discuss logistics. I showed up for the meeting a few minutes late, thinking there would be a bit of joking around at first, but everyone was dead serious, and hard at work when I arrived. There had been confusion over which boats were going, and where we were going, but this was dispensed with in seconds. All of the Division 2 boats that had said they would go elected not to. The decision was also made to bypass Terceira. I was a little disappointed, but agreed with the decision. When the idea was first discussed, we had thought Terceira was closer.

Our idea had been to arrive by around noon, swim and picnic until after dinner, and run all night to St. Miguel. Unfortunately, this didn't work for a number of reasons. To arrive in Terceira by noon we would have to leave here by around 4:00am, which is impossible (we're just not ready). Also, the weather isn't such that people are thinking about anchoring and swimming. Today was cool and windy. I don't know what the exact winds were, but it felt like 20 knots or more. That said, I've looked at the weather report for tomorrow, and it looks good. The whole trip is on hold until we speak with our "official" weather forecaster tomorrow, Mr. Walt Hack, but I will be very surprised if there is an issue.

The bottom line: we're anticipating a 2:00pm (GMT, which also happens to be Horta time) departure for St. Miguel. We're planning to run at 9 knots, and it's only a 150 mile run. We should arrive around 10:00am on Friday.

We will be traveling with the same boats as on our trip from Bermuda: Crosser, Goleen, Grey Pearl and Que Linda. Emeritus will not be accompanying us due to stabilizer problems. A few hours before we arrived in Horta, their stabilizers locked up completely. A technician was to arrive here today, but at 7:00pm, they had not yet arrived. As I had anticipated, there was some discussion about Emeritus. Bob is a highly independent person, and prefers running alone. No one ever said it, but I suspect we were all thinking the same thing. If we leave without Emeritus, the odds are he will make the run alone. I can't conceive why someone would bypass the extra safety offered by traveling as part of a group, but then there are people on my boat who can't understand why Roberta and I are paying for a hotel room when we have a perfectly good bed waiting on the boat. Sometimes people like their independence. That said, I REALLY want to find a way for Emeritus to catch up with the group. Aside from the fact that I like having him around, it is safer if we travel together.

Other topics at the meeting:

- ➤ The Division 1 and Division 2 boats were on completely different routes on the last leg. We would like to avoid having this happen again. Tomorrow, we will choose a waypoint just after St. Miguel, and have both divisions plan to run the rhumb line (a straight line) between that point and Gibraltar. This ensures that we are on the same track.
- ➤ The Division 2 (slower) boats will leave Horta, assuming the weather is right, on Saturday. Division 1 will stay in St. Miguel until Monday, and then start for Gibraltar. This should put us on the same track, arriving at roughly the same time.

There was a party that had been scheduled for tonight. It was a pot luck on the dock, and was described as being "Bring your own bottle." I didn't see a lot of people drinking, and the whole event seemed a bit serious. The departure tomorrow has us focused on preparations.

Sans Souci represented itself well at the pot luck. Our chef Phil, made some amazing Thai Pot-stickers. Roberta and I are on the Atkins diet, so we couldn't eat them. As Phil was carrying them out of the boat, I asked Roberta if it was ok to cheat and "have just one." She said she had already cheated and had one, so she supposed I could do the same. Phil made at least 50 or so pot-stickers. Roberta and I ate one each, which left 48. Two minutes after Phil carried the pot-stickers out to the group, I completely caved and ran for the table. I had to have another one. No luck. They had completely evaporated. We are not roughing it too badly on Sans Souci.

Those of you who read my report yesterday may remember that Roberta and I were to have a meeting today to discuss whether or not we should consider selling Sans Souci in Europe and buy a new boat in the U.S., rather than shipping Sans Souci back. We spent a couple of hours with the Nordhavn people, and I'm not sure what we accomplished. Roberta and I still need to talk some more, but my sense was that we have an emotional attachment to the 62, and as much as we like their new models, it would be hard to own a different boat. It was tough to conceive of giving up that big front deck, or the upper deck in the back.

It may have become a non-issue anyhow. We were thinking about the huge cost to ship Sans Souci back from Europe. This number may shock some of you. I know it shocked me. Guess what the cost is to ship Sans Souci from France to Seattle? $102,000.00!! Yes. You read that right. I called Dockwise Yacht Transport (http://www.dockwise.com/?sid=28) , the  shippers, to ask if I would be able to get a refund if we were to cancel the trip. They said "Sure, but only as a credit against a future trip. There are no cash refunds" Ouch.

It will be strange moving aboard Sans Souci. We had seven people on the last leg, and only five of these people are continuing on with us. Garret and St. John have moved to Autumn Wind. We are now being joined by two young men, Eric Leishman and Mike Ronquillo (an EMT), as well as Roberta's parents, John and Nova Heuer. Tomorrow we'll check out of the hotel, turn in the rental car, and move aboard.

Speaking of change, today I received an email asking me to pass along a message to Marty and Marge Wilson, aboard Karma. I spoke of them a few days ago. They are the couple who are half way through their second circumnavigation on a Nordhavn 62. Purely by coincidence, we were parked next to them here in Horta. Roberta and I have enjoyed meeting them, and have been looking forward to getting to know them better, but as I went out the door to pass along the message, I realized that Karma had left. They are now on their way north to Newfoundland. I'm sure we'll meet again, but have no idea where or when. It felt really strange for some reason not to see their boat.

The only other thing I can think of to report is that Roberta, her parents, Phil and Garret, have been working hard to paint our logo here in Horta. It looks great! We still have some touch up to do tomorrow, but we're proud of it, and hope to see it again someday. I on the other hand, wasted the afternoon messing with the satellite television tracking system. I finally decided that we are still too far from Europe. I've been thinking we're almost there, but we still have 1,200 miles to go! And, that's just to Gibraltar. Roberta and I have at least another 1,000 miles to go to our boat slip in France.

NAR Fleet leaves their mark in Horta.

OK – one more thing. Tomorrow I'm planning to drive the boat as we leave port. I've driven Sans Souci thousands of miles, but have been self conscious about running it in the marina in tight corners in front of Rip (our Captain) and Kirk (from Nordhavn). I know that they'll both be thinking "we could have done it better," but I need the practice. Hopefully there won't be much wind. Sans Souci is heavy, and doesn't move much with the wind, but I'm pretty rusty…

Talk to you tomorrow, from at sea!

Day 39 - At Sea, on the way to San Miguel

Division 1 of the NAR fleet, with the exception of Emeritus, left Horta at 4:00pm GMT, headed for St. Miguel, another island in the Azores. As I write this, it is 8:00pm, and we show 121 miles to our destination. We're running at 9 knots, and anticipating arrival around 10:00am tomorrow morning.

Thus far, all is smooth, but our departure on Monday for Gibraltar looks dicey. Here's the weather forecast I just received:

"...There is some indication that Monday/21-Tuesday/22 will bring some 25+kt SW-W winds and waves above 10ft to the Azores waters and eastward to 20W-15W. These conditions could impact directly on the scheduled vessels' departure Monday/21st for Gibraltar..."

I'm not sure what this means for our Monday departure. The Division 2 group is scheduled to leave on Saturday, and pass by San Miguel sometime on Sunday. By Monday when we depart, they should be 150 miles or so in front of us. The goal is for us to get on exactly the same track, and close the distance a little each day, catching up to them just as we arrive together in Gibraltar. Hopefully the outlook will improve. We have always known this third leg had the potential to be the roughest, but hoped for a positive surprise. Given that the last leg, which we thought would be the smoothest, became a very rough passage, it seems like we are owed good weather. Fair is fair.

Our departure today was not without incident. Just hours before departure, one of our boats chose to continue without one of their crewmembers. I do not know what was behind the surprise crew change, but it was quite an event, as a very large pile of bags suddenly appeared on the dock, and the person involved started going from boat to boat seeking a ride. I do not know what ultimately happened, or what will happen with him.

Sans Souci also had a crew change during the final hour in Horta. One of the Division 2 boats had a gentleman with a kidney stone problem during the Bermuda to Azores leg. After a few days of pain, the gentleman involved, one of the boat owners, believed himself cured. A visit to an Azorean hospital indicated otherwise. He underwent (I believe it is past tense) a minor medical procedure, and will need to miss this next leg. As this left the boat in question with only three crewmembers, we agreed to transfer Eric Leishman from Sans Souci to the other boat. We now have eight persons on board.

I am happy to report that our departure was without incident. I did take pictures of our logo, which we painted on the dock, and will post that picture later tonight or tomorrow.

Earlier this morning, Phil accidentally spilled a can of black paint on it. He had a scary hour as he hurriedly repaired the damage. As you will see from the photo, no permanent damage was done. I drove the boat away from the marina, zigzagging through a minefield of sailboats that were anchored within the approach to the marina. The wind was light, so I wasn't really tested. Yesterday, I watched a 130 foot powerboat, without a stern thruster, side step into a 135 foot opening, with multiple sailboats rafted together in front and in back, of the space he was assigned. In non-boater talk, I'll compare it to parking a car. It's as if he had to parallel park a car, in a space that was only marginally longer than he was. A car simply could not do it. We had 20 knots of wind at the time, directly on his nose. Dozens of us stood on the dock for the entire 20 minutes it took him, admiring his valiant efforts. I've had situations approaching strange marinas where I've been asked to accomplish similar feats. I know what I can and cannot do, and for now, choose to anchor out in these situations.

Many of you have written to me in the last couple of days asking that I send them a manual for arriving crew that was put together by Scott Strickland of Strickly for Fun. I have asked Scott for it a few times, and do expect that I will get it – but, I'll have to keep bugging him. I had a printed copy in my hands yesterday, and wished I could have had a copy prior to this trip. I tried to get a copy immediately, but Scott wanted to "de-personalize it" prior to giving it to me. As soon as I get it, I'll post it immediately on the web site and alert everyone to its existence in my daily update. Scott and I are different people, and that came through in my reaction to his "rules and regulations." He laid down very strict guidelines for crew. There was even a rule requiring that play with a Game-Boy was to be done outside, on the rear deck. Aboard Sans Souci, we were much more laid back, perhaps too much so. The document will be valuable for all boaters who download it, and customize it to reflect their individual preferences. It will force us to think through what we consider to be appropriate crew conduct, and ensure that our wishes are clearly communicated.

Yesterday, I wrote a paragraph for my daily update, which I deleted moments after I wrote it. I was thinking about how many miles the group had traversed: 18 boats, each having already crossed 3,000 miles of ocean. That's 54,000 miles collectively. I then added the following sentences to my paragraph: "And, prior to the rally, many of these boats converged on Florida from as far away as Alaska, crossing at least another 50,000 miles collectively. All of this without major mechanical difficulty or injury." My point was that although I have spoken at length about mechanical problems on the various boats, I wanted to make sure that my comments were read in the context that we are talking about a LOT of boats, and a LOT of miles. Although there have been mechanical failures, these boats have redundant systems. None of the boats would have been "in need of coast guard rescue," with the possible exception of Uno Mas, which lost its stabilizers in high seas. Having said that, I'm reasonably confident they would have been fine, but the point could be argued.

The reason I deleted the paragraph is that I remembered an incident that occurred just prior to the rally, which I have not mentioned previously. The only injury, to anyone in the rally that I have commented on, is Phil's cut finger, and I wish that were the whole story.

The day before Roberta and I arrived in Florida for the start of the rally, Lillian Montague was killed in a tragic accident aboard Boundless Grace, a Nordhavn 47. She and her husband Ron were in transit with their new boat, from Stuart Florida to Ft. Lauderdale, where they were to join us for the rally. They had anchored off of Palm Beach, and were leaving a crowded anchorage in 25 knot winds, when their stabilizer tangled with the mooring rope of a nearby sailboat. The sailboat was at anchor, and was uninhabited. When Boundless Grace's stabilizer fin became tangled with the sailboats mooring line, the sailboat was pulled to Boundless Grace. Lillian saw the sailboat approaching rapidly, and positioned herself to fend it off. She became pinned between her own boat, and the sailboat, and died from her injuries.

I chose not to mention the incident, as several people on Sans Souci knew the Montagues well. Kirk worked with them to commission their boat. Garret accompanied them to the Bahamas (their shakedown cruise), and threw off their lines in Stuart, only to be called to watch over the boat the next day as the police began their investigation.

Some of you may have the May issue of Passagemaker magazine. Boundless Grace is showcased on the front cover. Bill Parlatore, the editor-in-chief of Passagemaker, was aboard for the Bahamas trip. He arrived in Horta today, and will be aboard Strickly for Fun on this next leg. I spoke with him today, and was given an early copy of the next issue of Passagemaker that contains a two-page editorial he wrote about the incident.

It was a very tragic accident, and a reminder of how cautious we must always be around boats. Trouble, when it comes, can arrive rapidly, and one can never be too careful. If there is any lesson from what occurred, it is this: "NEVER put yourself between two boats, or a boat and a dock." These are heavy boats. Sans Souci weighs 120,000 pounds, and the Nordhavn 47 weighs over 80,000 pounds. When Crosser had trouble getting away from the dock in Bermuda, and a group of us were pushing her against the wind, I know that I was remembering this earlier incident, as were others.

The Montagues were just starting their retirement and this rally was to be the beginning of their new life aboard their new boat. Reading the Passagemaker article today was so sad…

Day 40 - At anchor in Sao Miguel

Division 1 arrived in Sao Miguel this morning at 8:30am. The 150 mile ride from Horta could not have been smoother, or calmer.

Last evening's only excitement was provided by Chris and Sonaia from Goleen. Sonaia elected to make the crossing on Crosser, in order to sample life on another boat, in particular to take advantage of their masseuse. Throughout the evening Chris and Sonaia spoke often via VHF radio, including on one occasion, a prolonged romantic discussion that had everyone glued firmly to their radios. As their conversation was ending, Braun from Grey Pearl sternly warned them that all VHF communications were to consist only of rally business. Later, in the middle of the night, my father in law John broke the news to Rip that Ray Charles had passed away. In memorial, Sans Souci broadcast a selection of Ray Charles songs to the fleet.

Arrival in Sao Miguel is on track to take longer than the passage to get here. We weren't allowed to enter the harbor until cleared by the marina office, which was supposed to open at 9:00am, but didn't really open until nearly 10:00am. Then we discovered that they had no space for us. We were asked to anchor and send in tenders with the ships papers.

For some reason, when we left Horta, we had to check out with immigration, and then had to check back in today here in Sao Miguel. The Azores are part of Portugal, which is part of the E.U., so once we are into the E.U., it seems to me that we should be in the E.U. and no further paperwork necessary. Not true. Here in Sao Miguel it was as though we were entering the country for the first time. I had to stand in line at four different offices, and clearing customs consumed about three hours. Back when Nordhavn was helping us, it took only about 10 minutes.

While I was ashore working with customs, Rip and team were back on Sans Souci trying to find an anchorage. Sans Souci was the last boat into the outer harbor of the

Marina, and our other four boats took the last available spots. After searching for an hour for a safe anchorage, they decided to come into the marina anyhow, and pulled along side the fuel dock. This gutsy move freaked out the local authorities who promptly called the cops. Thank goodness for Sonaia, from Goleen, who speaks Portuguese. She convinced the police that Sans Souci had hydraulic problems, and could not anchor. She then asked everyone on our boat to look busy, so that our cover story would work. The police left after we promised to make our repairs and get out to anchor as quickly as possible. After enough moorage was found in the marina that two of our boats could come in, we grabbed one of their anchorage spots. As I write this, Grey Pearl, Crosser and us are at anchor. The marina has said that they will not ever have space for Crosser, but that Grey Pearl and Sans Souci may be admitted tomorrow (to raft together against the sea wall).

Sans Souci and Grey Pearl, rafted together in Sao Miguel.

Everyone on my boat complained about the situation, except me. I love being at anchor, and could stay here for days. We can swim, hang out, or tender in as we please. Roberta, her parents and myself just spent a couple of hours on the back deck drinking some wine and talking. The Grey Pearl team floated in their tender behind the boat for a while to chat. Crosser brought us cookies (peanut butter!). Roberta and I had to watch her parents eat them while we starved. Soon we will tender into town for dinner, and it will be fun to explore.

Overall … Life is good. We may be in the marina tomorrow, or we may not. I don't care. The sunset is gorgeous, and we have three days to explore a new island.

I may not do an update tomorrow or the next day – depending on if anything interesting happens or not. The Division 2 fleet does not leave Horta until Saturday, and I do not know if I will receive regular updates from them. On Monday we will start on 1,000 miles of what could be our roughest ride yet. But, that feels a lifetime away.

Days 41, 42 and 43 - the final leg - 903 miles from Gibraltar

I knew I was in trouble 15 minutes after heading to sea, when Roberta said: "Are you wearing your patch?"

I wasn't, and it takes a couple of hours to kick in. I'm REALLY seasick; hence this will be a short update. I have a lot to say, but can't sit up long enough to say it. I've been lucky thus far, other than the first day out of Fort Lauderdale. Hopefully, this will be like then, and a few hours from now I'll be fine.

Because there are people who have family here on the fleet, who I am confident are curious how their loved ones are faring, I'll give a quick update, just to say I have spoken to both fleets, and everyone is well. I seem to be the only semi-casualty.

There are a few mechanical problems to report. Seafox has lost all stabilizers. I spoke with them just before departure, and they were worried that they might have a problem with them. Autumn Wind is running without their autopilot. I'm VERY happy not to be on their boat. The Nordhavn 62 runs horribly under hand steering (my opinion). You can do it, but it's exhausting. I heard they are doing one hour turns at the wheel.

Talk to you tomorrow (I hope!)

Day 44 - 807 Miles to Gibraltar

Thank you to all who wrote to me about my seasickness. I am feeling MUCH better now. I'm still not 100%, but at least I'm up and about.

Our stay in Sao Miguel was great! Any cruiser should consider stopping there for a few days. On the negative side, it is a huge island, with large cities, but on the plus side, we found several great restaurants, including decent Chinese and Mexican food.

Our first night at anchor, inside the Ponta Delgado seawall, merits some comment. The area for anchoring is small and crowded. We were anchored just west of a shallow rocky area. Where we were anchored was fine, but there wasn't much room for anchor drag should the wind come up. As Murphy's law would dictate, that's exactly what happened. We had hard rain and 30 knot winds most of the night. I was asleep at the time, but was woken by the unmistakable sound of anchor drag. It was only a short burst, followed by what sounded like the anchor grabbing. Rip and I took turns watching our position all night, and were pleased that the boat never broke anchor again.

As visibility was bad due to the rain, I used a radar trick that many of you may already know, but that I'll mention anyway in case someone doesn't. I set the radar at close-in range, in this case .5 miles. I then put up a VRM ring (a small ring, which can be sized to any size you want), to exactly touch the shore. This allowed me to know, at a glance, where our boat was in relation to shore, and if we had moved or not. Ordinarily I choose points of reference on land, but with the rain, my ability to do this was limited.

After our night of rain, the marina called to say we could come into the marina, and raft against the wall. Sans Souci was to park with Grey Pearl tied-up on our port side. In front and in back of us, would be double-parked sailboats. This is the same situation that existed in Horta, where I watched a 130' powerboat park in virtually its own length. Rip and Kirk each told me this was my big chance to improve my driving skills. I asked what would happen if I goofed up – and, they said "Nothing but an insurance claim". Winds in the marina were at 20 knots, on our tail.

Prior to owning Sans Souci, I owned a 44' twin-engine "normal" planing boat. In my old boat, 20 knots of wind was a huge deal. The dual engines helped with parking maneuvers, but the boat was so light in the water, that even light winds made parking a challenge. I had forgotten how heavy and how low-windage Sans Souci is. The thrusters easily overcame the wind, and parking was really as easy as using the thrusters to just side-step into the parking place. All not only went well on arrival, but I also pulled the boat out of the marina in similar winds two days later. Rip did an outstanding job of inspiring confidence, and convincing me I could do it. I don't know that I'm quite ready to do complex maneuvers without him to bail me out when I get into trouble, but look forward to trying.

Bob Rothman aboard Emeritus was stubborn about his desire to run alone, as we all expected him to be. I heard a rumor that he is a pilot who holds the record for the most single-engine solo flights across the Atlantic. After refusing to commit to any of us when he would depart, he snuck out of Horta at 6:00am, and is on our same track, but 150 miles or so in front of us. I doubt we'll catch him before Gibraltar. We did speak with him this morning, and he explained that thus far his only difficulty was that his rudder had been bitten in half by a 17-foot shark. We're confident he was teasing.

On a much more serious topic, we had a brush with semi-disaster here on Sans Souci last night. The holding tank refused to pump overboard. Because we had been in a marina, we had our holding tank set to "hold" so that no toilet water would pump overboard. Our intention was to start dumping once we were the legal distance from shore, but when the time came, the holding tank refused to pump. After an hour of thinking about life without toilets for five days, Rip was able to unfreeze the system via a manual pump in the lazerette.

As we were patting ourselves on the back for bailing our selves out of trouble, another alarm went off – this time telling us that the vacuum system for the toilet systems had failed. On Sans Souci, the toilets work the same (almost) as most commercial airliners. Waste is sucked from toilets, to a tank beneath the main engine, where it is macerated, and then pumped into a holding tank, to await further disposition. We have plenty of spare parts on board, but not a spare waste vacuum pump. This triggered another round of panic that once again calmed as we were able to get things going after allowing the vacuum pump to cool down.

Our toilets are slightly different than the ones on airplanes, in that the toilet bowl MUST be left with some water in it, or the toilet can not form a proper seal. We're still not certain this happened, but apparently someone flushed, and didn't verify that water was left in the bowl. We have a light in the pilothouse that tells us the pump is running, but a barstool was blocking its view. After a few hours contemplating five long days without toilets, you can bet that we will be monitoring that light in the future. If anyone has ever had their system fail, with a large crew, on a long passage, and had to deal with this, I'm curious how they handled it. Buckets? If this happened to you, email me (kenw@seanet.com), and if what you send is "discreet" enough, I'll include it in my daily update. Hey, I know it's not a pleasant topic, but, I'm curious what life would have been like. We still have 50 years of boating life to go. I suspect we'll encounter this situation again sooner or later…

One last note on this topic… While I was in a panic trying to solve the problem, Roberta's mom asked what was happening. I explained to her that we might not have toilets for five days, and she said "ok." I asked why her reaction was so mild. She said it wasn't that big a deal. "We'd deal with it." This shows the difference between her, who was raised on a farm, and me who lived in a city.

Here's a question I received yesterday:

"... There seems to be a recurring theme (on several boats) with the stabilizers. With what seems to be tech support at each of the previous stops, there does not appeared to be a fix. Is there any discussion amongst the group about the source of the problems or any indications of what is causing the recurrence? Or am I over reading the issue? Regards, and many thanks for an enjoyable and entertaining blog. John Coyle MV Neptune"

Stabilizers appear to be the BIG issue, and they are often discussed, although, I've heard more discussion than proposed solutions. On this morning's roll call, Goleen mentioned that they had now developed a small stabilizer hydraulic leak. Most of the systems that have failed are Naiad, but statistically Naiad is the dominant stabilizer brand in use. I believe that there are only three boats with ABT Trac stabilizers, including Emeritus, which had a significant failure. I'm not sure why there have been so many problems, or what the solution is. I did discuss it with Dan Streech of Nordhavn, and he attributed it to older stabilizers being less reliable than those being installed today. Perhaps this is true. I have no way of knowing. My personal gut reaction is that stabilizers do take a beating, and that this has been a long trip, with lots of beam sea activity. We've worked the stabilizers hard, and they have had (mostly minor) maintenance issues. As of now, there is only one boat running without stabilizers. Given that we have run over 50,000 miles of sometimes hostile ocean, things may not be as bad as they sound.

Today, there was some discussion of the merits of the new "digital" stabilizer systems. Braun, on Grey Pearl went for the expensive upgrade, whereas I passed on it. Braun swears by it, and appears to be running much smoother in following seas than we do. A couple of weeks ago, I made the decision to get the upgrade after this trip, but then spoke with Marty Wilson on Karma who said the upgrade had done nothing for him, except to de-stabilize his system. Currently, Sans Souci has had exactly "zero" problems with stabilizers. Now, I'm thinking to leave well enough alone.

This update is getting long, so I'll quit after passing along one more experience.

We were invited aboard Crosser for cocktails on Saturday night. Crosser is the largest boat in the rally, and is NOT a Nordhavn. It is a custom McQueen and this is its inaugural voyage. David Stone and his soon-to-be-wife have designed and built it over the past five years. I was eager to go aboard, as I had heard rumors that I would be blown away, which I certainly was. It really is in a different league. Incredible artwork, spacious bedrooms, a piano in the living room, a massage table built into the master suite, an eight person hot tub on the roof, heated marble floors, etc. It's not a boat that a retired couple could run alone, but it did feel very "homey." Check out their website: www.mycrosser.com. Sandy said they plan to live aboard for the next five years, full-time, just exploring the world. What a great life! Roberta and I have talked about living full-time on a boat many times, and even once set aside three years for a circumnavigation – but it's something that is easier to talk about than do. Maybe someday…

Talk to you tomorrow!

Crosser

213

Day 45 - Tooooo far to Gibraltar (547 miles)

Chef Phil's demeanor just before departure summarized how we all feel. He was sitting quietly, but looked gloomy. He kept asking how many days we would be at sea, and we kept telling him it would be five full days. He asked if there was anything we could do to shorten the trip. We would say "No," and he would think about our answer for a few minutes before asking again – "How many days exactly will it be?" The concept of five days just couldn't sink in.

We now have two of our five days behind us, and the three that are left feel like a lifetime. Everyone is sleeping, when not on watch, just to pass the time. Last night on our watch, a lonely voice came on the radio to say "Anyone for chess?" No response. The voice came back later – "Anyone play poker?" An hour later, a voice said "Anyone want to discuss the weather." That one got a taker, but the conversation lasted only about three minutes before that too became boring.

The weather is not doing much to brighten our moods. Yesterday, I thought I was back in Seattle. Grey and dingy. For a while, we drifted through fog that existed both outside the boat, and inside our heads.

Kirk has been doing what he can to energize the boat, but stubborn sullenness seems to have set in. He has now requested that each boat provide 30 minutes of entertainment after roll call. Sans Souci has decided to do a talent show tomorrow night. I'm hoping that the seas are calm. I'll put the music up loud and have Roberta's parents square dancing on the front deck. Thus far I can't think of a personal talent to exhibit. Perhaps I can count to 20 in hexadecimal or something…

Goleen is at least making an effort. They announced a fishing derby for the day. Only Grey Pearl agreed to put lines in.

The seas are improving. They're far from smooth, but not bad at all. Kirk just jumped on the radio to announce a group swim. That may kick off activity. It will be a while though before we can gather everyone together. Our boats are spread out over nearly an 8 mile distance. My guess is that we should be together in an hour or two.

It's strange to think that in just three more days the rally will be over. I'm very curious to get everyone's schedules post-rally. Roberta and I have now firmed up our schedule. We will spend a week in Gibraltar, for various small repairs. Then we'll slim the crew back to just Roberta's parents and us. We'll then do a two-day around the clock burst of cruising to get to Formentera (near Ibiza). After Formentera, we will have another 800 or so miles to cover, but can take three weeks to do so, and stop at all our favorite places in the Med. Around the end of July we'll park the boat near the France/Italy border where it will rest, until November, when it will be freighted to Vancouver. Hopefully we'll get one or more of the other boats to cruise with us for some portion of the run. We're surrounded by fun and interesting people, but we've been so busy crossing the ocean, we've not had time for fun. Some mellow island hopping is what everyone needs to remember why we love boating.

As I write this, it is 1:20pm GMT, and we are at 36.57N by 16.54W. We project arrival in Gibraltar on Saturday morning around 8:00am GMT. Division 2 is almost exactly 100 miles ahead of us, on the same track, and Emeritus is approximately 10 miles to their port side. We are running at 9 knots, and the slower fleet at 5.5 knots.

On this morning's roll call, no one had anything to report. No mechanical problems. No excitement.

My internet connection has gone flaky. I do have some pictures to upload, but am having a heck of a time doing so...

P.S. - Here's an email I received which answers yesterday's riddle:

"...in a similar situation, I have lined the toilet with trash bags. Good luck.

-Mark Hayes"

Day 46 - 389 Miles to Gibraltar

It is 2:30pm GMT, and we are 329 miles from Gibraltar, and the end of the rally.

For the past few hours, we have been trying to catch Goleen. Chris Samuelson, owner/Captain of Goleen, is setting the pace for our group, and wants to outrun bad weather. Chris' interpretation of the weather reports is clear, and unambiguous – "The weather is nice, so let's go as fast as we can and get into port, before the weather turns nasty." The seas are smooth today, with the wind behind us. But starting tomorrow, the wind could start reversing directions, which will make our voyage a LOT less fun. Chris put an exclamation point on how nasty things could get by reminding us that our marina is "around the corner" from a beach that is rated as the top beach in the world for windsurfing.

Our race towards Goleen started when Georgs, a reporter aboard Goleen, called to ask if we would mind catching up to take pictures. Each of the boats has been taking their turn. Crosser is the fastest boat, and quickly covered the three miles to reach Goleen. Que Linda, Grey Pearl and ourselves have had to work harder to narrow the distance. Braun Jones aboard Grey Pearl had my favorite line of the day when he called (via VHF radio) to Georgs on Goleen – "Georgs, could you pass along the following statement to Chris," he began. Then in his most serious voice he said: "I've been doing some math here on the Pearl. After a couple of hours of studying my arithmetic, I've arrived at the following conclusion: Two objects proceeding along the same course, moving at the same speed, never converge."

Sans Souci maintained our pace so that Grey Pearl could get its picture taken. Even after Braun's radio comment, it was at least another hour before the Pearl was close enough for pictures.

When Georgs called me to the radio, I assumed he wanted us to start crawling forward for pictures. He did want that, but made an additional request. He wanted to speak with

217

Michael, our Emergency Medical Technician. It was reported yesterday that Bransom had stumbled on the swim step and bruised the side of his foot. No one took this seriously, and many jokes were made about the matter at last night's roll call (several people offered to cut off the offending member). Apparently we joked too soon. Bransom had a painful night, and his toe was expanding at an alarming pace. After Georgs described Bransom's foot situation, Michael said that it was possible that Bransom may have broken his foot, and that he should lie down, with his foot elevated. He could then get an x-ray in Gibraltar. A Doctor riding along on Crosser, who had been listening in, concurred with Michael's assessment.

I thought that that was the end of it, but then we started thinking that perhaps we should send over some ice packs, pain killer and anti-inflammatory drugs. Michael spoke with the fleet Doctor, Dr. Hare, who is traveling with Division 2. After a brief discussion, a "care package" was agreed to. We all suspect that Bransom is fine, and have heard that he is sleeping peacefully, That said, we're bored, and his foot could be broken – so the decision has been made to transfer the care package to Goleen, and perhaps send over Michael – whether Bransom will be happy to be awoken or not. What else do we have to do? And, our documentary maker, Bruce Kessler, doesn't have much in the way of undersea medical rescue footage, so we're hot in pursuit of Goleen.

Now that we have a semi-serious medical emergency, we have been able to persuade Goleen to drop speed, and we are approaching them rapidly. Rip has made up a transfer bag, which looks remarkably like what it is: a blown-up garbage bag, attached to a long rope, with an Evian water bottle at the other end. I am uncertain why Evian was selected over Perrier, but suspect that it was not relevant one way or the other. As we are still moments from intercepting Goleen, I will pass on to other topics and report back in a few paragraphs.

At this mornings roll call, all boats reported in fine – including Emeritus, which is so far ahead of the fleet that we have given up all hope of seeing her prior to arrival in Gibraltar. At the 8:00am roll call, we were 389 miles to Gibraltar (running at 9 knots). Division 2 was 322 miles from Gibraltar (running at 7.5 knots), and Emeritus, running alone, had only 254 miles to go (at 9+ knots).

The sea has not only been smooth, it has also been quiet. We haven't seen another boat for a couple of days. Bob, on Emeritus, reported seeing groupings of fishing vessels, which could mean nets in the water. After Autumn Wind's run in with a net, I'm not looking forward to being anywhere near a fisherman. On the chart it shows some undersea mounds that rise to within 25 meters of the surface. Perhaps these collect fish, and explain why the fishermen are out so far. The fish MUST be somewhere, as they certainly have been avoiding our fleet. No one in either division has caught a fish in days.

We did stop for swimming yesterday but the sea, which felt smooth under way, was much rougher standing still. Aboard Sans Souci, we were rolling back and forth at a rapid pace, and everything was flying in every direction. Our swim-stop was hastened by the need to get going again before someone got hurt. Several people dove off the top of the boats, which was highly dangerous, as the boats were being tossed from side to side with each wave that passed.

And, while I'm still killing time as we close-in on Goleen…

Today, I was looking at the Nordhavn site, and discovered that they have daily commentary from journalists, two of which are traveling with Division 2. I've enjoyed reading them, and seeing what our friends up ahead are up to. I started to excerpt comments from the commentaries, but thought you might prefer reading them yourself. Check out the following link: http://www.nordhavn.com/rally/underway/commentary.htm

I mentioned yesterday that Kirk had been encouraging activities, to keep us all motivated. Last night, Grey Pearl lead the evenings activities with a trivia game. They made the mistake of focusing on TV trivia, primarily Gilligan's Island and I Love Lucy. Roberta and Phil seem to have mastered this particular subject and were on the microphone responding before the questions were finished being read. One question stumped everyone though – "How did they ever get off the island?" After Grey Pearl admitted that they didn't know, I surfed the internet for the solution. Curious? The answer is that they didn't. The series ended without a final episode, although it was followed later by three "made for TV" movies, which had them off the island and back on.

After trivia, David Stone (from Crosser) and I decided to play chess. On a side note, my Dad and I have a game going at ALL times. I travel most of the time, and chess allows us to chat every day, even with me in the middle of the Atlantic, and him in California. We play on www.atlanticchess.com. The cool thing is that sometimes we make only one move per day, and other days we are able to finish whole games. The game between David and myself was even stranger. We called moves to each other across VHF. It was a great game, consuming nearly six hours, while boring the rest of our fleet who were forced, for hour after hour, to hear comments like "Rook at my Kings Bishop 3 to your Kings Bishop 4". I lost, but had a blast!

Meanwhile, back to Bransom's foot...

Whoa! That was scary. I've put pictures on the website, under Photos – Part III (http://www.trawlerweb.com). Check them out.

Here's what happened....

Rip stood on the front of the deck, as Kirk brought Sans Souci within 20 feet of Goleen (I was busy taking

pictures). He then pitched his Evian bottle towards Goleen, but missed. Do no ask me why both boats were running at full speed SO close together. We should not have been. Rip's short throw was the least of our problems. Goleen's wake grabbed Sans Souci and started our stern swinging. To avoid our stern striking Goleen, Kirk turned the wheel towards our starboard side, putting us on a collision course with Goleen. Fortunately, Goleen dropped power and allowed us to pass IN FRONT of her. From my perspective on the front deck, it seemed certain that a collision WOULD occur. When asked to estimate how close we came, the distances ranged from 2 feet to 6 feet, all of which were TOO close.

Rather than risk getting anywhere near each other again, we dropped the throw bag into the water, and Goleen picked it up with their boat hook. I'll be very curious to see what pictures and video Goleen has of the incident. We've since spoken to Bransom who reports that the painkillers are working magic.

After the drop, a LONG multi-boat discussion ensued, as we all spoke about the best running speed for an on-time arrival in Gibraltar. Que Linda kicked off the discussion by stating that if we continued running at over 9 knots we would arrive at 3:00am GMT on Saturday morning. This caused us to review tide tables, current tables, wind patterns, our most recent weather reports, etc. for Gibraltar. At the completion of the conversation it was decided that our "correct" speed should be 8.2 knots. Goleen is now just a speck on the horizon, reflecting Chris' desire to get there as quickly as possible.

Lastly…

I've been receiving a TON of email, and apologize that I can't respond to everyone. I'm a computer programmer, not a writer. I tend to agonize over paragraphs for hours, and sending out my daily emails is taking more time than it should. That I've actually managed to write something nearly every day for 45 days demonstrates that square pegs can be put into round holes – but, it's slow and time consuming. Thank you to everyone who has written! Please be assured that even when I don't respond, all email IS being read.

Here is a small sampling of yesterday's mail, with my responses:

Q. *"…I was wondering if it would be possible to share with your E-mail list one of my most recent listings. A 2000 model 57' Nordhavn named "Elin". She has only 1100 hrs on her main and 140hrs on her wing. Properly equipped and ready to go. One of my very good clients has thoroughly enjoyed her and is now ready to move into a larger motor yacht…"*

A. This is fine with me. Good luck with the sale! I see that you have posted some great information about the boat under "Open Discussion" on http://www.trawlerweb.com

Q. *"… I have enjoyed your web site a great deal. I was curious about not hearing much about Spirit of Zopilote. At the start of the crossing we were told that a documentary was being made of the trip. Is this still true? Could you update us on this? Thanks again for your great postings! Ken Olsen"*

A. Originally, I had thought that Bruce, and his boat Zopilote, would be accompanying us on the entire rally. He and his wife Joan are flying from place to place, meeting us whenever we are on land. Their boat is still in Florida. At each stop they gather all the film from each rally boat and make a copy. They also shoot interviews with the crews. Editing of the documentary is already underway. An effort will be made to obtain TV distribution for the documentary, but no one knows what will come of this. I assume I'll get a copy, and that they will be available to be ordered, but it's too soon to say.

Q. *"Ken: What is the patch of choice for combating Mal de Mer? Have you tried several kinds and what do you find most effective? Any side effects such as dry mouth, etc What does Dr. Ware recommend? Being a boater without a totally cast iron stomach, I do need help from these meds. Comments and inputs would be very much appreciated. Thanks Rod Sumner P.S. - I think I speak for all of us following their dream via your excellent web blog in saying a heart felt thank you for the time, expense, expertise and honesty you have shown with the Sans Souci web site. Many thanks and keep up the reporting of the great adventure..."*

A. Most of the really effective anti-seasickness drugs are prescription. See your doctor. My patch is Scopalimine (or, Transderm). It works well for me – but, was a disaster for Roberta. She's reasonably small – and it gave her a bad stomach ache, confusion, and dizziness. I definitely have dry mouth. It's frustrating because you are perpetually thirsty – but MUCH better than seasickness. Other drugs we have along are: Bonine (Meclizine) and Promethozine.

Talk to you tomorrow!

Day 47 - 148 miles to Gibraltar - at this time tomorrow we'll be on land!

I'm sitting at the table in Sans Souci's pilothouse, studying a map. As I look out the port side window, Portugal is only 50 miles away. I can't actually see it, but I know it is there. If I could look straight ahead for 150 miles, I would see our destination, Gibraltar, a British territory. If I shift my head slightly to the left, Spain is only 80 miles away. If I tilt my head towards the starboard window, Casablanca (Morocco) is 100 miles away. Last night, the Canary Islands were only a two-day run south of us. I tried to convince the crew that we should stop in the Canary's. From there, we could have run to the Sahara Desert in a few hours, then turned back northeast, and still arrived in Gibraltar in advance of the big July 5th rally party. No one indicated any interest, and I suspect I would have been thrown overboard had I pushed the topic. From my seat in Sans Souci's pilothouse, there are a LOT of different countries and cultures surrounding us. I wish I had time to explore them all.

As I was typing this paragraph, I looked out the starboard pilothouse window and noticed that Que Linda has come along side. I took the opportunity to grab my camera and shoot some pictures of them, and then curious as to why they were running so close, only about 50 yards away, I called Hal on the VHF radio. "We wanted to surf the net," he responded. I had forgotten that we are always on the internet, and have a wireless internet system on Sans Souci. Hal was using our internet connection from his boat! I couldn't stop chuckling when I realized this. We are the world's first floating internet café! More history made…

Speaking of funny things - Goleen did an hour-long comedy show last night that was hilarious. Everyone on Goleen participated, and we all had a great time. There was one strange moment however when Goleen suddenly went quiet about 10 minutes into their performance. They were on the radio one minute, and then suddenly disappeared mid-sentence. They still had not come back on the radio after 10 minutes of silence and were not answering radio calls. Just as we were starting to think we should turn Sans Souci towards them to see if they were in need of assistance, they popped back on the radio, without explanation, and recommenced their comedy hour – from the beginning. I still do not know if it was a prank, and part of the show, or temporary radio problems. I didn't like how spooky it felt to have them just disappear. Within seconds of their return, we were all laughing so hard the earlier mystery was immediately forgotten.

Last night, it caught us by surprise when we overheard the Division 2 boats talking on the radio. At the time they were about 40 miles in front of us. As I type this, we have cut this distance in half. We're still a bit out of range to comfortably hold a discussion, but expect to be able to chat back and forth on the radio before this evening. They should start showing up on radar within the next few hours.

Chef Phil sat with Roberta and I for a while during our 8:00pm to midnight watch last night. Our conversation drifted towards the rally, and whether or not it had changed our lives. Everyone agreed that it had, but no one could quite say how. For Roberta and I personally, it has stretched what we think we are capable of. For four years while our boat was in France, we sat only 80 miles from Corsica, but never went there. We talked about it endlessly, and have all the marine maps, cruising guides, etc. But Corsica always seemed SO far away that the trip just kept getting put off. Had we not done the rally, we were going to "make the leap" to Corsica this year. That 80 miles sounds like nothing to me now, and I'm embarrassed to admit that we thought it was such a big deal. Roberta and I were even saying last night that we would be willing to make an overnight run with just her and I on the boat. We don't have a particular trip in mind, but know that we never would have considered such a thing in the past. I'm sure that there have also been bigger-picture attitude changes that are more subtle, and that even we may not understand. Boating from place to place is very different than taking a plane. I compare it to walking a city, rather than just driving through it. There is more of a feeling of "really being there." I had predicted that the distance would feel huge to me, but it doesn't – the world feels much smaller than I expected. I have a sense of the world that couldn't have come from a map or book.

Overnight, the seas decided to remind us "who the boss is". The wind rose to 20 knots, and sent 9-12 foot waves crashing into our port side, for hour after hour after hour. There was no danger, and there was no sleep. About every 15 minutes a wave would hit our port side hard, resulting in a large bang, as though someone had just slammed the side of the boat with a massive sledgehammer. The stabilizers worked well, but even with most of the roll eliminated, there was plenty of movement left in the boat. Standing or walking without pacing your movements to the roll of the boat was impossible. I think we still would have been able to sleep had Shelby, our dog, not been so frightened. Every time a wave would hit, her eyes would go wide, and she would start running circles and crying. Much of last night was spent trying to convince her that all was well.

This morning, the seas are calm, and life is good again. We've just received our slip assignments for Gibraltar, and are looking to see where the advance team put us.

I have no update to give on Bransom's foot. The only comment at roll call was from Chris on Goleen, who said that "He has taken his drugs, and drank his wine, so he is currently unavailable for comment." Michael Ronquillo, our Emergency Medical Technician, was sitting here in the pilothouse, and started to panic. We calmed him down by saying that Goleen was "just kidding." And, they may have been…

Our radio has just come alive again, and it's Division 2 I'm listening to. They have a regularly scheduled 2:00pm Chick-Chat (their name, not mine). Roberta is downstairs taking a nap now, and it doesn't take long for us guys in the pilothouse to determine that they are unlikely to discuss beer or sports, so we change channels.

Tonight looks to be stressful. After days with no other boats, we are expecting to see them coming at us from every direction. I doubt anyone will get much sleep as we spend the night dodging freighters, and start thinking ahead to arrival.

That's all I can think of for now – so, talk to you tomorrow!!!!

P.S. - A couple of days ago I published a picture of a very strange "thing" that we captured while swimming. I think it's seaweed, but Roberta and Phil say it is a creature. Is anyone reading this list a biologist? Can you tell us what it is? If so, email me at: kenw@seanet.com – thank you!

Anybody know what this is???

Day 48-Arrival Gibraltar

This update is being sent out by Ken's dad. I just got off the phone with Ken. He told me the hotel in Gibraltar has no adapters to hook up his laptop to the internet and asked me to give a brief update on what is going on. The last hours of the trip were the bumpiest, with 40 knot winds directly into the bow of the ships with very high waves breaking over the bow of the ships. He has posted pictures to give you an idea of just how rough it was. I am soooo glad I wasn't there. All of the ships are now docked in Gibraltar and everyone is safe and well.

They will be in Gibraltar for nine days. The "End of Rally Party" will be July 5th. Knowing Ken like I do, I'm sure he will in the next couple of days find an internet cafe and give a much more detailed report. Ken said that as rough as it got, his only fear was that someone would get hurt trying to move around in the boat.

Sans Souci plows through the waves!

228

Day 49 - The End (Gibraltar)

Our final day in Gibraltar was perfect. The weather was horrific, but there is more to the story…

Roberta and I had the 8:00pm to midnight watch. As our shift began, we were about 150 miles from Gibraltar, and all was calm. But then I opened my email, to find this note from Walt Hack, our weather analyst:

"…The weather god has again intervened in the developing pressure pattern today and Saturday, and will indeed swing the local wind for the Gibraltar Strait passage to EASTERLY! However, he is being kind and keeping the wind intensity to at/below 20kts, and the wave heights at about 5ft or less…."

Thus far, the wind has always been behind us, or on the side. Generally speaking, I don't like wind from ANY direction. But, the worst possible direction is to have the wind blowing straight at you. We have run 4,000 miles with the wind behind us, to the side of us, or behind us, with much of it in the 15-20 knot range. As I read the report, I was thinking, "OK, it will be a bit bumpy, but no big deal."

During our shift the wind did flip around to the front, and increase to 20 knots, as predicted. Also as predicted, we encountered the Division 2 boats. We first saw them from about 8 miles away. As it was dark, all we saw were their lights on the horizon. The way that they were spread out, had I not known better, I would have sworn that we were approaching a city. Throughout our shift, the radio was alive with chatter. Our division had only five boats, so radio communications were infrequent. Division 2, with eleven boats, was much more active on the radio, plus now they had our boats to speak with. Normally during Roberta's and my shift, we put a "book on cassette" on to help pass the time. For the first time, it was impossible to do so, due to the non-stop radio chatter.

As we approached Gibraltar, we were surrounded by freighters. Chris, from Goleen, had predicted that it would be a stressful night, and that no one should plan to sleep. All boats wishing to enter the Mediterranean from the west must pass through the Straits of Gibraltar, or run thousands of miles south around Cape Horn. Throughout most of this rally, seeing another boat was a rare and exciting event. We now found ourselves surrounded by freighters in every direction. My radar screen was almost worthless, and appeared to have contracted some form of measles (little white dots everywhere). Because of the merger of our two groups, there were 17 dots on the radar, representing our rally boats, and then at least an equal number that were big freighters, or enemy targets as we had taken to calling them. Our boats were huddled together in a tight pack, in the hopes that this might make us more visible to the freighters.

Without Chris, I don't know how we could have safely entered the strait. Chris has a device on his boat, which shall definitely be on my shopping list the next time I upgrade Sans Souci. He has AIS, which is a radar enhancement that gives you information about any ships that appear on your radar. All boats over 100 feet are required to transmit AIS information. Chris was seeing each freighter's name, heading and speed. His AIS system was also computing how close the ship would come to our group.

Chris has no lack of self-confidence. Whenever he observed an enemy target that was in our path, he did not hesitate to call them and let them know that he considered this inappropriate. Chris sounded incredibly intimidating as he put freighter after freighter through the same drill. He would ask them their heading and speed (which he already knew), then ask where they came from, what they were carrying and where they were going. He would then ask if they saw our fleet. Keep in mind that Chris is aboard a 57 foot boat, speaking with a foreign crew, on a city-sized freighter, in his impeccable British accent. After a few minutes of verbal sparring, Chris would ask the freighter to change their course so that we might pass by safely. My favorite was an exchange last night where the freighter immediately agreed to make a turn to starboard. This wasn't sufficient for Chris, who then demanded to know exactly how many degrees, and when the turn would commence. We then watched in amazement as this freighter and another large freighter maneuvered to avoid striking each other, after having changed courses to avoid coming too close to us.

Knowing that Chris was clearing boats reduced Roberta's and my stress to a level where we thought we were going to bed after our shift ended at midnight. And, in fact we did, although we were wrong to think we would be sleeping.

Uno Mas makes her way through the head seas into Gibraltar!

I do not know how high the waves were. My sense is that they really weren't that large - perhaps 5-7 feet. However, they were very frequent. I timed them, and a wave was hitting us around every 2 seconds. Side to side rolling was not an issue, but the front of the boat was pitching up and down in an ugly manner. It was uncomfortable enough that sleep was impossible. The front cabins of Sans Souci had emptied, as everyone drifted to the main salon of the boat, where the pitching wasn't quite as bad. From time to time we would hear something somewhere crash to the floor, even though we thought we had everything tied down.

As Roberta and I were fitfully trying to sleep, the wind was getting nastier. We were in our bunks downstairs, and noticed that the pitching was getting worse. Before going to bed, Roberta had asked that I close the hatches in case water came over the bow. I didn't think this was likely, but I was very wrong. At 5:00am GMT, we took a huge wave over the bow and suddenly had a huge amount of water get past the closed hatches. The television and two satellite receivers that sit in one corner of our cabin have survived through thousands of miles in good times and bad, often with the hatches open, but now they were inundated with sea water, even though the hatches were closed. I had closed the hatches but not locked them. 99% of the time this would have been fine – but, this was the other 1%. They were toast, and not the only victims. A fair amount of sea water had entered our cabin. Roberta was not very happy with me…

It was time to get out of bed and see what was happening. The 62 is well engineered for high-seas, with handholds everywhere to help you move in a bouncing boat. For the first time, movement was nearly impossible. As we groped our way into the main salon, the first thing I saw was Roberta's mom stretched out on the floor of the main salon. John, her dad, was trying to get her a pillow and blanket. Neither of them looked very happy. Phil was stretched out on the couch looking VERY uncomfortable. Michael was in a chair, trying to cover himself with a blanket.

I went up to the pilothouse to see what was happening. The winds had increased to 35 knots sustained, occasionally rising to 43 knots. Wave height was higher but not high. I'd guess at perhaps 6-8 feet. We were pitching violently, burying the nose every few waves, and I could see several other boats around us, all of which were also struggling with the wind.

Kirk was at the wheel, with Rip standing beside him. Kirk was grinning ear to ear, which surprised me. His comment was "This is nothing. I've seen much worse heading north in the Pacific." As I thought about it, I've also been through much worse. We were rocking, but nothing bad was going to happen. Within a few minutes the euphoria caught on, and I cheered up. I heard someone on the radio shout "Ride'm Bronco" and someone else say "Wheeeeeee!" We were getting slammed, but it was well below the threshold of what a Nordhavn could take – so, why worry about it?

No one on our boat was seasick, and the hatches were now correctly closed – so, attention shifted to getting some great pictures before the wind died down. Photography was quite a challenge, as the sea spray was such that there was no way to go out on deck. Michael Ronquillo assisted me. He would open a side door to the pilothouse between waves, and hold it open for just a few seconds, during which I'd snap a picture, and then pull back as he slammed shut the door. I have some very cool pictures that I'll be uploading over the next few days (if I can get a decent internet connection). Hopefully someone got similar ones of us!

Grey Pearl makes her way in towards Gibraltar.

The high winds lasted another five hours. A few times Chris called us to say that he had found calmer water by hugging the shore. We thought about it briefly, but were having fun and the picture taking was good – so, we stayed with the wind. He called us several times, confused about why anyone would voluntarily put themselves through such weather.

It just felt like the perfect ending to the trip. Had we slid in on flat water, the voyage would have felt like it didn't have a proper end.

Around 10:00am GMT the wind dropped to a more rational 20 knot level. Jim Leishman came on the radio to tell us all to follow him to the "Rock" for picture taking. I advocated mutiny on my boat, and going straight into port. After five days at sea, I wanted to be off the boat. Losing another couple of hours to pose for pictures sounded like the wrong idea.

We stayed with the group though, and wound up having a great time. The sun came out, and the water was smoother. A camera boat was sent from shore to take pictures of the boats arriving, and we decided to give them something fun to take pictures of. I was in a humorous mood, so I put the song "YMCA" blaring from the front deck speakers, followed by "Electric Avenue." Roberta's parents went out on the front deck and danced their hearts out. Autumn Wind and Grey Pearl pulled along side of us, with their crews applauding. We also attracted a customs boat, with officers who looked un-amused, which pulled up along side of us. They left 15 minutes later, without contacting us, having decided we were crazy, not dangerous.

As usual, Roberta, her parents and I moved into a hotel, which has proved somewhat disastrous. The hotel, called The Rock, is allegedly the nicest hotel in Gibraltar. It's not bad, but I certainly wouldn't recommend it. The worst has been that I couldn't get a power adapter for my computer, and they don't have internet anywhere in the hotel. They couldn't even provide a phone cord so that I could dial into the internet. Meanwhile, back on the boat, the marina has wireless DSL. The crew is surfing the net at DSL speed, while I have finally gotten a flaky 28.8 slow modem connection working here in the room. There is a good chance I'll be booting the crew off the boat so that Roberta and I can move back to the marina.

The rally officially ends with a huge party on July 4th. Most of the boats will be leaving on July 5th. Roberta and I only have another three weeks before we have to be in Seattle, and want to deliver the boat ourselves to Cap D'Ail, near the Monaco border (approx. 1,000 miles). I'm a bit nervous about the first leg, from here in Gibraltar to Formentera, which is approximately 400 miles, or a 48-hour run. It will be Roberta's and my first ever overnight run (other than the rally), and we'll be doing it with just Roberta, her parents and I. We would like to do this next trip leisurely, so we are planning to leave Gibraltar early - meaning within the next few days. This will not go over well with the rest of the rally group however, as we already have a bit of a reputation of being anti-social because we have been staying in a hotel while in port, so I suppose it doesn't matter...

Before I end, I should tie up some loose ends.

> Bob Rothman and Emeritus never rejoined our group. He traveled the entire distance from Horta to Gibraltar alone, arriving the evening before the rest of the group. In a very pleasant surprise, he tendered from boat to boat as we were arriving in Gibraltar to say hi to each arriving boat.

> During our final roll call, one of our boats did not respond. It was the boat just behind me, so I went to the back deck and looked to see if it was still there. I instantly knew something was wrong, because it was sideways sitting still in the water. As were thinking we needed to turn back to help, a call came on the radio saying they were fine and that we should go ahead. They said they would catch up soon, and ignored questions on the radio about what happened. In port, I got the rest of the story, which I shall repeat without the boats name, as they were a little embarrassed. They ran out of gas. All of us have been running from a day tank, and transferring in fuel as needed. Sans Souci's day tank is only 300 gallons, so it's easy to run out of fuel if you forget to transfer fuel in. All they had to do was transfer a little fuel and they were back running. Oops.

➢ I've received many questions asking how we were able to do internet from the middle of the Atlantic. Sans Souci, as well as Goleen, were equipped with Fleet 55/77 units. These provide "always on" internet connectivity, but are expensive to use, and fairly slow. Our service was about half the speed of a normal dial-up modem. The nice thing though was that we were always on, and could surf the net at any time. The downside was that the cost for my internet connection for the trip will be around $7,000! Keep in mind that we had eight bored people sharing the connection. It's still a lot of money anyway you look at it.

➢ A few people did get sick during the final approach, most notably Teri on Strickly for Fun. Once into port, Teri taped a t-shirt to the side of their boat that was hilarious. It was a t-shirt Lugger had passed out to the rally participants that had some stats on the trip. It originally said: "30 Vessels, 3,800 miles, 1 power source – Lugger." Teri decided that there were other important stats to focus on, and added to the shirt how many patches she wore, how many pills of varying sorts, and a  more personal message – FOR SALE (SEE WIFE). I put the picture of the shirt under the Photos – Part III, Misc pics section (http://www.trawlerweb.com)

➢ Also on the website: I posted a picture of a "thing" that we found during our swim 150 miles out. Thus far, I've received three responses, all of which thought it was something different. One person guessed at coral, one as a sargassum fish and the third as mature Squid eggs. I still don't know which is true…

➢ I haven't forgotten that everyone wants me to upload the Guest Manual that was put together by Scott Strickland. I saw him today and he absolutely promised to get it to me within 24 hours.

This is my last official rally email. I have a ton of pictures that I would like to upload, and will, as soon as I can get a high-speed connection. Check the site from time to time for them.

I haven't decided whether or not I will post anything as we run the next 1,000 miles. If I do, it will only be one or two updates, just to let people know we are surviving. If you do not wish to receive these, go to the website, click on My Account, and choose the option for "Do not send Email." I will also send to the list information on how to obtain the video from the trip – assuming that it is for sale someday.

Lastly, I wish to offer a HUGE thank you to the following people, plus to all the other people who deserve to be here, but whose names I've temporarily forgotten:

> The people at Nordhavn. Dan Streech, Jim Leishman, and their team.

> Milt Baker!!!! I'm not sure of his relationship to Nordhavn, but he put together the 500 page operations manual that was so amazing. I will be asking Nordhavn for permission to post it, as it would be invaluable for anyone thinking to cross the Atlantic.

> Bruce and Joan Kessler, the documentary film makers, who were given an impossible task, and yet I am confident will produce something great. They have already circumnavigated, and a real highlight for me was getting a tour of their Spirit of ZoePilote.

> The rally participants, who were an awe-inspiring group. Many of them are continuing around the world from here, and I'm very jealous of them.

➤ Our crew – Dan Streech, Christian Fittipaldi, Capt. Rip Knot, Kirk White, Garret Severen, St. John Oneill-Dunne, Chef Phil Strable, Michael Ronquillo, Roberta, and her parents.

➤ All of you! I have received an overwhelming amount of mail about my updates. These have really inspired the entire crew. Thank you, thank you.

➤ All the other people in the rally advance team (Jennifer, Amy, etc) who made this rally possible.

History has been made. This was the first Cross Atlantic rally by powerboats, but it will not be the last. Hopefully many of you who are reading this will make your own crossings, and I look forward to reading your logs someday!

Thank you,
Ken Williams
Sans Souci, 6209
http://www.trawlerweb.com

P.S. - Chef Phil sent me a message which follows...

=============== *Through the eyes of a chef - by Chef Phil* ===============

As chef on board the Sans Souci, I want to give my "take" on this amazing experience as we are about to reach our final destination of Gibraltar. I've been spending the last few days thinking about all that has happened. It feels like this whole experience has been much like a roller coaster ride.

First you buy your ticket to ride the roller coaster with a little anxiety and a little excitement about the thrill of the ride. Then you get in line and both the excitement and the anxiety builds. There still is a chance to back out but you tell yourself you've made the commitment and you should follow through with it. As you get up to the front of the line you start asking yourself what have you gotten yourself into? But still, you convince yourself, you can do it. And then you get in the car (boat) and they lock you in. Yikes! There is no turning back now. Now you are asking yourself questions like "what was I thinking?" As the car starts to move you still have anxiety but you are also proud of yourself for sticking with your commitment to do something

238

challenging. The car starts to climb the first big hill and again you wonder why you decided to take on this challenge of the unknown. And then, weeeeeeeeee!, you are off and running and you are laughing and smiling and saying to yourself that this is the best experience ever! And then you find yourself saying, "come on… bring it on, gimme all you got!" It is at that point that you know you can survive almost any challenge because you overcame your fears and lived to tell about it. And when the ride ends what do you do? You say, "come on, let's do it again!"

It literally seems like ages ago that I arrived in Ft. Lauderdale with Ken & Roberta and began the task of provisioning. There were so many unanswered questions back then in my mind about what it was going to be like preparing food in a kitchen (galley) that was constantly moving. Working in a kitchen-in-motion was not a new experience to me since I have been working for nearly a year now as chef on The Silver Lariat, a private railcar. I guess I was expecting much of the same. There are little tricks that I have learned on the train about how to minimize spillage and what you can and can't do. But I had no idea that the "rocking motion" on a boat would be amplified at times which included not only left to right but up and down, back and forth and every combination there of. On a train the motion is best described as "rocking", on a boat it can be a combination of anything depending on the conditions of the sea. At times you just have to wait out a roll to continue what you were trying to do. And that could be as simple as walking from one side of the galley to the other. I learned that the further you spread you legs apart while standing chopping vegetables the better chance you have of continuing to work when the rolls come along.

Another part of this experience was learning and accepting the fact that you are sharing a small living space with 7 other people with 7 different personalities. One learns to be humble and go with the flow. Which was also the case when preparing food. I was lucky and I would say that most of the meals I prepared was to the liking of most everyone. It was fun to "spoil" everyone with 3 complete meals each day especially after I learned that many of the other boats in the fleet didn't have such a luxury. I was told that I had the hardest job on the boat but I'd have to say I had the best job on the boat. To be able to cook meals for 7 very appreciative people and to say that I crossed the Atlantic in a motor yacht is something I am so very proud to be able to say. Asked if I would do it again knowing now what I didn't know before my answer would be a resounding, YES.

But with that said, I can say I've done it and I don't need to do it again!

After we reach Gibraltar I look forward to exploring parts of Europe before returning home to Seattle. If anyone out there is looking for a chef with "international experience under diverse conditions", I'm your man. Time to revise my resume.

Thank you Ken & Roberta for an experience of a lifetime!

Chef Phil Strable
philipjon@comcast.net

Game Over – The Final Chapter

Greetings all...

Roberta's and my cruising has come to an end. It's sad as I sit here looking at the boat, and looking out at the Mediterranean, and knowing that it will be at least a year, or even two, before we take to the seas again.

Why might it be two years? Those of you who have been reading my updates for a while will remember that Roberta and I have considered selling Sans Souci, so that we could have Nordhavn build us a new 62. After spending a few months on Sans Souci, we've decided we would like the interior laid out a bit differently – mostly to enlarge one of the guest staterooms. After thinking for a while about selling Sans Souci, which is still an option, our current plan is to keep her and do an interior remodel. Hopefully this can be completed in time for cruising season, but you know how those things go...

Before I begin my last update, one bit of business:

Over the next few weeks, the website will be going through changes (http://www.trawlerweb.com) Now that the cruising is over, I am going back to my life as a retired computer guy. I've been keeping myself busy coding on a do-it-yourself website builder (http://www.websiteconstructionset.com/). It's just a hobby, but there are 400 or so websites that have been built with it, and after two months of neglect, it needs my full-time attention.

I'm turning over management of this website to a gentleman, John Sytsma, who volunteered to take the site over. My hope for this site is that it can continue to be somewhat what it is, with a slightly wider focus. There are a lot of couples out there cruising the world, who could use a forum for exchanging information, both technical and fun. Nordhavn has a great site, but it's for owners only. I am

renaming this site to: http://www.trawlerweb.com. Both the old and new website addresses work, so use whichever one you like.

My goal for the site is that it can provide valuable information to people who are cruising. There is a real need for cruisers to share information on destinations, insurance, maintenance, boat customization and electronics, anchoring tips, etc. I'd also like to provide a forum for other boaters to share their trip reports.

I have no interest in making money off the site. I do not want to sell advertising on the site or accept sponsorship money. My only goal is to enhance yours and my boating experience, through creating an online community of people with similar interests. It costs me nothing to keep the site alive, but it can profit all of us immensely. The website is meant to be a hub for the globally distributed community of trawler owners, or potential owners, who seek information or have information to share.

My hope is that John will do a solid job of running the site. Ultimately though, its success or failure will depend on whether or not all of you who are reading this contribute to the discussion. I leave it up to you as to whether or not this is something you would like to do. If you would like to drop participation, simply go to the website and choose "Do Not Email" under the "My Account" section.

All that said, we can now go back to my update. A wise man once said, the best place to start is at the beginning, so let me start with our departure from Gibraltar…

Last Thursday morning, July 1st, Roberta (my wife), Roberta's parents (John and Nova), Shelby (our dog) and myself left Gibraltar for Formentera. Our plan was to stop for one night at Puerto Banus, a port only 35 miles east of Gibraltar in Spain, and then run the 48 hours required to reach Formentera, an island off Barcelona Spain. Formentera is one of several islands in a group called the Balearic Islands. We had Sans Souci in the Balearic Islands a couple of years ago, so it would be a home-coming of sorts.

On July 14th, a delivery crew will be meeting us on another island in the Balearics - Mallorca. The delivery crew will take the boat to France where it will sit for four months until it will be transported, via Dockwise Yacht Transport, to Vancouver, near our home in Seattle.

I was nervous leaving the dock at Gibraltar. I've pulled Sans Souci away from the dock countless times, but have never felt comfortable doing so. Roberta and I give the appearance of competent crew going in or out of a port we are familiar with, but in strange surroundings, it can be a completely different story. The rally made life simple. We had seasoned veterans aboard ship at all times. Even on those occasions where I drove us into port, others took care of the myriad little details that need to be done for an arrival or departure.

We timed our departure to leave before everyone else was awake. We figured this would help us cover-up any departure errors we might make, and also help us sneak out of town. Even though we finished the rally, the "final" event (banquet) was still four days away, and we needed to get cruising. When you have only ten days for cruising, weather delays can quickly ruin a vacation. I already have a hard time explaining why we shipped Sans Souci to the U.S. from Europe, only to drive it back to Europe where, after we get our ten days of cruising, it will be shipped right back to the U.S. Each of those ten days is precious to us.

Our departure was not to be as private as we wanted. As soon as I started the engines, all the neighboring boats woke up. As it turned out, this gave us a chance to say one more round of goodbyes to all our friends, and was really nice. The departure was anti-climactic. All went well …

It felt strange to be alone! After 49 days with a group, we were suddenly floating free.

Immediately after leaving the dock, I looked at the computer, and noticed that it still showed us at the dock. It was not receiving updates from the GPS. We had to float for a few minutes while I rebooted the computer. I keep saying that I'm going to make up a checklist for leaving port, and this was a reminder of why I need to get this done.

Leaving Gibraltar harbor, we immediately encountered a tender with some very serious looking, and very armed, military types aboard. They circled Sans Souci close-in giving us a detailed inspection. It took only a few seconds to recognize these as American soldiers. We smiled and waved, and tried to look as harmless as possible. Roberta shouted for me to get the camera, which I refused to do. I have a general rule against photographing heavily armed serious looking people, although I did sneak a shot as they were leaving us. They never did wave or lose their stern dispositions. As we looked at where they were going we realized what was up – they were the advance team for an approaching American submarine. These are serious times, and they were protecting the sub. Good.

Proceeding east a few miles later, we noticed on the map a large rectangle drawn. No note on the map told us what the significance of the rectangle was. In front of us we saw a commercial fishing boat pulling a net. This led us to believe that the box on the map denoted a fishing zone. Was the box on the map an indication of a fishing zone? It stretched from shore to about 10 miles out, and was about 5 miles wide. To go around it would add at least a couple of hours to our journey. I started doing research, and found nothing that helped. A cruising guide said to give fishing boats a wide berth and to not assume they follow the rules of the road. Nothing told me how far behind the fishing boat its nets stretched, which is what I really wanted to know. 50ft? 100 Meters? 5 miles? How does one know? We took the conservative route and went the two hours out of our way.

243

The run to Puerto Banus is a short one, only about 50 miles. We were nervous about entering port, but our worries were unfounded. I had signed up for the only slip available, an 8 meter wide berth, at $650 per night. As expensive as it was, we had to drive to Puerto Banus days earlier and personally beg for it. We had faxed, telephoned and emailed – only to be told the port was full. In person, we were able to work something out. Getting into the berth was simple, even with a bit of wind. Plenty of space, and the slip next to us was open. Puerto Banus is the nicest port I have ever seen! Imagine a better version of St. Tropez – or, if you

haven't been into St. Tropez, I'll describe it this way: the city frames the port. The port is popular with the jet-set, and mega-yacht folk. There are at least 50 great restaurants you can walk to. There are upscale shops, discos, supermarkets, internet cafes, all within an easy walk. There is also a wild nightlife. Tens of thousands of people flock to the port each night for dining and dancing until dawn.

The port had only accepted us for a day, but we didn't want to leave. This sent me back begging to the nice lady at the capitainerie, who consented to two more days. Contrary to the ports reputation as impossible to get into, we had found a loophole. The mega-yachts own their slips, and go to sea for weeks or months at a time. Their slips are held open just in case they want to come back, but are rented when the office knows that the owner isn't in danger of coming back. $650 per night for a boat slip is irrational, and not something I would normally pay – but, after 47 days on the rally, a little luxury sounded better than you can imagine.

We also weren't looking forward to our next run, which we knew would be tough. Those of you who have been reading my posts for a while know that I am a "day boater" – I don't like to go anywhere that is more than about a four hour run. We now needed to run 48 hours, with effectively just Roberta and I on board. Roberta's parents were not part of our watch schedule. Neither has any knowledge about boats, and wouldn't know what to do if anything should go wrong. We assigned ourselves alternating four-hour watch schedules, and set in for the long haul.

Our first problem wasn't long coming. Nova was making dinner (spaghetti) when the stove quit. At the end of the trip, coming into Gibraltar, we had run out of propane, and flipped to our backup propane tank. I made the changeover, and noted that the backup tank was reading empty. I went back to the galley, and the stove was back on, but suspected it wouldn't be for long. I had Rip look at the tanks, and he confirmed the tank reading, but told me not to worry, as he had personally filled both tanks, and knew that regardless of what the gauge said that it was full. Ignoring instrument readings can be problematic, as we were finding. I do believe that Rip filled both tanks, but the fact of the matter was that we appeared to be out of propane. Oh well... it would be a nuisance, but certainly wasn't a huge deal.

Around 2:00am, on my shift, with just John and I in the pilothouse, we hit a weird one. There was a blip on the radar, but we couldn't see anything. It was an absolutely black night. It was about two miles out, and we assumed it was a sailboat running without lights. But then I tweaked the radar and realized that I could see eight or so of the blips, running in a slightly arced line, spaced about a quarter mile apart. For those of you who want to look at a map, we were at: 36'31N by 3'33W, about 12 miles off shore. They were curving to the right, blocking my path, and roughly matching a line I could see on the map, that I assumed was an underground cable. I wanted to cross them, as I was reasonably certain that it wasn't a net – but, I wasn't 100% certain that it wasn't a net. What to do? I circled for a bit, and messed with both radars to try to see if I could learn more. On our smaller radar I couldn't make them appear no matter what I did. On the large radar they were unmistakable. I shut down the small radar, in case it was some sort of interference between the two radars. Nope – no difference. Something was in the water. I woke up Roberta, who grumpily said I should just turn right – go another five miles out to sea – and, forget about it. The dots stretched for at least another 10 miles, but we kept them on our left. I don't think it was a radar glitch, as it wasn't a straight line – but was it a net? I don't know. There were no lights whatsoever, and I never saw anything.

Our ride was bumpy, but not a problem. The wind seemed to know which way we were going and stayed on our nose. We had about four hours that were really bad – where we were really slammed, but nothing that scared us.

What did worry me was fatigue. With Roberta and I doing four hours on, four hours off, I was having trouble sleeping. Roberta would send me downstairs to sleep, and I would lie there not able to sleep on command. I did one night-time shift alone and noticed myself drifting towards sleep a couple of times. I reminded myself that this could be fatal, and forced myself awake. I set my alarm clock, built into my cell phone, for 15 minutes later – and, kept setting it over and over again through the shift. The next morning I told everyone I wasn't doing a night-time shift again without someone along to keep me awake. Many people do watches alone without falling asleep. Others, particularly sail boaters, sometimes go to sleep and just don't worry about it. These people are nuts, in my opinion, and have also been known to run, or anchor, without lights. Scary and dangerous.

We had a couple more encounters with commercial fishing boats. Roberta decided to experiment with passing a half mile behind one. Nothing bad happened. This emboldened us, and when we encountered a fleet of 10 of them blocking our path coming into Formentera, we just drove straight through them (keeping a respectful distance behind the individual boats)

We approached Formentera in 25 knot winds, at 9:00 in the morning. We were tired and wanted to go to sleep. Anchoring looked like it would be a miserable experience. I had phoned virtually every marina on the near-by larger island of Ibiza, all of which had no space available. Finally I called Formentera's sole marina that surprised us by saying they had an available slip. The cruising guide warned that it was a small marina with frequent entry and exit of high-speed ferries, and not very protected from the wind.

Our smooth exit from Gibraltar, and entry/exit at Puerto Banus had emboldened us. I was convinced we could get into port, no problem, even with the wind. I was wrong. Just entering the port took a half hour, as ferry after ferry came shooting into the port entrance. Each time that I would think I was aligned, a ferry would come blasting out, or another shoot up behind me. I finally picked my window and shot into the port.

Inside, the port was a mess. There is a small turning bay, perhaps 150 feet across. On the right is a ferry dock, with room for four or five ferries. To the left there were various boat docks, and straight head there were some more boat docks. I was directed to proceed through the turning bay, just past the first dock on the right. In the bay was one ferry arriving, one departing, a 50' sail boat that was struggling with the wind, and drifting out of control, plus a couple of other smaller boats that seemed to not know where they were going. The wind inside the marina was showing as 22 knots. I was dodging the other boats, while looking to see what I had to do to get to my dock. Unfortunately, the narrow entrance to the dock I wanted to get to was further narrowed by a couple of sailboats rafted together at the end. Quickly, I ascertained that this wasn't happening. The entrance to the dock would be nearly impossible without wind. The wind put it over the top. I shouted to Roberta "Let's get the hell out of here!" Her response: "You can do it. Just take your time." I believed her, and maneuvered a bit more, trying to avoid the out of control sailboat, which seemed to now be under control, but still in my way. After a few more futile efforts to align myself, I called to Roberta – "This can't be done. If you think you can do it, the controls are yours." She gave me a disgusted look, and grabbed the controls. I went towards the back of the boat, to have a look at the situation there and within 30 seconds, realized the boat was pivoting! I ran back to the front, where Roberta was and shouted "What are you doing?" She said "This is impossible – we have to get out of here. We're drifting into the wall. If we don't get out now, we're going to hit" That, and the fact that she walked away from the controls, got my attention quickly. I did drive us out of the marina, but it was one of the hairier things I've ever done. The marina was not surprised when I called back to say "Sorry. I decided to pass on the slip. I cannot get in." I now understood why it was the only available slip within 50 miles.

Anchoring was sounding a LOT better. Formentera is a strangely shaped island. The northern part of the island is a long sandbar, a 3-mile long sandbar. Given that sandbars have two sides, this means six miles of beautiful beach, and many miles of awesome hiking. Unfortunately, the sandbar is low, so there isn't much protection from the wind, but there is some. The sandbar runs north to south, and boats tend to anchor on the east or west side, based on the wind. Not only does this provide some sheltering from the wind, but it also has you blowing offshore should you break anchor. Each side has beachfront restaurants. It was an east wind, so we chose the west side, and anchored. It wasn't bad at all, and we asked ourselves why we ever considered going into port. We were alone, due to the wind, but this didn't last long. With each hour, the wind dropped, and new boats arrived. By 1:00pm, the wind was down and the beach was packed. We napped then tendered ashore for a wonderful lunch, and hike on the beach.

As were tendering to shore our first time, the first sail boat we passed had a couple of young men (hunks) standing on the back deck, totally nude, showering. Dress codes are extremely loose in the Med. I was a little nervous that Roberta's mom might freak out, but all she said was "Can't we slow down a little to see if they turn around?" I told her not to worry that she would see LOTS more similarly dressed people over the next few days. Roberta's dad later made his only comment on the situation, saying "Ken, do you think they sell any copies of Playboy on the island? I can't imagine they do. This is much better."

We had three incredible days on Formentera. The only excitement was tendering to shore. On the second day, the wind flipped directions. All of the hundreds of boats moved to the other side of the sandbar. The winds had come back up. This was not a problem for us at anchor, but the waves were breaking on shore. We could see everyone at the restaurant enjoying their lunch, but I didn't want to take the tender to shore, with the breaking waves. Everyone was hungry, so they convinced me. We all got in the dinghy and tried, but failed. Back to the boat. We then noticed the restaurant tender going boat to boat taking people to shore. To get to the beach they were surfing the waves, lifting the engine, and driving fast up onto the sand. We signaled the guy and did it – exciting! Roberta's parents didn't like it though, as it was tricky getting out of the tender and very wet.

 On a related topic of wind at anchor, I should mention our flopper stoppers. We've had them for years, but only used them a couple of times. On the east side of Formentera, we were anchored with a 1.5 meter swell. This made it miserable on the boat. The flopper stoppers (there is a picture of them on the website (http://www.trawlerweb.com) act like stabilizers at anchor. Roberta and I made a command decision to force ourselves to really master their deployment, after years of avoiding their use. It took some practice, but what had taken hours the first time, we now have down to minutes. I would now consider dropping them a normal part of our

anchoring process, unless the water was absolutely flat, and would never own a boat without them.

After a few days, we moved to an anchorage at nearby Ibiza. Sometimes I like quiet bays to anchor in, but as we had no ability to cook aboard ship, I was seeking a protected anchorage, with a good restaurant. We found the perfect place for this at Ensenada de la Canal on Ibiza (Playa Mitjorn). Great restaurants and a fun beach.

The restaurant did have a tender, but we decided to do our own tendering. The local tender guys tend to be a bit crazy, and I was convinced I could do a better job. The waves were breaking again (too much wind), but I had studied their technique, and had my own ideas. I would get close enough to shore, to be just where the waves started breaking, raise the motor and jump into the water. I would then lead the boat as close to shore as I dared, and ask everyone to jump out. The bad part of this idea was that Roberta and her parents were exiting the tender in knee high breaking waves. This wasn't horrible, and Roberta and I thought it was kind of fun, but her parents were not amused. Leaving shore, I goofed once, and we took a large breaking wave straight over the bow of the tender, soaking everyone, and filling the tender. Roberta and I were laughing hysterically. Her parents were not.

I loved it there, but it was clear that Roberta's parents did not like the twice-daily trips to and from shore. They were real work. The wind was moving, so it was time to find a new anchorage. I asked Roberta's parents whether they would rather go to another anchorage, or if I should see if I could get into port in Mallorca early. They jumped on the opportunity, and I agreed. As much as I love life at anchor, being on shore sounded good.

We had a nine hour run ahead of us to Mallorca, and I was burnt out on long runs, so I looked at the map to see how to break up the trip. I found a port on the east side of Ibiza that would get us a couple of hours closer and called them. They had a slip!!! We headed out immediately. Wow! A very cool marina, called Puerto Sta Euralia. I had no expectations, and was extremely impressed. We had no trouble getting in, with one small exception.

In the Med, everything is the Med Tie. There are no finger docks. Everyone parks side to side, with only fenders to separate them. Your bow is held in place by a line that extends to the bottom of the marina, and your stern is tied to the wall by your own stern lines. The bowline, when you arrive, is dangling from the wall at the back of your boat. You back to the wall, someone jumps off, grabs the rope, jumps back aboard, and then walks it to the front of the boat, where you winch it tight – and, you are done. Roberta's and my normal procedure is that I back the boat to within about 20 feet of the wall, then she takes control, and I walk back to collect the bowline. We have a redundant set of boat controls at the aft deck (as well as several other places on the boat). For an unknown reason, which I need to investigate, the aft controls would not work. Roberta pressed the button and assumed she had control. She shouted up at me: "I've got it" and I ran downstairs. We were drifting slowly backwards at the time. She then shouted: "I can't get control!!!!" Oops. We were going to hit the wall. I ran back up and goosed us forward just in time. As usual, a crowd had gathered to watch us park. The 62 is an unusual looking boat, which is in some ways a pain. I am often confronted by a curious crowd which wants to learn more about the boat while I am trying to tie lines. In this case, the crowd that was preparing to ask questions, instead watched Roberta and I look very confused as we bailed ourselves out of trouble. Oh well...

By a stroke of luck, Sta Euralia is the same city as one of my favorite restaurants on Ibiza – the Bambudhha Grove. We taxied to dinner, and had a great time.

The next morning, we set out for a seven hour cruise to Mallorca, which we decided to shorten by picking up the speed to 9.5 knots. In just six hours we were entering the port at Puerto Portals, in Palma. Puerto Portals is incredible! I had thought Puerto Banus was great, but now am reconsidering which I like better. It's not quite as big, or hip – but - it's quieter, and much classier. We had no trouble getting into our slip, and the people are very nice. We've mostly cruised the coast of France, with only one previous trip to Spain. I've been growing more impressed with it by the day, and wish I had more time. We don't. We have only four days here at port in Mallorca, waiting for the delivery crew – and, our time on the boat will be over. Thus, my log has reached its end.

Thank you again for having "accompanied" Sans Souci and myself on this long quest. We have crossed the Atlantic and then some. I thanked everyone in sight with my last update, so I won't bore everyone doing that again - but I did forget one important thank you --- to Sans Souci herself. She has brought us nearly 5,000 miles, through some calm seas and some very rough seas, with virtually no problems. I asked last night at dinner if anyone was ever scared. Neither Roberta, nor her parents, could remember one moment when they felt in danger. That says a lot. I doubt I'll ever cross another ocean, but am thrilled to have done so. Who knows, maybe I'll reconsider someday?

Ken Williams
Sans Souci, 6209
http://www.trawlerweb.com

Rally Participants

Uno Mas in calm seas.

Sue & John Spencer, Roy Rouse. Not pictured: Clint Spencer (Leg 1), Chris Mather (Leg 2)

Satchmo crew poses for a photo op.

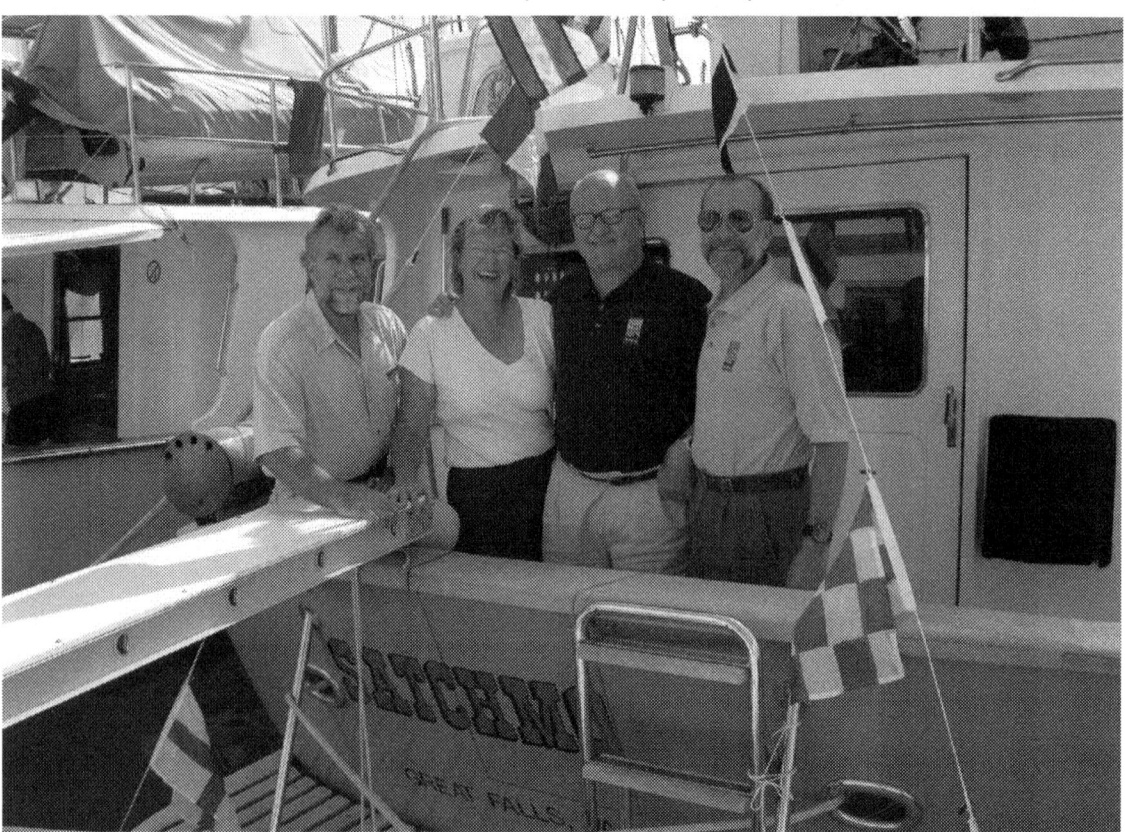

Steve Soltysik, Ellen & Bill Bane, Calvin Kendig

Envoy with paravanes deployed for stabilization.

Don Bunnell, Barrie Smith, Wayne & Patricia Davis. Not Pictured: Janet Smith (Leg 1)

Egret plows through a wave while her crew smiles for the camera!

Front Row: Scott & Mary Flanders – Back Row: Cecil Newsome, Dean Wiley

World Odd@Sea crew welcomes this adventure with open arms.

John & Dulcie Harris, John & Pam Chatting, Steve Lawrence

Stargazer crew waves to the camera.

Bill Carpenter, Will Perras, Michael Perfit, Kevin Keith

Strickly for Fun crew flying high!

Bill Parlatore (Leg 3), Teri & Scott Strickland, Frank Sain (Leg 3)

Not Pictured: Jon Ehly (Leg 1 & 2), Christine Ehly & Sean Ehly (Leg 1), Georgs Kolesnikovs (Leg 2)

Sundog crew poses on the Portuguese Bridge.

Back: Lee Roman, Dave Hill, Robert Greenbaum   Front::Robert Schaper
Not Pictured: Adam Greenbaum (Leg 1)

Four Across crew poses on the Fly Bridge.

Eric Leishman (Leg 3), Doug Seaver, Will Seaver, Jennifer Alloway, Charles Metcalf (Leg 1 & 2)

Que Linda on the hook in Bermuda.

Hal & Linda Wyman, Chris & Staci Wyman (Leg 3), Wayne Almquist, Bob Owens

Not Pictured: David Wyman (Leg 1)

Goleen sits at the dock in Bermuda.

Bob Senter (Leg 1 & 2),Sonaia H. Maryon-Davis, Bransom Bean, Chris Samuelson
Not shown: Kate Brunel-Cohen (Leg 2), Jon Ehly (Leg 3), Georgs Kolesnikovs (Leg 3)

Emeritus sits at the docks in Bermuda.

Bob & Janis Rothman, Matt & Caroline Inman

Sea Fox heads out to sea.

Dennis Sturdivan, Tom Selman, Dennis Fox, Rod Semrad (Leg 1 & 2)

Not Pictured: Julie Fox (Leg 1), Kurt Krogen (Leg 1), David Fox (Leg 1)

Grey Pearl and the Rock of Gibraltar.

Braun & Tina Jones, Maralee Costino (Leg 3), Steve Kellenberg (Leg 3) Jose Gutierrez
Not Pictured: Mark Wildman (Leg 1), June Crafton (Leg 1 & 2), Mort Taubman (Leg 2)

Autumn Wind crew posing on the Portuguese Bridge.

Bill & Arlene Smith, St. John O'Neil-Dunne (Leg 3), Patrick Hemphill, Garrett Severen (Leg 3), Mike Ronquillo, Eric Leishman (Leg 1 & 2), Jackie & Josie (Dogs)

Not Pictured: Brad Smith (Leg 1 & 2), Georgs Kolesnikovs (Leg 1), Bing O'Meara (Leg 2)

Sans Souci makes easy headway as she closes in on Gibraltar.

Phil Strable, Rip Knot, Ken & Roberta Williams, St. John O'Neil-Dunne (Leg 1 & 2),
Mike Ronquillo (Leg 3), Kirk White (Leg 2 & 3)
Not Pictured: Dan Streech (Leg 1), Christian Fittipaldi (Leg 1), Garrett Severen (Leg 1 & 2),
John & Nova Heuer (Leg 3)

Crosser and crew enjoy some flat seas.

Back Row: Richard Doering & Linda Rice-Doering, John Burgess, Beverly Monigal
Front Row: Anita & Dale Neifert, David Stone, Sandra Howarth
Not Pictured: Patrick Hemphill (Leg 1 & 2)

Atlantic Escort cruises into Bermuda.

James Leishman, Brad Smith (Leg 3), Kari Ware (Leg 2 & 3), Kevin Ware, Jim Leishman
Not Pictured: Justin Zumwalt (Leg 1 & 2), Dave Shuler, Scott Shane (Leg 1), Peter Swanson (Leg 2),
John Wooldridge (Leg 2), Brad Kovach (Leg 3), Peter Janssen (Leg 3)

Rally Staff:

Joan & Bruce Kessler, Amy Zahra, Jenny McCauley Stern, Milt & Judy Baker